FUNDAMENTAL

EDUCATION

★

UNESCO

EDITORIAL COMMITTEE

KUO YU-SHOU,
Chairman

MARTINEZ BAEZ

HENRY W. HOLMES,
Editor

ALBERT CHARTON

MARGARET READ

ISAAC L. KANDEL,
Advisory Member

CONTRIBUTORS

MEKKI ABBAS

H. B. ALLEN

MARTINEZ BAEZ

A. N. CABALLERO

CHAO YUEN-REN

ALBERT CHARTON

R. M. CHETSINGH

A. G. DICKSON

B. H. EASTER

EMANUEL GABRIEL

V. L. GRIFFITHS

HOPE HAY

ELLEN HELLMAN

F. L. K. HSU

J. D. R. JONES

T. J. JONES

ISMAIL KABBANI

I. L. KANDEL

BEATRICE KING

HENRI LABOURET

F. C. LAUBACH

J. A. LAUWERYS

H. O. McCONNELL

MARGARET MEAD

C. K. OGDEN

MARGARET READ

I. A. RICHARDS

H. A. SALMAN

ELENA C. TORRES

R. W. VAN DIFFELEN

WANG CHENG-SU

QUINTIN WHYTE

MARGARET WRONG

FUNDAMENTAL
EDUCATION

COMMON GROUND
FOR ALL PEOPLES

★

REPORT OF A SPECIAL COMMITTEE
TO THE PREPARATORY COMMISSION
OF THE UNITED NATIONS EDUCATIONAL,
SCIENTIFIC AND CULTURAL ORGANISATION
PARIS 1946

NEW YORK
THE MACMILLAN COMPANY
1947

CONTENTS

Chapter I. INTRODUCTION

PAGE

The origins of the present document; its scope and
purpose   1

Chapter II. NOTEWORTHY EXAMPLES

Accounts of Fundamental Education in action in selected areas; difficulties and achievements . . .   14

Chapter III. GENERAL CONSIDERATIONS

Articles and excerpts on major issues of theory; the
controlling concepts of Fundamental Education .   144

Chapter IV. POLICIES AND METHODS

Problems to be met in the attack on illiteracy; the setting and concomitants of illiteracy; the larger aims
of Fundamental Education   215

Chapter V. SUGGESTED LINES OF ACTION

Possible steps for Unesco in forwarding the world-
movement for Fundamental Education . . .   288

Appendix   306

Index   319

v

FOREWORD

This volume, a first fruit of the labours of the Education Section of the Preparatory Commission's Secretariat, was prepared for the First Session of the General Conference (November-December 1946) in explanation of the proposed plan of work in the field of Fundamental Education. Inevitable printing delays prevented its being submitted in full to the Delegates, but the first and final chapters were issued as a separate pamphlet for the Conference, with an introductory statement covering the contents as a whole.

The volume is now presented to a wider public, not as a considered treatise on the question, but as a working document. It focuses attention upon a world movement of increasing magnitude, in relation to which Unesco may perform a number of helpful functions. This movement frankly faces the existence of immense numbers of people who lack the most elementary means of participating in the life of the modern world. Such a situation is not only a threat to peace and security, none the less real because indirect, but also a barrier and a challenge to science and culture. Unesco has good reason, therefore, to take Fundamental Education as one of its primary fields of interest.

Abraham Lincoln, in his famous metaphor of the house divided against itself, gave it as his judgment that a nation half slave and half free could not stand. The same may well be true of the world. Where half the people of the world are denied the elementary freedom which consists in the ability to read and write, there lacks something of the basic unity and basic justice which the United Nations are pledged together to further. Fundamental Education is only part of the wider and fuller human understanding to which Unesco is dedicated, but it is an essential part.

JULIAN HUXLEY,
Director General.

. . . that since wars begin in the minds of men, it is in the minds of men that the defenses of peace must be constructed:

that ignorance of each others ways and lives has been a common cause, throughout the history of mankind, of that suspicion and mistrust between the peoples of the world through which their differences have all too often broken into war; . . .

that the wide diffusion of culture, and the education of humanity for justice and liberty and peace, are indispensable to the dignity of man and constitute a sacred duty which all the nations must fulfill in a spirit of mutual assistance and concern; . . .

and that the peace must therefore be founded, if it is not to fail, upon the intellectual and moral solidarity of mankind.

FROM THE CONSTITUTION OF UNESCO.

CHAPTER I

INTRODUCTION

The Origins of the Present Document

Like a simple but impressive pattern which recurs within a more elaborate design, the theme of Fundamental Education is brought forward again and again in those discussions which have thus far advanced the programme of Unesco. And the pattern has itself developed, as these pages will show. The attack on illiteracy is not the whole of Fundamental Education; other elements, spiritual as well as material, appear as factors in the problem.

The development of the idea is evident both in the proceedings of the Preparatory Commission and in the work of the Secretariat. The record is revealing.

Within half an hour of the signature of the Final Act establishing the Organization, 16th November, 1945, Sir Alfred Zimmern, then acting as Executive Secretary, speaking before the First Plenary Meeting of the Commission, expressed his conviction that Fundamental Education should become one of the major concerns of Unesco. With respect to the long-term programme of the Organization, Sir Alfred said,

If I sense aright the feeling of the Conference—the purport of the resolutions put in, for instance, by the United States Delegation and speeches made by numerous delegates . . . [it] is that in the field of education the direction in which the new Organization would wish to direct its labours is in helping . . . the countries . . . which are faced with large masses of human beings living in conditions not only of poverty but of ignorance,

I

and of removable ignorance. It seems to me we cannot act too quickly in selecting the direction in which we propose to place our work; and the subject that occurs to me . . . is 'Illiteracy among adults and the means to be taken throughout the world to combat it.' That is a subject which interests a large number of our member states . . . it interests a number of states which have very few illiterates amongst their metropolitan populations. . . . If we could decide here and now to take this up, . . . it would give our National Commissions in the various countries something immediate to work on and make them feel our sense of urgency . . . and that we were really going to turn into action the provisions that we have made about removing poverty and ignorance and helping the poorer sections of the world community. (Applause.)

In addition to the general approval with which these remarks were received, the delegate from Mexico, Dr. Jaime Torres Bodet, and the delegate from Brazil, Senor J. J. Moniz de Aragao, spoke more specifically of the urgency of the task. Dr. Torres Bodet voiced explicitly what appears to have been the sense of the meeting, "that this should be one of the subjects to be dealt with in the first Session of the General Conference of this Organization."

It need hardly be said that this single incident in the earliest days of Unesco has an historic background in the development of the social theory of education; nor is it unconnected with the evolution of the social sciences or the long effort of mankind to achieve an ever larger measure of freedom and of self-control. This is not the place, of course, for any part of this greater human story; but it is worthy of note that in the discussions of Fundamental Education as an interest of Unesco, as indeed in the discussions of other urgent tasks of the Organization, there was evident a sense that the issues involved and the action to be taken had critical significance in the light of history.

Even before the first meeting of the Preparatory Commis-

sion it had been said that if the new Organization was to
succeed, it must raise the level of general education in the
various societies of the world. The Hon. Nils Hjelmtveit,
Minister of Education of Norway, speaking to the Conference of Allied Ministers of Education, had pointed to the re-
moval of illiteracy as a necessary first step in countries where
illiteracy existed. He went on to say, "We must give depth
and breadth to the education of the common people if we
are to lay a firm basis for democracy within the individual
nation and for understanding and collaboration among the
peoples of the world." Here was a preliminary but weighty
statement by a responsible Government representative.

Government proposals of a formal character were received
on this topic within a few weeks after the Secretariat had
begun its studies. In February, 1946, a Memorandum was
submitted on behalf of the Iranian Government by Mr. G.
A. Raadi, representative of Iran on the Preparatory Commission. It argued the importance of universal education as
a means toward peace, security, and social justice and presented a working programme for Unesco in this field. The
concrete proposals of this Memorandum will be considered
later in the present document. It is significant to note here
the argument that "great masses of men in many parts of the
world are deplorably frustrated and deprived" in respect to
education, and that "this condition creates a disequilibrium
incompatible with peace, universal goodwill, and mutual
understanding among nations." It is further of interest to
note that one of the steps recommended by the Iranian Government as deserving of "special attention" in the discharge
of this "primary function of Unesco" is . . . "The search for
the social and economic causes of . . . wide-spread illiteracy."
Thus illiteracy is presented, not as an isolated fact, to be
treated out of connection with its causes and its setting, but
as one element in a complex human situation.

At about the same time—February, 1946—a Memorandum was received from the Mexican Delegation under the title "Organization of an International Campaign against Illiteracy." The major proposal of this Memorandum and its valuable information on the situation in Mexico will be taken into further account in another place. What is especially pertinent at this point is the statement that . . . "ignorance is not an isolated social fact, but one aspect of a condition of general backwardness which has many other features, like paucity of production, absence of industrialization, insignificant exports, poor transport and communications, deficient capital and income, bad conditions in regard to food, clothing, housing, and public health, and a high death rate." The complexity of the problem is again asserted; but the Mexican Memorandum goes on to argue that "the United Nations . . . cannot afford to wait for [the] slow evolution . . ." of a complete economic and social solution of the problem of ignorance, but that Unesco must, in the interests of peace, organize immediately an international campaign against illiteracy. An issue of major importance was thus brought formally before the Secretariat.

In addition, also in February, 1946, at the Fourth Session of the Preparatory Commission, the Cuban delegate, M. Luis Perez, urged the view that "the primary aim [of Unesco] should be action which benefits the greatest number and touches the lives and welfare of the masses of men and women in all our lands. . . . [It] should be directed primarily to reducing inequalities in education, science, and culture within each nation and community and between the various nations and communities which form the United Nations. . . . That is what we mean by human betterment. . . ."

Encouraged by these memoranda and expressions of opinion, as well as by the obvious interest displayed by most of the delegates, the Education Section of the Secretariat included in its suggested programme a recommendation for the appointment of a Commission on Fundamental Education; and the Section also presented to the Education Committee of the Preparatory Commission a special paper on this subject. This paper was drafted in May, 1946, discussed late in that month with the Education Committee, and subsequently revised in the light of the comments made by members of the Committee.

In presenting the recommendation for the appointment of a Commission on Fundamental Education, Dr. Kuo Yu-Shou, Senior Counsellor for Education, explained why this new term was chosen. One might speak (he said) of "Illiteracy", "Mass Education", "Basic Education" or "Popular Education." One should, however, think not only of an attempt to liquidate adult illiteracy but also of the problem of providing elementary education for all the young people of all the world. The expression "Mass Education" corresponded to some degree to what the educational staff of Unesco had in mind but evoked unpleasing connotations of educational methods which paid insufficient attention to individual differences. The phrase "Fundamental Education," which at least has the merit of indicating an education on to which more could be built, seemed to have fewest disadvantages. It would be used to indicate a field of activity which would include and go beyond mass education, adult literacy campaigns, popular education, and the provision of primary education.

The special paper referred to above was discussed with the Education Committee of the Preparatory Commission on the 25th May, 1946. The paper proposed, in effect, the preparation of the present document, and it outlined a procedure for that purpose. It also presented the views of the Education Section of the Secretariat as to the reasons for choosing this field for early consideration and action.

The reaction of the Education Committee was favourable. In an interesting examination of the proposal advanced by the Secretariat, it became clear that no one concerned would be content to regard literacy as an end in itself. Like any tool, literacy may be used for bad purposes as well as for good ones. The whole content and direction of education come into question; and the utilization of education as a means toward war and conquest—as lately in Germany, Italy, and Japan—cannot be forgotten. The importance of work with youth organizations was emphasized. "In the next ten years," said Professor Paulo Berredo Carneiro, of Brazil, "the youth between 15 and 20, trained by Mussolini and Hitler, will inherit the reins of government. . . . The essential problems of youth have not yet been touched. . . ." And M. Henri Vallon, of France, referred to ceremonies as "a means of using collective feeling to the advantage of youth." Others spoke to the same effect, yet all admitted the urgency of effort to spread, in the widest possible way, the values to be achieved by education broadly and humanely conceived. These points of view are reflected in the final proposals of the Secretariat for its entire programme in education and also in its development of the idea of Fundamental Education, as described later in these pages.

The records of the meetings of the Preparatory Commission held in July, 1946, contain various references to the project in Fundamental Education, as finally put forward in the first draft of the Program prepared by the Secretariat.

The comments of the delegates show marked differences in the approach to the problem, but they show no conflict of opinion as to the basic merit of the undertaking. Said Dr. Alf Sommerfelt, of Norway, ". . . People ask 'What are you going to do? What can you do?' Therefore I think it is necessary for the future of Unesco to take up something that people at large can really understand, which can be an element in the work for peace. . . . At first we must concentrate upon one project which will really catch the imagination of the world. . . . Personally I would be in favour of a campaign against illiteracy. . . ." Dr. J. Idenburg, of the Netherlands, emphasized the need of a spiritual objective for popular education and of co-operation with church agencies. This was instanced again by Dr. I. J. Haarhoff, of the Union of South Africa. The President of the Preparatory Commission, the Rt. Hon. Ellen Wilkinson, pointed out that religion, as such, lay outside the jurisdiction of Unesco, whereas cooperation with church bodies in education remained entirely possible. M. B. Drzewieski, of Poland, spoke of the importance of psychology in dealing with educational problems; and he pointed out, as did other delegates, the great need of improving the social and economic conditions of teachers. Dr. Esther Brunauer, of the United States, called attention to the need of proceeding co-operatively within the framework of the United Nations, without thought or hint of pressure or compulsion. There were other reactions to the idea of Fundamental Education, none in opposition, during the course of an extensive discussion of the proposed Program.

In this document, which covers all the undertakings then proposed for consideration, the following passage concerns this topic:

A. Commission on Fundamental Education. It is proposed that twelve to fifteen world authorities in combating illiteracy, in furthering primary education in less developed countries and in conducting mass education, prepare summaries of their experiences and observations in these fields as related to Unesco's place in such programmes. A small committee of such experts would then edit this material and propose a programme of action concerning fundamental education by Unesco to the First General Conference. These summaries and proposals would be published in the autumn of 1946 as an essential preliminary step in the on-going programme of Unesco in Fundamental Education.

It should be made clear that the immediate action proposed was not the establishment of a Commission but the enlistment of a group of competent persons who could bring together and edit a body of materials useful to the General Conference or to any Commission in this field which the Conference might decide to establish in the future.

This proposal was listed among the educational tasks of Unesco to be undertaken forthwith. Concerning all these tasks, the Education Committee said, "We believe them to be of educational significance, representative of the broad scope of education, demonstrative of Unesco's relation to other agencies, and affording opportunities for growth in the right direction."

Proposal "A" was adopted at the seventh meeting of the Fifth Session of the Preparatory Commission, on Tuesday, 9th July, 1946.

The Secretariat was thus enjoined to seek the services of a number of persons experienced in the main phases of Fundamental Education; to obtain from them written reports and reactions; to bring these materials together under editorial supervision; and to propose a programme of action for consideration by the First General Conference.

The present document is the result of this effort on the part of the Education Section of the Secretariat and of its collaborators.

Dr. Julian Huxley, Executive Secretary of the Preparatory Commission of Unesco, writing of the problems "which need to be given a place in Unesco's educational programme in the near future," expressed as follows the conception of Fundamental Education which had emerged from the discussions mentioned above:

First, the attack on illiteracy. This demands a high priority in view of our general principle that the lightening of the 'dark zones' of the world must claim a major share of our efforts in all fields. It demands it also, specifically, because literacy is a prerequisite for scientific and technical advance and for . . . better health, more efficient agriculture, and more productive industry; for full intellectual awareness and mental development; for . . . democracy and national progress; and for international awareness and knowledge of other nations.

On reflection, however, it is speedily seen that . . . mere literacy is not enough. It needs to be linked with the general system of education, and, with illiterates above school age, . . . with general social education, notably in relation to health, agriculture, and citizenship. That is why, in Unesco's programme, literacy campaigns have been merged in a more comprehensive study of Fundamental Education.

. . . Literacy is not enough, for by itself it by no means guarantees the benefits mentioned above. . . . Certainly for some people literacy has meant . . . merely . . . new ways of filling time, . . . new forms of escape from reality—in the shape of cheap newspapers and magazines and . . . films—instead of sending them to the stored treasures of art and wisdom or promoting a fuller enjoyment of reality and a deeper understanding of nature and human life.

Nor is literacy . . . necessarily going to lead to democracy, or, if it does so, to a right development of society. Nazi Germany demonstrated all too clearly the way in which one of the most thoroughly literate and highly educated peoples of the world could be led into false ways and undemocratic developments; and in democratic countries the manipulation of the press and the debasement of literature and the cinema is all too possible. . . . Again, knowledge may easily be incomplete and information distorted, and these are among the most potent sources of international ill-will.

Thus, here, we are again brought up against the need for study from the widest possible angle, with all the consequences and implications of the project in view; and the value of an organization which, like Unesco, is by its constitution many-sided and concerned with all the higher activities of man, is once more demonstrated.

The Scope and Purpose of the Present Document

The general setting within which Fundamental Education has been envisaged by the Secretariat and the Preparatory

Commission can best be understood by a careful reading of Chapter II of the Final Program Report, the chapter entitled "Unesco and Education." In this chapter the programme of action to be suggested in the document here presented is numbered 8 in a series of 13 projects. It is among those projects which are conceived as a means of adjusting education to present needs.

To quote in part the statements introducing the project in Fundamental Education:— "The Charter of the United Nations points out that stability and well-being are necessary if peaceful and friendly relations among the nations are to be created. Such conditions imply advances in economic and living standards as well as the universal acceptance and observance of fundamental human rights and freedoms. . . . Where industrial development has not gone far, the most important and urgent issue is felt to be that of providing for the whole population that minimum education which would enable them to make better use of the tools and equipment of a scientific age . . . to promote better standards of life in larger freedom . . . to play their rightful role in the comity of nations. . . . The present educational inequality between nations represents a danger to the peace of the world, which cannot become One if half of it remains illiterate. . . ." Unesco, accordingly, (it is proposed) "should launch upon a world scale an attack upon ignorance, by helping all Member States who desire such help to establish a minimum Fundamental Education for all their citizens."

The purpose of the present document is to suggest ways in which Unesco may proceed with an enterprise so vast yet so urgent, so difficult yet so inspiring, so complex yet so challenging in the breadth of its human appeal.

The persons who took part in the task of preparing the document are named in an Appendix, and the part each of them played is there briefly indicated. Much of the work was done, of necessity, by correspondence and by conferences of individuals or smaller groups; at no time was it feasible to bring the entire group together for prolonged discussion. Fortunately, the object in view had about it no character of finality or completeness, nor could it have. Fundamental education is an on-going process. Unesco is a new agency, preparing to help in fundamental education from a new, a global point of view. Choice was to be made of means—not for doing everything that could possibly be done, but—for "launching," where it might be desired, an "attack." The choice of means was itself to be suggestive only, since it is the General Conference that must take final action as to the programme to be adopted. Fundamental education had to be grasped and presented in its essentials as an actual undertaking in the world of reality; but all the facts about it would not have to be assembled by November, 1946. The major difficulties to be encountered would have to be analyzed; the objectives already announced, and the objectives conceivable for Unesco, would have to be reviewed and classified; but only the history of the world, of education—and of Unesco—could provide the last word on such matters. In this understanding of their task, with humility but not without hope, the group concerned began the work of preparing the present document.

Chapter II gives *instances* of fundamental education which are at least worthy of thoughtful attention. *It makes no pretention to completeness.* Presumably the examples given are sufficiently varied to cover almost all the problems and issues of fundamental education as an effort of nations, associations, and devoted individuals. Chapter III consists of analyses and reflections on these problems and issues. Chapter IV deals with problems of a somewhat more practical kind; that is, with problems of policy and of method. In all three of these chapters articles solicited by the Secretariat have been used, or excerpts from such articles; and memoranda gathered in various ways have also been woven into the text. In general, the facts adduced and the views expressed have been attributed to the persons from whose contributions they were derived; rarely has the Editorial Committee offered comment or judgment of its own. In one respect, however, the Editorial Committee was forced to use its own discretion; for not all the material submitted could be included in these pages, and it therefore became necessary to decide what would best serve the final purpose of the document and be of most use to the General Conference.

The final chapter is the work of the Editorial Committee, as amended and approved by the Secretariat. It is here that a programme of action has been drawn up for consideration by the General Conference.

The hope that has sustained a multitude of eager teachers in many lands, a hope that shines in the life and words of Comenius and Pestalozzi and Horace Mann, a hope that is corrected but not defeated by modern science—this hope has upheld also those who have served in the definition of this programme. The admission of difficulty, of danger, of the stringent need for judgment in the choice of means and policies, cannot obscure the vision of a new possibility—that the yoke of labour may be measurably lifted "from the worn neck of the race" and that education may yet help the great masses of mankind "to rise and look about them and have knowledge ere the grave." Without peace this cannot happen; but unless it happens, peace can have no deep and enduring foundation.

Our ancients said, "People are the foundation of the nation. If the foundation is firm, then the nation will enjoy tranquillity." I apply that to the whole world. If the foundation is firm, then the world will enjoy tranquillity. But three-fourths of the world's people to-day are underhoused, underclothed, underfed, illiterate. . . . Now as long as this continues to be true we have a very poor foundation upon which to build the world.

JAMES YEN
as quoted in *Tell the People*
by PEARL S. BUCK, N.Y.,
The John Day Co., 1945, p. 11.

CHAPTER II

NOTEWORTHY EXAMPLES

The Materials for This Chapter

On the 12th June, 1946, the Secretariat sent to fourteen persons known to be experts of international reputation in fundamental education a request for what was called a Survey Paper. With the request went a Memorandum explaining what the Secretariat had in mind, namely, the preparation of the present document—provided, of course, that the Preparatory Commission should later decide to approve the project. Each of the persons approached was invited to send in his contribution strictly in his individual capacity and in no sense as a representative of his Government.

Emphasizing the possible significance of what was asked, the Secretariat said in its letter, "We know that to compress a lifetime of experience and a mass of knowledge into a brief statement is an onerous and trying task. Our hope is, however, that you will agree with us regarding the value of the work we are attempting to do."

The Secretariat asked for full rights in the manuscript submitted. The Memorandum listed, as suggestions only, a series of questions which had been raised in consultations held up to the date of the request.

In addition to this request for articles, the Secretariat asked at the same time for briefer reports from a number of other experienced persons. *It was quite impossible to obtain first-hand accounts of action in every part of the world.* The intention was to present a picture of Fundamental Education which would be fairly representative of the variety of its cir cumstances and the character of its main problems. The editing was to make the testimony of these workers and their reflections upon their problems into as coherent a statement as the material would, in the time allowed, permit.

Fortunately, the Editorial Committee was able to associate with it, either by correspondence or in person, several scholars and administrative officers of experience. These authorities were able to read the original articles and memoranda and add others of their own or comments on the situations described and the points of view expressed. The present order of presentation emerged from numerous consultations in the Committee and among the collaborators.

It should be noted that some of the articles had to be divided, so that they appear in part in this chapter, in part in later chapters. A very careful effort has been made to ascribe to its proper source and authorship each of the statements quoted or paraphrased. The Editorial Committee trusts that no confusion will arise through this use of the material and that no injustice has been done to any of the contributors. On behalf of the Secretariat, the Editorial Committee expresses its deep gratitude to those who have given time and thought to the preparation of the materials here presented.

The reader will observe that the references to passages quoted (or given in substance without exact quotation) occur as parentheses in the text itself, not in footnotes. Each reference consists of the name of a contributor, the number of his contribution as listed in Appendix B of this volume, and (if necessary) a page number. The page number refers to the official mimeographed copy of the contribution as retained in the files of the Secretariat. Articles here printed in full, or nearly so, are on file in the form in which they now appear.

The Arrangement of the Chapter

The Editorial Committee recognizes the pertinence of a comment by one of its collaborators on the arrangement of materials in this chapter. He says (Kandel, 1) that he would like to see, if possible, a division according to stages of advancement rather than according to geographical location. He notes that the problem in Jamaica differs from that of a segregated group in Africa not because the former is in an American region, the latter in an African region, but because the basis of the attack on the problem would have to be differentiated by the circumstance of segregation in the one case, more fully developed relationships in the other. In an article given in full in the next chapter (Read, 1, p. 8) criteria for distinguishing among areas according to their stages of advancement in literacy are indeed proposed; and other contributors similarly make distinctions among areas on various grounds.

It did not seem feasible, however, to present the materials of this chapter in the more scientific way suggested. The materials at hand were too specifically and closely related to conditions obtaining in specified areas. To take these materials apart and re-group them on the basis of a sociological analysis was a task which could not be undertaken in the time at the disposal of the Editorial Committee. Nor is its inherent difficulty, regardless of time, to be ignored. Judgments as to the advancement of an area cannot be made except on the basis of very full information and after precise definition of the criteria to be used. At this stage, therefore, it seemed best to present the materials of the present chapter geographically.

The Editorial Committee hopes, nevertheless, that the articles contained in Chapter III, and the materials of this volume in general, will be helpful in making such distinctions among areas as may be needed for well-defined *opera-*

tional purposes. The outcome to be desired is action, whether on the part of the peoples concerned, the governments involved, or Unesco—or all of these. It is inevitable that fuller information and analysis will be required and that factual reports and conceptual formulations should be constantly renewed; but some action—action as wise as may be, as fully informed as possible, yet *action*—is the ever-recurrent plea of those who are giving their lives to the actual work of fundamental education in the remoter and needier areas of the world; and their plea should not be gainsaid for the sake of refinements of technique or documentation.

The Purpose of the Chapter; Its Relation to Later Chapters

In Chapter II the intention is to tell the story of some of the typical efforts now afoot in various parts of the world. Some statistics are given to show how many people are involved and to add such other quantitative data as the materials at hand would permit; but the statistics offered must be regarded in general as tentative and subject to correction. Exact knowledge must come through further research, which is in itself a task of considerable magnitude and difficulty. Aside from statistics, the kind and quality of the work now being done should appear with some clarity from the materials in this chapter. It will reveal also the forces at work and the institutions and classes of persons concerned—governments, churches, voluntary agencies, communities. The chapter is meant to be positive in tone, without obscuring problems and difficulties. The basic issues involved in fundamental education are treated more systematically in the articles which form the body of Chapter III, and more technical problems are discussed in the contributions which are presented in Chapter IV. The present chapter is designed, therefore, to serve as far as possible as a background for the later discussions. It is intended to be informative, although there is much further information which could have been helpfully used if it had been available. The reader is asked to note that certain nations and areas of great extent and major political importance could not be represented in this account of fundamental education in action.

I. A GENERAL VIEW

With respect to literacy and illiteracy throughout the world—remembering always that fundamental education is larger than education for literacy alone—it is possible to present a general view in statistical terms that are relatively recent and perhaps as reliable as the nature of the problem, at the present stage of our attack on it, will allow. The statements here given (Laubach, 1, pp. 2, 3, 4) are based partly on a table printed in *Education for Victory* (Vol. 3, No. 22, May 21, 1945), a journal issued during the war by the United States Office of Education. The sources of the table are named in a brief foreword to the table: they go back to 1929 for some data and come down as late as 1944 for others.

It is not easy to determine the illiteracy rate of each country, for each country has a different standard. The State of New York calls a man literate if he writes his name. "A resident of New York State who casts his first vote by war ballot is relieved thereby of the responsibility of furnishing proof of literacy when he later votes as a civilian," reports the *New York Times,* although new civilian voters must present evidence of their ability to read and write English.

Some consider a man literate when he can read a few sentences in print; others require him to read and write letters. This makes a great difference in statistical reports. In Lithuania, for example, the statistics would be twenty-one per cent higher if we included only those who can read, than it would be if we included those who could both read and write, for they have 421,000 persons in their population of 2,000,000 who can read but cannot write.

Even if we decide to include writing in our literacy requirements, our basis for judging is very inexact and will depend upon the temperament and handwriting of the one being examined. Some handwriting would defy the skill of any reader. Dr. Chaturvedi of India proposes that a better test would be to dictate one hundred common words from a basic word list and ask the student to write them.

(1) The statistics indicate that illiteracy approaches the vanishing point in the countries of Northern Europe—Denmark, Norway, Sweden, Finland, the Netherlands, Switzerland and Germany, which have claimed a literacy rate of over ninety-nine per cent. Recruits in the army of the United Kingdom indicated an illiteracy rate of only one per cent. A more recent estimate, however, puts the illiterate *and semi-literate* in the British Army at 20 per cent "of present-day recruits"—September, 1946. On the other hand, the countries of Southern Europe have a high rate of illiteracy—Italy, twenty-seven per cent; Spain, forty-six per cent; Portugal, fifty-four per cent; and Bulgaria, fifty-five per cent. . . .

(2) The United States of America and Canada have about the same literacy rating as England and Northern Europe. The most recent official statistics of the United States of America indicate that three per cent of this country are still illiterate; that is about four million people cannot read or write. However, the American Association for Adult Education disputes these figures, it declares that sixteen million people above the age of ten years are illiterate. This difference is due to the widely different definitions of literacy. The census of the United States of America regards anyone as literate who can write in any language. The American Association for Adult Education contends that an American ought to be literate in English, at least to the standard of a fourth-grade child's literacy. Among American-born whites, illiteracy is only one and one-half per cent, but among American-born Negroes, it is sixteen and three-tenths per cent. Among foreign-born Americans, illiteracy is more than nine per cent. Among the children of these foreigners, illiteracy is low; as low as it is among the children of the native white Americans. The foreigners send their children to school. According to the American Association for Adult Education, at

least fifteen million people in this country never went to school, and fifteen million others can barely read or write. The statistics of Canada indicate that three and seven-tenths per cent are illiterate. The provinces of Quebec, Nova Scotia, and New Brunswick have a much higher rate of illiteracy.

Next to Europe and English-speaking North America, the highest literacy rates are, very surprisingly, in the small islands of the South Pacific, where only one century ago the people were in the main extremely primitive. This is wholly due to the teaching of the missionaries. In Samoa, only four per cent are illiterate; in the Gilbert and Ellis Islands, six per cent; in Hawaii, fifteen per cent; on Guam, twenty-two per cent. New Zealand and Australia, both of which are overwhelmingly white at the present time, are only five per cent illiterate.

(3) Latin-American countries come next, in order of literate countries. Argentina has the highest rate, with its population almost wholly composed of immigrants from Europe. Its official illiteracy rate is thirteen per cent. British Guiana and Chile are each fifty per cent. Brazil seventy per cent; Cuba, fifty-two per cent; Puerto Rico, fifty-five per cent; and Mexico, sixty-two per cent.

Dr. Rycroft's book, *On This Foundation,* perhaps gives the best literacy statistics available for each of the South American countries. When these are weighed by populations of each of the countries, we find that the average literacy rate of South America is still only twenty-nine per cent. We do not have complete available census data for the Indians of Latin America, but statistics of Peru are perhaps fairly representative of all Latin America. The illiteracy rate of Peru in 1940 was forty-two per cent. Where the Indians live, the illiteracy rate is over eighty per cent, and where the Spanish-speaking people live, it is under thirty per cent.

(4) Asia as a whole is eighty to ninety per cent illiterate. This is not true of Japan, which claims an illiteracy rate of less than one per cent. It seems that this "literacy" was not sufficient in many cases to read newspapers. A postwar investigation showed that a knowledge of 400 Japanese words was called "literacy." In 1930, India was ninety-two per cent illiterate; in

1940 eighty-eight per cent were illiterate. The figures for Siam were sixty-nine per cent illiterate in 1935; in the 1941 census, fifty-two per cent were indicated as illiterates. The statistics of the Dutch East Indies show that their population is ninety-five per cent illiterate.

A great campaign has been going on in China. They claim to have reduced their illiteracy rate to eighty per cent. It is impossible to gather accurate statistics, especially under the present chaotic conditions in that country. The other countries of Southern Asia, with the exception of Burma, have a higher rate of illiteracy than does China; Baluchistan, Afghanistan, Iran, Iraq and Arabia have an illiteracy rate of more than ninety per cent. The total illiteracy rate for the continent of Asia probably ranges between eighty and ninety per cent. But in the great population areas of China and India, it is rapidly decreasing at the present time, because of the huge campaigns being conducted in those countries.

(5) Africa has the lowest literacy rate of all the continents. Among the coloured population, it is from two to ten per cent in various countries. In many parts of that great land, literacy campaigns are getting under way, and the next fifty or seventy-five years may show the same marvellous transformation that we saw in the Pacific Islands during the nineteenth century. Nearly every one of these campaigns has been started by missionaries, who are now teaching illiterates in more than a hundred different languages. Egypt has an illiteracy rate of ninety per cent; the Bantus of South Africa, eighty-eight per cent. For the rest of the continent, no census is available. In many sections the illiteracy rate may well reach ninety-nine per cent.

II. THE AMERICAS

Documents are available on the problems of fundamental education in several American countries but in too few to give any comprehensive picture of the situation in the American hemisphere as a whole. The general view of illiteracy given above makes it obvious that no American country is without serious problems in this field. Students of comparative education are aware, for example, of the extensive and growing literature on the education of Negroes in the Southern section of the United States. Myrdal's *An American Dilemma*, which is a landmark in the immense effort that has been made by American Foundations toward sympathetic understanding and wise action on the Negro problem, is in effect largely a study of Fundamental Education. Out of the material submitted for our present purpose we can present only a few extracts on the circumstances in the central portion of the two American continents.

Incomplete though it is, this account has a special significance. The countries concerned are, with one exception, Republics of relatively recent origin, and their efforts present a picture of what independent peoples, aided by awakened governments and by good neighbours, can do to advance their lives through fundamental education.

COLOMBIA (Caballero 1, pp. 7-14). Describing the educational work carried out by the Colombian Ministry of Education "during the last few years," this contribution reports:

We organised and succeeded in carrying out a series of study visits to all parts of the country. Wherever we arrived, we gathered together all the teachers in the public schools. Before the end of one year we had been in direct contact with 8,000 school teachers, out of the 10,000 in Colombia. We talked to them, we heard their complaints, we discussed in small groups the different school problems. We then visited them in their schools. We met the children of all regions. School teachers and children of the more distant parts of the country felt, many of them for the first time, that the forgotten corner where they lived was also a part of the national consciousness. They felt that the central government was coming out to them to listen to their problems, to help them, to give them the kindness and understanding they had lacked till then.

On the return from each of these visits the Ministry would

put into practice some of the proposals that were considered most urgent: the fundamental reform of syllabuses for elementary and secondary education; the establishment of close contact with health authorities; the creation within the Ministry of the Bureau of School Architecture, to prepare and distribute plans for buildings of different types, according to climatic conditions and the resources at the disposal of local authorities; the establishment, as centres for cultural diffusion, of a pedagogical museum and library at the Ministry, and of similar institutions at all provincial capitals; the setting up of children's libraries and the presentation to all teachers of a small collection of textbooks on all subjects.

Teachers' Training. It was most important to train a new type of school teacher who would bring to the school the "modern tendency" that we preached in our visits. The comprehensive view of the country that we had obtained made us realise the urgency of giving each school a deep social significance. All plans had to start with the health of the children. It was threatened by various factors; deficient nutrition, total absence or a low standard of personal hygiene, endemic diseases caused by ignorance or carelessness on the part of the family or local authorities. To face this terrifying situation it was necessary to make of each teacher a social worker; a sentry who would sound the alarm to public organisations wherever these conditions were found and interest the whole community in the problem. It was also urgent to give him an esthetic conception of his school —cleanliness and good taste in conditions of simplicity, or even poverty—a happy atmosphere and at the same time the discreet control of an active teaching influence, which might be described as the teaching of common sense, without pedagogical terminology, closely bound to interests and realities related to the age of the child and local conditions.

It was necessary to help them with books, maps and charts, etc., drawing materials, lectures, educational campaigns by means of radio and cinema. It was on an extensive programme of this nature that we focussed our activities.

In order to achieve our purpose more effectively, we directed our attention to two objects: one, the immediate problem of improving the quality of present school teachers, the other, the long-term problem of providing the teachers of the future. To attain our first object we decided to bring to the capital without delay the best school teachers from different parts of the country and give them one year of intensive training in the general principles of our new proposals, taking advantage at the same time of the long personal contact afforded by their stay in the city to improve our knowledge of the necessities and realities of the Colombian School. We organised training courses for teachers of both sexes, from which were sent out the best elements that help us to-day in different parts of the country. As a continuation of this we organised vacation courses of one or two months that took place in the main centres and as a result pedagogical assemblies were organised and committees of school teachers and parents were set up.

The long-term activities could only be achieved through the setting up of a new type of Teachers' Training College. This resulted in the creation of the National Teachers' Training Colleges.

The rural Training Colleges for schoolmistresses have been highly successful. The schoolmistresses in charge of these colleges fully understood the deep social significance of these institutions and the aims of the Ministry. We urgently needed rural schoolmistresses, with not so much book-learning as close contact with their environment and interest, above all, in the health and moral character of their children. They had to be interested in agriculture, in domestic and school tasks. They had to have understanding of children, and to be able to exert an influence on the grown-ups, who in our villages and countryside so often lack the most elementary training. We required schoolmistresses ready to carry on their tasks in the most remote corners of the country, and we believe now that the many hundreds of young girls being trained in our rural colleges may soon be the admirable teachers of the near future. Their practical training has taught them how to be good housewives as well as schoolmistresses, how to make their own dresses and clothes for others, how to prepare a meal, how to nurse the sick, to advise mothers and children, and they are now ready to carry out a great programme, to bring all this to the country villages from which they came.

The Spirit of the New Programmes. The programmes for primary education were tried out for two years and have now been approved as final. They are based on the conditions and environment of the countryside and of each school, and are suited therefore to all the districts of Colombia. The first subject of study is the life at home and at school. The second year is devoted to the study of the life of the community (the street, the village, and the town). The third year covers the municipality and the district. The fourth, the country as a whole. The fifth and sixth years are devoted to vocational training. Throughout this programme the school endeavours to develop ethical and hygienic tendencies as well as social solidarity.

In the secondary school, a broad basis of general culture is given to the pupils, avoiding all premature specialisation, but stressing the importance of the four great branches of learning: mathematics, natural sciences, language, and social studies (geography, history, civics and philosophy).

A great importance is also given to physical and moral education, to drawing, handicrafts, music and singing, all of which are studied throughout the whole school life.

Will this new type of school be able by itself to transform the moral and spiritual structure of our collectivity? Schools, as they are usually understood, are not so far reaching. The family and social environment determine as a rule the ways of children, more than the school itself. But the school that we aim at having will tend to embrace the life of the home and the whole community. It is a school with a definite social tendency and its action will not be confined to the four walls of the school.

At the same time, we conceived school reform as a joint social activity in which everybody should participate, all the Ministries, all private and public organisations, and the citizens as a whole. In fact it is not possible to think that any official or private body or any thinking citizen could view the question of education with indifference. We must all take an interest in this great task, whether moved by a generous impulse of public spirit or by an instinct of self-preservation.

That is why we realised that we would never obtain full results in school reform unless all citizens felt concerned in it. That is why, while we were working on concrete improvements, it was such a joy for us to travel throughout the country on our propaganda missions. Wherever we arrived, we used to call together, not only school teachers and parents, but also the public officials, and explain to them in talks, animated by a sincere conviction, the meaning of the activities we were carrying out.

Municipal and district councils were requested to give preference to public health and education in their budgets. We mentioned public health first because with disease and hunger the school is not possible. We insisted on good school inspection, but we insisted still more on school medical inspections. We insisted from the beginning on the punctual payment of the teachers and increases in salary, and now and again we insisted on preference being given to primary education, as it was not right to provide for secondary schools and scholarships when the fundamental elementary education was not available for all those who required it.

We told parents how important it was that they should be in touch with the school and all its activities. We asked them to study for themselves the items of the local budgets earmarked for education, and to intervene every time there was a danger of these items being treated as a dead letter. They had the right to insist on their children's getting not only the instruction provided in the past, but the wide social and technical education required for the present. We in the government now make the same demands that we used to make from outside it, as it is not a question of calling good what we had previously classified as bad, but of awakening the public conscience, and for this purpose it makes no difference whether one is a public official or a private citizen.

It would not be true to say that all the schools of the country are now filled with the new spirit in education, but no one now takes a pride in remaining aloof from the progressive forces in education. Even those who may at heart favour a system contrary to freedom, to liberty within order, and wish to see pedagogical systems of a dogmatic and inflexible character, will hide these tendencies. What we can say is that the new school is no longer uncertain of itself.

If much has been achieved, still more remains to be done.

Elementary education is now free and compulsory. In five years the education budgets have increased by 500%. Travelling schools circulate all over the country. School boards, radio, cinema and official publications are contributing to the ambitious programme of popular education. In spite of this, the number of illiterates is still extremely high. It is estimated at not less than 45% of the population. The Government has therefore a long way to go to reach its objective.

Budget. Following our system of administration, the budget for elementary education is divided into three parts. The State pays for the 16 National Teachers' Training Colleges, and their subsidiaries, and gives the necessary material to the 12,000 public schools of the whole country; the 14 departments (provinces) pay the school teachers in their areas, and each one of the 800 municipalities has to pay for the school buildings. In theory there should be no objection to this system. In practice there are many municipalities that cannot afford to build or keep their own schools, and there are several departments that do not include in their budgets the sums required to increase each year the number of school teachers in their districts. At the same time, we have national, departmental, and municipal school inspectors, a fact that often causes friction and introduces disorder in the schools.

This consideration, as well as others, has made most ministers ask for a radical change in the administrative system for the creation of a more centralised budgetary system and a more efficient educational organisation. In the meantime, the national government and the departments are approving considerable sums for the building of schools, helping school restaurants, the services of which are completely free, helping the state secondary schools, and giving grants to many private schools.

The Education Budget is to-day over 24 million pesos, of which 8 million come from the national treasury, 12 million from the departments, and over 4 million from the municipalities. The whole country is devoted to a vast cultural campaign.

Educational films, popular concerts, open-air theatres, art exhibitions, book fairs, popular scientific lectures have developed considerably in the last few years.

The national radio, well equipped and directed, is carrying out a series of programmes to inform the people of the activities of each one of the ministries, and devotes considerable time to good music, plays and literature. It is an excellent weapon for the advancement of civics, science and art.

Agricultural Education. In the last few years the Government has given preference to agricultural and industrial education. We created the National Council of Agricultural Education, composed of the Ministers of Education, National Economy, the manager of the Bank of Agrarian, Industrial and Mining Credit, the presidents of the Federation of Coffee Planters, and the Farmers' Association, and three members nominated by the Government.

One of the first steps taken by this National Council was to address itself to all the local legislatures of the country, requesting them to pass legislation enabling the provinces to co-operate with the national government in the immediate establishment of vocational and agricultural schools. A new section of the Ministry was created recently for this purpose. The Minister brought from Puerto Rico an expert to train teachers in agricultural education.

Industrial Education. In 1936 this was given a new impulse. A Chilean expert directed it into new paths, and in 1939 a special section was created for him in the Ministry. A general conference of directors of industrial and vocational schools met at the end of last year and resulted in the new programmes that are now being carried out.

It is of interest to note that this type of conference has always been called whenever a change of plan or of policy was to be decided upon. When the Minister considered that it was necessary to change syllabuses, he called for an assembly of heads of training colleges, and later, one of heads of secondary schools.

The Minister has also created two Technical Councils: one for elementary and one for secondary education. The latter is advised by delegates from private schools and the national university. The director of the central Teachers' Training College is also a member of this important body, which directs the training of teachers in secondary schools and training colleges, in natural science, social science, mathematics, and languages.

The Ministry has created a new department, that of Commercial Training, to direct the 600 establishments that provide this kind of training in Colombia.

The article closes with an interesting account of the new National University of Colombia and its "University City."

A further report (Laubach 2, pp. 1, 2) from an American Protestant missionary lists as obstacles to the programme of Fundamental Education in Colombia the lack of governmental funds—resulting in lack of schools in many areas, lack of equipment, and low pay for teachers; next the failure of many teachers to develop a spirit of unselfish service; and finally the absence of incentive to learn on the part of illiterates. The remedies proposed are the stimulation of religious faith, governmental publicity and legal compulsion (as in Mexico), and practical projects which will make clear the value of literacy. "When the men realise that in order to learn better farming methods they must know how to read, they will have an incentive to study."

ECUADOR (Laubach 3, pp. 1-3). The report in this case is from the campaign director of a mission-sponsored, nationwide effort for literacy.

Guayaquil: One of the first steps was having the newspapers co-operate in printing coupons to be filled out by persons who knew of illiterates so that literary workers could call on the illiterates and register them in classes. 140 of those coupons were turned in. Then it was arranged for the *Union de Artistas y Escritores* (Artists' and Writers' Union) to organise a Literacy Committee. It was felt that it would be better not to start with a church-sponsored committee, so neither the Protestant nor the

Roman Catholic church was an official organiser of the Committee. The *Union de Artistas y Escritores* called in other organised groups to get behind the movement, such as students of pedagogy, Normal Schools, Labour Unions, the Office of the Co-ordinator of Inter-American Affairs, Washington, D.C., and others. Then, when they were sufficiently interested to carry on, the *Union de Artistas y Escritores* let them continue alone. Laubach charts were printed by Reed and Reed with a note at the bottom of each stating that they were being printed *free*. When they were ready, Alan Reed called on one of his most important competitors and told him what they were doing and asked if he wouldn't be interested in helping. He agreed to print posters if they could find good designs. A contest sponsored by the *Union de Artistas y Escritores* was held and the best posters submitted were printed; the most famous one is the green and black one which says, "Make a great and powerful nation by teaching people how to read." The Literacy group was called *LEA* (which means "read" *L*iga para la *E*nsenanza de *A*nalfabetos). Another group then printed half a million stamps (2 cts each) which were put on letters sent out by the Electricity Company and other groups; they helped keep literacy before the public.

In the first five months after Dr. Laubach's visit, there was very little action because the government had to examine the system, submit it to teachers, and wait for reactions to experiments. Therefore, we asked government officials if they would mind if a small group went ahead with literacy on their own account, since they would not have as much prestige at stake if the method did not prove a tremendous success. The government agreed to this.

A census was taken to find out the number and location of illiterates, a carnet was given to official workers in the campaign, municipalities printed handbills advertising the benefits for literates, such as "One illiterate less is one citizen more." 25,000 were sent out in cracker boxes to the remotest parts of the country. Another 25,000 were packed in with soap cakes, so that in every section people began to be aware of the need for a literate nation.

Quito: The campaign in Quito was started through the *Union Nacional de Periodistas* (journalists) and it has been very successful. Their charts were printed in the newspapers and a great deal of space was given to articles on the progress of campaigns, etc. They gave new literates a diploma of citizenship, signed by the Minister of Government and a certificate was given to people who had taught one or two illiterates to read. After a three months' period a ceremony was held with municipal officials present, in which these documents were given out.

The *Union Nacional* claims to have taught about 60,000 people to read in two years; that is probably an exaggeration, but gives an idea of the work being done. One man, Arturo Celi, has taught 100 people to read.

The government decreed that about one-half million sucres a year would be given to literacy work; 180,000 went to Guayaquil and 380,000 to Quito. Another decree was that citizens between 18 and 50 would have to prove that they had taught some one to read during the year or pay a teacher to do so.

Last week they held "Alphabet Week" during which newspapers ran articles devoted to literacy; every day was set aside for some special phase of literacy. A poster contest was conducted, and part of the proceeds of a movie theatre during one day were given to literacy.

There are some people who are opposed to literacy campaigns. For instance, a man at the Rotary Club said once that if we taught these people to read, they would try to get more wages and stir up a great deal of trouble. The answer was that they at least would not use shyster lawyers to plead for them, but could understand for themselves what was going on.

Now, our great problem is the transitional stage. The people are learning to read and they must be given material to read so that they don't forget what they have learned.

One answer to that would be to have the newspapers print one quarter of a page of the daily newspaper especially for new literates. Headlines just like those on the front page could be used, and there could be three emphases made in very simple Spanish: International news, national news, and local news.

Also articles could be run on agriculture, health, nutrition, or even Aesop's fables. Mats could be set up by someone trained to write this type of material. This would be a full-time worker.

GUATEMALA (Laubach 4, pp. 1, 2). A brief report from a missionary director of literacy campaigns contains the following items:

Among the chief causes of illiteracy are listed (1) lack of church emphasis on the importance of the Bible; (2) a one-crop (coffee) economy which requires only illiterate labour; (3) a feudal peonage system; (4) Indian masses (Quinchés, 500,000; Cakchiqueles, 400,000; Mams, 330,000) which create a language-literature problem. Among incentives to literacy are listed (1) preaching on the authoritative character of the Bible; (2) government stimulation of industries requiring literacy; (3) government use of barracks, prisons, and hospitals as centres of literacy campaigns. Patriotism as a sustaining motive is said to have failed in the first governmental campaign in the capital city; merit points toward promotion for teachers who do overtime work is recommended. New readers are forming clubs to subscribe to newspapers, which reduces the price to each subscriber. Literature in various Indian languages is being produced by missionary effort. A governmental "normal-word" method has been found to be slow; a modified Laubach method rapid. Primers in the latter are available in Spanish and in five Indian languages. Audio-visual aids are used: town court-houses have radios with loudspeakers for town squares; posters invite to Lay Conferences; educational films from the Co-ordinator's Office are appreciated by rural audiences.

HAITI (Gabriel 1, pp. 1-4). In this island Republic conditions in the rural schools (first established in 1875 under a Bureau of Public Instruction) had gradually become deplorable. "There were no school-houses really adapted to the purpose; there was little equipment or none; no books, paper, ink; teachers' salaries on the average were $5.41 a month." Then a revolution occurred. A brief review brings the story of this change, in bare outline, down to 1946.

At the dawn of her independence, proclaimed in 1804, Haiti was concerned to make provision for the education of an intellectual "élite" and created lyceums and colleges, from which were to be drawn the teachers, government officials and employees who would assure the functioning of public services and guarantee the future of the young nation.

Later on, the Constitution of 1843, revolutionary and democratic in its origin, made provision for the creation of primary schools, urban and rural. But more than a quarter of a century elapsed before the setting up of the first real rural schools. These schools had the same syllabus and the same objectives as the urban schools. Their ultimate aim was to produce secondary-school graduates and also to show to the world that the Negro was able to reach the highest degree of culture. These schools functioned on that basis up to 1932, without having changed in any notable degree the living conditions and the mentality of the Haitian peasant.

In 1924, during the American occupation of Haiti—an unfortunate political event, offensive to Haitian pride—some farm-schools were created. As is implied in their name, these schools were intended to promote agriculture and to renovate the rural districts by imparting a functional education with an agricultural bias to the young Haitian peasants. Seventy school-houses in concrete, providing one or two classrooms, were built. A well-aired workshop was annexed to each school. A tract of land of a size varying from one to ten acres was attached to each school and thus made it possible for the pupils to put into practice the theoretical lessons on agriculture given in the classroom and to experiment with new crops. In the workshop wood-work and metal-work were executed; the pupils could thus repair farm tools, build a fence or a poultry-house, construct home furniture, repair a door or a window, build sheds. The morning was devoted to academic instruction and the afternoon to farm work and workshop activities.

These farm-schools were strongly opposed by the politicians because of their practical curriculum and their American origin. They succeeded, however, in implanting themselves in the Haitian rural community, thanks to their usefulness and their efficiency. It is fair to say that their success is mainly due to the ability and devotion of the teachers trained at the Central School of Agriculture, also an American creation.

In 1932, the nationalistic government of President Vincent decided to pass over to the department of Farm-Schools, renamed at that time the Division of Rural Education of the National Service of Agricultural Production, all the existing rural schools, which up to that date had been controlled by the Ministry of Public Instruction. The budget of these schools, the majority of which were functioning somewhat irregularly, was transferred from the Ministry of Public Instruction to that of Agriculture. They were closed to allow reorganisation; a new teaching staff was recruited and trained; school-houses were built or improved or repaired; the curriculum became similar to that of the farm-schools.

Now there are in Haiti approximately one hundred farm-schools and more than three hundred rural schools with an enrolment of thirty-five thousand pupils and a staff of six hundred teachers.

These schools give an elementary education spread over a period of six years. Furthermore, the pupils undertake practical work in agriculture, including the following items: methods of sowing, cutting, storing, grafting; cultivation of the main crops of the country and of certain foreign plants; raising of chickens, goats, pigs, and even cattle in some regions. The manual arts curriculum includes basketry, weaving, clay modelling, woodwork, tin work and blacksmithing. Besides these crafts, the girls do sewing, cooking, laundry, home management, and child care.

The school-children undertake, as well, activities aiming at the moral, social, and material improvement of their community. They group themselves in clubs called 4C for the education of the "Cœur" (Heart), the "Cerveau" (Head or Brain), the "Corps" (Health of the Body) and for the improvement of the "Community"; they also join the Boy Scouts, the young farmers' clubs and the co-operative societies. Parents' organisations and adult associations are co-operating with the school in its educative work.

At this point we present a brief statement (Charton 1, pp. 1, 2) on a situation in America which is not that of an independent Republic but of a French Colony. The contrast in policy is of interest; but the problem is fundamentally the same.

THE FRENCH WEST INDIES. The French West Indies, Martinique and Guadeloupe, have been linked with France since the seventeenth century, since the era of the Islands, since "Old France." Ancient countries of slavery, liberated by the crusade launched by the men of 1848, the West Indies were the scene of a colonial experiment made on the political as well as the intellectual plane, which is now at its final stage.

The educational and cultural problem appeared there in extremely simple forms, which did not give rise to any real debates about the nature and the substance of the question. After 1848, the French West Indies became without any reservation a part of the home country. Assimilated politically, the inhabitants of Guadeloupe and Martinique, white, creole, and coloured, enjoy the same civil and political rights, without any distinction as to origin and race. The establishment and the extension of the French primary school constitute one of the elements and one of the consequences of this political assimilation. The West Indians want to be French citizens. French civilisation and culture, propagated by the Catholic religion, the school, and the practise of political rights, have become for them a state of nature, a political and sociological reality.

For there is no conflict of cultures. When the French took over the French West Indies in the beginning of the seventeenth century, what was the composition of the population? Some surviving Caribs; a powerful African element; French planters, land-owners and "bourgeois" who founded families and gave birth to the creole elements of the country; coloured men, mulattoes of different shades, particularly numerous in Martinique and much less numerous in Guadeloupe; and out of this mixture there came an expansion which created a very high density of population and even a problem of over-population. All those inhabitants of the country are linked together by the French influence and the French language, which may have the characteristics of a dialect or of a "patois" in its popular form but is not faced by any competing language. The West Indies speak French, even when it is a French patois.

Consequently, the problem of primary education is a matter of extension of popular education and of adaptation of education to the needs of the country. The population of the islands is essentially rural; but it is primarily concentrated in big boroughs and composed of agricultural workers. Insufficient means of communication in a mountainous country, poverty and over-population are the main features of this country. For a long time, the education of the people was neglected, the villages kept isolated; consequently, the percentage of illiteracy is enormous.

However, since the Third Republic, France has been carrying out in the West Indies the same policy in primary education as in the home country. Special difficulties were met, results did not always correspond to our effort; it appeared to be necessary also to direct the primary school system more towards meeting the needs of the country and fitting into its economy. The West Indies are tropical countries, and they must look towards neighbouring islands having the same social and economic structure for closer relations, which are beginning to be established.

Primary education has been very greatly developed. Guadeloupe, with a population of 304,000 inhabitants, had a school population of 26,612 in 1944, that is to say, if we admit a ratio of school population of one-tenth, the school attendance is 89%. In Martinique, with a more diversified population estimated at 260,000, the primary school population is 27,800. It seems that this figure covers approximately the entire school population for a minimum school requirement.

Here is an experiment in colonization, which has nearly run

its course. The extension of French primary education, truly popular, to the whole population of a country, is a decisive fact in the West Indies. To a certain extent, it is to consolidate this situation, this incorporation into France by political right and through the school, that the First French Constituency, at the request of their representatives, decided that Martinique and Guadeloupe were from now on, like Reunion and French Guiana, territorial departments of Overseas France.

HONDURAS. A brief report from a mission source reads as follows (Laubach 5, pp. 1, 2):

Schools of this mountainous Republic with a few exceptions are still using the traditional system. Generally, buildings are inadequate, often one room; benches without tables are used; there is a lack of materials and teachers' helps. Teachers find life hard in the villages, which lack modern conveniences. Thus, good teachers obtain city positions.

The present Minister of Education is progressive. He is attempting to revolutionise the entire system. Periodical visits to larger centres for conferences with teachers, new school programmes, changes in laws regarding public education, a rural normal school recently opened, a national campaign against illiteracy, are on his programme.

The government programme on literacy in 1945 benefited 30,000 who received certificates of recognition for work completed. In many sections it failed, due to lack of co-operation. All teachers of primary schools, and pupils of fifth grade, are listed in regulations as teachers of a determined number in the campaign. Rotarians are distributing Reader's Digest pamphlets of Dr. Laubach's method but volunteers are lacking as teachers.

Reading materials for new readers are most urgently needed. The government has not provided for this. Villages and hamlets do not receive daily newspapers. Town libraries are few, non-existent in villages. Travelling libraries would involve personnel and means of transportation, in many cases by mule. Village schools could be used as reading rooms under the direction of teachers. Wider use of film slides should be made with projectors not requiring electricity. Outdoor movie programmes with portable outfits to move into given areas were most effective during the war. Effective use of silent movies could be made and would stimulate a desire to read by use of clear titles.

Athletic clubs exist and could be fitted into the general campaign. Other club work, except for Lions and Rotarians, is non-existent. Civic clubs should be organised with an agricultural and educational approach.

Latin-American programmes over a town-owned public-square radio are most effective. Greater use could be made of this method if radios could be more generally provided.

MEXICO. In this country, with an area of 2 million square kilometres, a population of 17 million people, a varied climate, and a fascinating history, the background of educational development would include the story (as in some of the American countries to the South, notably Peru) of ancient civilizations, as well as the story of the devoted efforts of Spanish priests. The more recent and more highly organized efforts toward popular enlightenment go back only to 1910, nearly a hundred years after the declaration of Mexican independence in 1821. This story is outlined in the following excerpt (Gabriel 2, pp. 5-9):

The obstacles to popular education during the first decades of Mexican Independence were numerous and insuperable. Conflicts between church and state, unfortunate selections of federal and state government officials, the loss of Texas, the war with the United States of America, all absorbed the energies and resources of the young nation. Until the Revolution of 1910, there was no concerted effort, no major action, towards the improvement of the living conditions of the great bulk of the people.

Benito Juarez sought to uplift the social and political thought of Mexico. His term of office was interrupted by the French invasion and the three years of Emperor Maximilian's rule. His short government constituted, however, one of the most beauti-

ful pages of Mexican history, which has been too often characterised by corruption and a complete indifference towards the
welfare of the masses. The death of President Juarez in 1872
ended the political career of a democrat with a broad spirit and
great ideals. After Juarez and, as a reaction against the good
undertakings of his government, General Porfirio Diaz, having
been elected President, exercised a dictatorial and autocratic
power during a period of 35 years. Progress was made in the
economic and financial sphere; but nothing was done for the
spiritual and material welfare of the rural masses. In 1894,
there were nineteen schools of Law, nine schools of Medicine,
eight schools of Engineering, twenty-six Theological Seminaries,
one school of Mining, eighty-one Lyceums, four schools of Fine
Arts, four schools of Music, several schools of Arts and Crafts,
many primary Normal Schools and a great number of urban
primary schools. This list of schools is sufficient to show that
the educational system was inadequate and did not attempt to
meet the real needs of a population which, at that time,
amounted approximately to twelve million inhabitants, the majority of whom were living in the rural districts, where no schools
were to be found.

In the State urban schools, instruction and acquisition of
knowledge were considered as ends in themselves, and no effort
was made to relate knowledge to the living conditions of the
school children or the urgent needs of the nation. Education
was very formal and the children left school with an artificial
culture which did not help them to improve the social and
economic conditions of the country. We should mention, however, the successful educational attempts made by a Swiss, En-
rique C. Rebsamen, who, shortly before 1890, established fairly
advanced experimental schools in the State of Vera Cruz.

Up to 1910, living conditions of the masses had not changed.
Cruelties which characterised the colonial times still persisted.
The Indians were kept in slavery, and no measure was taken to
satisfy their thirst for spiritual freedom and their great desire
to possess a tract of land.

Civil wars from 1910 to 1920 prevented the putting into effect
of social and educational reforms advocated by revolutionary

governments. Education still remained in a state of stagnation. Rural schools were virtually non-existent.

In the cities, the schools imparted a formal education to a limited number of children belonging to the middle and upper classes of society. The Revolution had not yet influenced, in any notable degree, the cultural agencies of the country. However, a Federal Bureau of Education was created in 1910; but this office could not accomplish much because it was in constant conflict with the inalienable rights of the States and the jealous autonomy of the communes. It was, therefore, subordinated to these political influences.

We had to wait until President Obregon came into power to see an end to this tragic state of affairs. He created the Ministry of National Education and appointed Jose Vasconcelos as Secretary of State. The latter was full of enthusiasm; he wanted to build an educational system which would embrace all cultural aspects of the country and which at the same time would meet the pressing needs of the masses. To carry out such a plan, he had no trained staff at his disposal. He had the brilliant idea of sending educational missionaries to the neglected and forgotten part of Mexico, that is, rural Mexico. The missionaries had to train inexperienced teachers and to help them in solving problems met during the application of the scheme of the Federal Bureau. First they undertook the task of surveying rural conditions and the needs of the Mexican masses. Their enquiry included the following items: educational conditions of the locality, necessity of a campaign against illiteracy, type of education to be worked out, economic conditions, crops, local industries, means of communication, current wages, languages spoken by the Indians, possibility of finding teachers in the locality.

The next excerpt (Torres 1, pp. 7-10) gives the personal experience of a member of the cultural mission constituted in 1926 by the Ministry of Public Education and Fine Arts.

In many respects the year 1926 was a favourable one for a rural education designed to help develop remote communities. Together with Prof. Moisés Sáenz, a group of three of us planned the organisation of the first six groups inaugurated officially by the Ministry of Education. All three of us had studied at Teachers College, Columbia University. We each had our own specialty but we also had a common background of the same school, the same studies and much experience in the same type of work in Mexico. We called to our aid many professional people, such as physicians, lawyers, agricultural experts, etc., and we even invited the painter, Diego Rivera.

We were inspired in this work by the optimism of those who had dreamed of establishing a system of education which would give a fair opportunity to each man to make for himself a normal and peaceful life. We were moved with the desire to give our fellow man the chance to enjoy the fruits of his labour, to contribute to the welfare of his community, and to take advantage of education to the extent of his capabilities.

The first six missions in Rural Education were dependent on the Ministry of Public Education and were not granted government funds. The necessary money was collected from unused funds originally intended for projects of the same Ministry. which had not been carried out. These circumstances, though unfavourable in the case of Mexico, did permit recruiting of personnel which was not subject to political influences of any sort.

Before personnel was employed, an analysis was made of the qualities desired in those people who were to lead the groups, as well as the lower-ranking personnel. The directors of the missions, without exception, were people of considerable training. The social workers were five graduate nurses, one professional social worker, and an American lady who joined our work with genuine missionary zeal. Each of the agricultural assistants, who came to us on the recommendation of agricultural experts, was well versed in the agriculture of the region where he was to teach. Teachers of physical training were selected in accordance with recommendations from the Secretary-General of the Y.M.C.A., all of them being young men under 25 years of age, well trained in sports, hygiene, first aid and scout work, and with a wholesome moral and spiritual outlook. Once our personnel was selected, we held meetings with the professional people who were to assist us, particularly in the training of the 24 persons responsible for the rural programme. At the same time, we selected an auxiliary group made up of people who did fruit and vegetable canning, curing of hams and meats, carpentry and plumbing, and who would be able to travel to each community as needed and requested by the people of the Missions.

The meetings of the organisers and professional people set as their object the establishment of uniformity of teaching and the attainment, as far as possible, of a degree of civic training for the people.

Agronomists and doctors were never in accord, but agreed to settle the differences among themselves rather than to carry on debates in the meeting itself.

The programme was a simple one: (1) improvement of conditions for rural school teachers; (2) improvement of agriculture through teaching of basic facts such as proper selection of seeds, methods of pruning and grafting of fruit trees, laying out gardens, modernisation of farm methods in plowing, fertilisation and rotation of crops; (3) preventing and combating contagious diseases and regional diseases, purification and proper care of water systems, springs, wells, etc.; (4) improvement of living conditions, household methods and infant care; (5) food canning and preserving, curing of furs and skins, construction of simple furniture, carpentry methods for houses and barns, whitewashing of walls, and general useful instruction in manual methods for conservation and repair of the house and farm buildings; (6) organisation of games and collection of regional games, dances, and music, with the end in view of encouraging their development.

Each mission held a six weeks' in-training course for its teacher-teams. Sixty teachers were divided into four groups, each of which was to receive the same training, passing successively through the courses given by the professional people charged with the induction. In this way considerable individual instruction was possible and students were able, because of the small classes, to discuss their problems and views in the classroom.

The original idea called for a four-year plan with yearly

refresher courses of six weeks of intensive study. At the end of each session each teacher received six books which he was to study during the course of the year until the subsequent course was undertaken.

The work in the small communities was rich in material content though informal in presentation. The method of instruction was pleasant and interesting. The student teachers came to acquire the position of companions to the professors instructing rural teachers, and in this manner the entire community worked voluntarily in groups according to their interests. The work was richly rewarded. Encouraged by the fine example of the mission workers, many people who were particularly adept in one craft volunteered to teach their fellow villagers. More and more rural schools were built and, as a result of improved teaching conditions, began to attract a higher type of applicant for teaching positions. Villagers and landowners began to offer assistance and co-operation to the mission and to the teachers.

The medical profession began to realise the importance and potentialities of this work, and supported the organisation of a Department of Rural Public Health, the rural divisions of which have, to date, gone forward with gratifying speed and efficiency. The Government itself, in an effort to secure the confidence of these people, established the *Banco de Credito Ejidal,* a farmers' land credit bank. The Ministry of Agriculture established in turn six rural agricultural institutes. Rural normal schools established well-defined programmes.

There were organised several Indian study centres with programmes particularly in the manual arts—carpentry, farming, animal husbandry. Young men and women from these classes progressed to the point where they could learn Spanish and from there went on to learn reading and writing.

All this work in rural education and rehabilitation continued, without great difficulties, until 1934.

A more recent governmental effort of national scope to combat illiteracy has sought to enlist the entire population of the country, from the President to the humblest person who has learned to read and who can teach at least one other person to do so.

These accounts of educational work in American countries are obviously scattered and incomplete. Vast regions—e.g., Brazil, Argentina—are not represented. Again the reader is asked to remember that this chapter can provide only samples of fundamental education in action. The cumulative effect of such direct reports as are available may lead, however, to general impressions of the work to be done, and of its difficulties, which will have substantial truth and value.

Even here in these first instances some of the larger problems of fundamental education declare themselves. It is not just the command of reading and writing that is to be sought; it is the command of living. And it is in the home, the fields, the local crafts, the local arts, the local political community, that the start must be made. Content counts heavily, as well as means and methods. Books, newspapers, pamphlets, the radio, films, and personal contacts are required, in addition to classes; and the message all these are to convey is of more importance than their mere operation. All available agencies that may and will co-operate can be included—governments, religious bodies, associations, individuals; and if the beginnings are to be found in immediate local realities, the outcomes to be sought lie both in the improvement of family and community conditions and in the widening of horizons toward new attachments, national and global.

III. AFRICA

Moving directly east from any of the American areas we have here considered, we should find ourselves in Africa. Problems of Fundamental Education in that great continent are presented in detail for two areas which show marked contrasts and also some similarities; these are French Africa

(French West Africa and French Equatorial Africa) and the Union of South Africa.

Our contribution on the first of these concerns itself, in its earlier pages, with French policy in all the colonies of the Republic. Our contribution on the Union of South Africa is confined to the situation in that one member of the British Commonwealth of Nations. At the risk of seeming to go into too much detail with respect to special and selected situations, we have ventured to present the articles concerning these two areas at considerable length. These articles show very precisely the complexity of the problems to be faced, basic differences of authority, and differences of policy; yet the problems involved are in some respects the same. The treatment of Fundamental Education in other continents may be somewhat abbreviated by reference back to these two African examples and to the American examples presented above.

As in the case of the Americas, we regret that we can give no accounts of fundamental education in action in several important areas of the African continent, especially the Belgian Congo and British territories other than the Union of South Africa.

Our French contributor (Charton 2, pp. 1-15), writes as follows:

FRENCH OVERSEAS TERRITORIES. In all the overseas countries which France has undertaken to develop and civilize, she has had, from the beginning, to face problems not only of primary teaching as a preliminary to secondary and higher education, but also problems of an education open to all social classes and groups of the population and intended to create the popular school, basic education, in the style of the French elementary school. In the early days of colonisation, French policy declared its civilizing mission and its determination to educate. This policy was put into effect, illustrated and developed by Galliéni in Tonking and Madagascar, by Faidherbe in Senegal, by Lyautey in Morocco. As the country is pacified, as roads multiply, as markets grow and peace and order are restored, schools are established and begin to function. They are to be found in the Algerian "douars" and the Kabyl mountains, in the outposts of the Moroccan Atlas, on the Saharan borders, amongst the huts of the African bush, in the rice fields of Tonking and Cochin-China, near the Cambodian pagodas, in the smallest villages of the West Indies and Réunion.

We find the popular school already there, in its conception, if not in its full extension, its objective and ideal already determined. It is the school open to all, to the Negro peasants, to the Algerian Jews as well as to the middle-class Moroccans, to the sons of Mandarins and of tropical Africa's tribal chiefs. Even when special schools have been built for notables, as in Morocco, or for the sons of chiefs, as in tropical Africa, the primary school itself is offered to the people and admits everyone irrespective of class or race; thus it is of the same democratic nature as the primary schools of France. Hence, the French educational system in Indochina, or in the West Indies, which extends without barriers from the village school to the University, has rightly been called the "Universal School" system, whereby the proletarian child has a chance of reaching the highest grade of university studies.

If the popular school has not yet attained the degree of expansion that was expected, the reason lies in certain facts, and is not a matter of principle. French colonisation is a recent event, except in the "old colonies." Algeria has been a French possession for hardly a hundred years. Most of the other French dependencies date from after 1870. Morocco, under the authority of the Sultan and controlled by France, was not completely subdued until little more than ten years ago. The great West African and Equatorial African federations, as well as Paul Doumer's Indo-Chinese Federation, date back to just before the first world war. It was not until the end of that war that France was able to organise the development and education of her big colonies on a large scale. It was then that, except for the old colonies and Algeria, where steps had already been taken, the first programmes for popular education were drafted, and the French Government realized the immensity of its educational task, the obstacles it would encounter, the special methods required, the fundamental objectives it must pursue.

The obstacles are many and native reactions vary with experience, and with the diversity of cultures and peoples; the obstacles were originally material questions of time and money. The popular school in Europe, the ambition and dream of the Eighteenth Century and of the Revolution, took the whole nineteenth century to achieve. It was impossible to accomplish overseas in twenty years what a century had failed to complete in Europe. Take the question of resources. The colonised territories are either new and unpeopled or ancient and immobilised; they had to be developed *in toto* and, first, in relation to the primary necessaries of life. The first task was to build roads, open whole areas, organise trade and manufacture, preserve the race and the population. In the early stages the school could only fit itself into this great task. Since 1848 the population of Algeria has increased from three million to eight. The population of Tonking has doubled since 1910. That of Morocco has risen from 5 or 6 millions to at least 9 millions since 1910. Tropical Africa, the perennial victim of so many scourges, has been saved from depopulation. The very fact of colonising means that a greater effort is called for, new generations to educate and bring up. Lastly, the great world crisis of the 1930's gravely affected the western powers' overseas possessions on account of their precarious exchange system and the narrow limits of their natural resources, which made it impossible for them to bear the cost of equipment and modern education without outside help or foreign loans. The world crisis, which thus greatly slowed down social progress both in colonial territories and in the countries of the Great Powers, came to an end in 1936, only to be followed by preparations for war and by the second world war, whose first results have created the present situation.

Next, let us consider the obstacles due to the nature of overseas people, to their social structure, their psychological make-up, their very aspirations. In her overseas territories France found a complete lack of educational system or else a traditional educational system congealed in religious formalities and incapable of promoting any truly modern educational activity. In tropical Africa life centred round the tribe and the village. In North Africa we find Koran schools, many of them wretched things, run by inferior teachers, with instruction limited to the reciting of a few verses from the Koran. In Indo-China, traditional education led up to the examinations for the recruitment of mandarins and scholars. But in the villages the teaching of a few Chinese characters remained consistently limited, sterile and mechanical. The economic and social environment was fixed and immovable, opposed to all change. In North Africa, as in Asia, we are dealing with civilisations that are temporarily static and, in the case of the rural masses, with populations thrust back upon themselves, with hardly any outside needs, confined within a family-based economy, their tempo of life determined by family, labour and the seasons, far removed from towns, modern cultures and modern life. It is therefore not surprising if in a number of regions we have encountered almost a refusal to be educated, at least a distrust of or lack of interest in the new school. There are still areas where the school, a foreign innovation, has neither been assimilated nor accepted by the people. It was necessary to win over the population, to meet them half-way, convert them to education, make the school a reflection of their way of life, establish it in houses they are familiar with, to teach in the language of the country and of the native village. Progress was naturally most rapid in countries already long developed, like Cochin-China, Senegal and the West Indies. Later the attitude of the people quickly changed, the school was a success: it lightened the darkness, created a focal centre, and opened the gates to another world. It qualifies, elevates, emancipates; it creates careers, aptitudes, fortunes. Now, people clamour for it, attend it more for the individual opportunities it offers than for the general progress it brings to the community. But twenty, fifty years were needed to bring about and speed up this development, which is even now unequal, progressing faster or slower according to the region. And it is the last world war with its widespread mixing of peoples, its technical and political revolutions, the unity it has given to men's minds, which today makes the peoples' request for popular education urgent and imperative.

How did French policy conceive primary education in the French overseas territories?

It was really inspired by two principles, seemingly different and even opposed by nature, but in reality complementary and coincident: the principle of assimilation and the principle of adaptation.

At first the policy of assimilation held the field and, although its development has had to take account of facts, it has nevertheless maintained its force and ambitions in certain regions. It was born of the ideas of 1789; it considers that all men, irrespective of birth and race, are equal before the law and before the future. Henceforth, colonising became an assimilation, a conversion of peoples to civilisation, their incorporation within the French nation.

This incorporation cannot be limited to an élite, to trained staffs or to the elements responsible for steering development; it must be carried to the very heart of the population itself; it must be general, fundamental. The aim is to create French nationals, citizens, overseas Frenchmen, French provinces. It is France overseas. The "Africans learn to be French," to quote the title of an English book on France's educational policy in French West Africa.

The school, particularly the primary school, is the main instrument of this assimilation. To-day, it is the French school that is imported and planted in overseas countries; the French school with its syllabuses and legislation, with the same chapter-heads as in the mother-country, with its schoolmaster, who at first will be French, but who will later be trained like the French schoolmaster in similar training colleges: the French school with its powerful assimilatory instrument, the French language and instruction in French. The native languages are discarded, even forbidden; traditional educational systems, where they survive, vegetate, lose their importance and authority. The Indo-Chinese themselves have asked for increased French schools to take the place of the old traditional institutions. In North Africa, the

Koran schools still stick to recitations from the Koran and are no longer of any real popular educational value. Important factors have greatly assisted the French school in its development and success. Even in the elementary grades it is of great advantage to pupils, for it trains and qualifies them for the new occupations and functions created by the development of the country. It opens the doors to careers and to even the most modest positions. The social transformations, the development of relations in economic areas opened up to new enterprise, encourage the practical use of French, make it a current language whose use is necessary, and which thus creates the need and the demand for schools.

Lastly, the French school, especially in tropical Africa and Asia, symbolises emancipation and liberation. It means access to the sources of culture and modern civilisation. It absolves the African, for instance, from remaining shut up in his own surroundings, the prisoner of tyrannical traditions; it signifies liberation and promotion. The reproach is rather that schools are insufficiently widespread, that they only cater for a minority and have not yet reached the masses.

But, along with this policy of assimilation and of developing a purely metropolitan education, France has also followed, by a series of often successful and fruitful syntheses, an educational policy that we may call a policy of adaptation or policy of nationalities. Certain facts, cultural, economic and social, dictate the conception and direction of popular education in overseas territories. In Asia we are faced with civilisations that go back thousands of years, whose history, language, literature and culture have been influenced by China and India. We are faced with nationalities in the making, seeking a national status for which modern culture is a valuable tool, a means of action, but which does not demand real assimilation. In North Africa, we confront a Muslim civilisation, which is also in the process of intellectual and technical modernisation influenced by the West, but which maintains its faith, its law, its right, its language of learning and its dialects, its habits, in a word, the world which the Muslim civilisation conceived and built for its believers. In tropical Africa too, and in Madagascar, there have grown up in the course of time original civilisations not fully based on concrete historical and national realities, which the natives themselves have created and which are strong enough to compose a complex human environment, capable of internal reaction and transformation. Nowhere, in fact, do we find "virgin soil." Can we, then, in the elementary school, sacrifice the natural, moral and social values of the country and its traditions? Can we denationalise, "distort" the people as it were, by eradicating their language and even their personality?

And there are other facts that make a policy of adaptation necessary. All the French overseas territories have to be equipped, modernised, "opened up" to world communication, but this opening up is carried out by zones in contact with each other and by developed populations. When dealing with masses, if education is to transform the ways of life and the economy of a race, must we not seek support from the environment, respect its traditions, utilise its language and make the school a moral and civic centre of activity, an instrument of internal progress and not a foreign importation, a complete innovation alien to the moral climate and conditions of the country?

Lastly, a more practical reason: how can we launch a real education of the masses in a new tongue that requires much practice, many teachers, a costly organisation? Is it not better to have a village and a people's school, which will destroy ignorance more quickly, which remains the local school, familiar, known, understood, useful? The over-learned, ultra-European school does not reach the masses. It runs the risk of being the school of a minority.

These, therefore, are the two apparently opposite poles, between which rest the achievements of French educational policies in overseas territories. For actually, the solutions adopted have been different according to the countries under consideration and the political, cultural and economic environment on which the system of popular education has to be based and developed; they have been adapted, too, to the reactions of the people themselves. Even in vast areas like tropical Africa or Indo-China, many separate formulas have been applied to different problems. The whole country does not always march in step along the same road. In tropical Africa there are differences between the developed areas of Senegal, the Lower Ivory Coast, Dahomey, and the Sudan and Chad savannahs. The Annamite problem is one of nationality and civilisation and cannot apply to the primitive peoples of the central Indo-Chinese mountains.

Hence, the primary popular school has developed in the direction of a more complete realisation of the facts, a fuller satisfaction of the true interests of the people. In parts where the formula of the French primary school has been maintained and developed, we have sought to give it a hold over the country, over the environment, to define its active part in real education, in improving the health of the rural population and their social and material conditions. On the other hand, in countries where the traditional or national primary school has been adopted or improved, we have tried, as in Indo-China, to give it a modern character and bring it into relation with the higher-grade studies conducted in the French school.

After this analysis, we propose to describe the popular educational policy in the main countries of the French Union, taking mostly into account countries we know from personal experience. We shall thus study first of all tropical Africa.

French West Africa. When we speak of French West Africa, it must be understood that the statements made no doubt apply also to other African territories under French control: French Equatorial Africa and the mandated territories of the Cameroons and Togoland, where political, economic and social conditions and the educational data are substantially the same. Despite many distinguishing features, colonial development in all these countries confers upon the gradual advancement of French West Africa a unity of direction that mainly derives from the very aims of French colonial policy in Africa.

What, then, do we mean by French West Africa? To begin with, it is a huge fragment of the African Continent, an immense scattered area extending from the Sahara to the great forests, from the Atlantic Ocean to Lake Chad, a country spread over many latitudes and governed by vast distances which, particularly in the remote interior, create isolated and geographically enclosed regions which roads and other communications are only gradually opening up.

It is mainly a country of scanty resources, still dominated by the forces of nature, compressed between the desert and steppe which threatens it from the north and an almost unpopulated forest belt in the south, an inhuman and hostile element which modern science is coming gradually to dominate and exploit. Thus it is a thinly populated area, with its fifteen million inhabitants spread over three million or so square miles, with immense empty spaces and its peoples and villages collected in a few privileged districts situated in the big river valleys and forest savannahs. Its population is still stationary, ravaged until the French came by the slave trade or domestic serfdom, its expansion checked by natural scourges—stillbirths and sleeping sickness—against which the campaign is not yet concluded; it is in fact an ethnographical complex of different peoples bound within the rigidity of contrasted forms of life, with its Tuaregs, its nomadic Whites, its coloured folk, its cattle-raising and sheep-rearing Fellatas, and its Negroes, originally peasants, but now also traders and artisans. A country of many races and tribes, refugee peoples cut off one from the other and between whom the roads and the French language and administration are at last establishing contacts. The babel of tongues is illustrated by the existence of something like 200 languages and dialects in French West Africa alone.

Such is the human and natural environment in which the natives of French West Africa pass their social, economic and cultural lives. What, then, are the main characteristics of those lives?

Economically, French West Africa is still in an elementary, often primitive state, life being confined to the district and limited to the effort to satisfy essential requirements still inadequately served. An exchange economy has resulted from colonisation, from the opening up of communications and the introduction of new exportable products. But when it comes to the native economy, there is a wealth of traditional elements the utilisation of which depends on education and practical measures. Agriculture and cattle-breeding are for the most part divorced, the Negroes being the tillers of the soil and the Fellatas the graziers. Agricultural implements are archaic. Tropical Africa cultivates with the hoe, and the plough, even in the form of the swing-plough, is little used. Harvesting is still by hand, and it is in this way that the products of the forest are gathered in. The Negro has no machinery; often he has no draught animals, no mill to grind his millet, no press to extract his oil. He works with his hands as in the earliest times. He has little or no money; he works for the community, the village. Cultivation is of the extensive type; the area of bush exceeds that of cultivated land, and fields are abandoned as soon as they are exhausted. Production is primarily for local consumption, and the principal products are millet, rice, maize, bananas and manioc.

How shall we define the various native communities of French West Africa from the social point of view? First, there are rural communities, scattered families living on their own soil and upon their own resources, with their patriarchs, their customs, their work in common and their domestic institutions, in which the woman is a labour hand, a chattel. Next, there is a hierarchy of institutions, of petty local authorities with village chiefs, communal heads and sometimes, along the Niger and among the "Moissis" of the Ivory Coast, certain traditional regional and provincial authorities, who have inherited power and lawful authority. Lastly, there are religious communities divided into two large groups, the Moslem group and the animistic group, with the marabouts and the brotherhoods and also with the communities of elders, fetishist leaders, and customs to regulate marriage, family life, hunting, fishing and labour.

Culturally, tropical Africa is not the clean slate, the *tabula rasa* so often described by Africans themselves who repudiate their past. There are Negro civilisations which impart a general style to African life, which comprise elements of original culture, Negro civilisations with their own folk-lore and mythology, their art, which has a genius of its own, and, lastly, with their own general reactions to the problem of civilisation. There are, however, enormous gaps in this all too elementary culture;

there is no educational system fit to assimilate and transmit the achievements of progress to future generations; there is hardly any literature or written language, an enormous dispersal, and closed cultural communities thrown back upon themselves and seeking no kind of unity or association with their neighbours and kinsfolk.

At the same time new classes are emerging upon this ancient and seemingly static background; fresh forces are active, thrown up by the school or religion, by economic pressure or colonisation. Among the new classes is a land-owning middle-class, peasants who have got on and grown rich by economic exchange, through the sale of their cocoa, coffee and ground-nuts. There is also an intellectual or "evolved" class who know French, officials and employees who have entered the administration or the new business community which has arisen from industrial exploitation, especially in the coastal settlements like Senegal and the Ivory Coast. Higher up are sections of an older bourgeoisie, consolidated as in Senegal by French culture and participation in political life.

In the next place, there has been a more or less rapid development affecting religious beliefs, a twofold movement. In the Sudan, in Senegal and in the Futa Djallon, Mohammedanism in its simplest form has made great strides in French West Africa, driving out the old animistic beliefs. Secondly, conversion to Christianity, mostly Catholic, has taken place as the result of missionary work in the southern colonies and areas in which animism still survived. Thus French West Africa is a sort of borderline between Islam and Christianity. Under this twofold pressure animistic beliefs are vanishing, as well as under the influence of European penetration and modern teaching; all the same, they still possess a strange power over the common man.

Such are the conditions which have from the beginning governed the problem of education, especially elementary teaching. There can be no question here of building upon a genuine native culture capable of maintaining a complete system of teaching and education. What is needed in all parts of Africa is a reinforcement from outside, French support, cultural and spiritual nourishment which will liberate and enrich the country. The big and formidable question of the cultural development and transformation of the African races as entities does not at present arise. We need cadres, a staff of administrative and economic assistants, teachers, employees, doctors, secretaries, artisans and skilled workers. These are being trained in French schools, which teach in French, for the service of the New Africa that France is creating. Elementary teaching really started in 1904. Although it has spread all over the country, to the borders of the deserts and great forests, although there is now a French school in every district and French teachers are carrying the teaching of French into the villages, while there are French-speaking groups and enclaves in every province, elementary teaching is not a genuine popular education, a fundamental education aiming at the development of the whole mass of the people and at the raising of their standard of living and economic level. Rather it is the teaching of a small minority, a means of picking out that band of "evolved" auxiliaries, of whom the country and its economy are in need. For this reason the educational system follows the successive stages of a pyramid: at the base are the elementary schools, urban and rural, the nurseries of a central or regional school; then comes a higher-grade school, each stage being recruited from the previous one. Owing to the dearth of trained staff, the humblest diploma is at a premium and the certificate of elementary studies is not a mere recognition of a minimum education, but a diploma which opens the door to jobs and to the new way of life. Naturally, this general and utilitarian teaching is given in French and according to French syllabuses, but they are adapted to local requirements and to the occupations and aptitudes of pupils.

The real problem of fundamental education and the teaching of the masses has arisen since the first World War and more especially during the 30's. Education, hitherto dispersed, excludes the greater part of the population. There is a gulf between the generations, between the "evolved" who leave their village or locality because they cannot turn their education to account, and the mass of the mainly rural population, which remains sunk in its traditions and its ignorance. There is the same disparity within the family, between husband and wife, the teaching of girls lagging far behind that of the boys. Although a few regions, like the coast of Senegal and Lower Dahomey, already have an established educational tradition and a substantial number of schools, the greater part of the interior knows only of the school concentrated in the capital, a mere annex to the administration, a French affair, existing for the Whites and not yet a naturalised African institution.

Education, after life itself, is the African's first and most urgent need. Side by side with the education of staffs, which leads on to an acquisition of general culture, to vocational training and the training of a class of intellectuals and technicians, there must be education of the Africans themselves, useful, concrete teaching to constitute a liberation and a practical tool. The two tasks, far from being mutually exclusive, are supplementary, for, if we are to mobilise the mute and passive millions of tropical Africa and to procure for them the satisfaction of their primary needs in the way of food, lodging and clothing, everything boils down to education. Some help, of course, comes from the forces of example, from emulation and the creation of new needs through the development of roads and railways, the arrival of new settlers and contact between the races. But Africa remains a country of natives, and its colonisation is to some extent the work of the natives themselves. The settler, the planter—and this is his excuse—is in most cases a witness, a model, an experimenter, in a word, a guide and educator. It is for education to combat scourges and epidemics and, especially in the case of women, to wage the campaign against stillbirths and on behalf of child welfare and elementary hygiene in the home. It is for education to transform everyday life, to extend food production, improve the standard of nutrition and housing, to secure a water-supply. The whole transformation and modernisation of rural Africa is a question of education: the use of the plough and of draught animals; the independent farm working for its own account and selling its surplus; the introduction of new and productive crops; the utilisation of the palm-groves instead of their destructive exploitation; even bee-keeping. It is for education to create a civic discipline, to apprentice a new society by co-operation and mutual insurance, to secure the social development of the family by prohibiting child marriages and reducing polygamy. Finally, it is for education to breed a kind of political and national conscience, to foster regard for a broader notion of society, to introduce the idea of country, of solidarity with France, the country of adoption. Education must provide Africans with experience in the administration of the affairs of the village or province, with their first apprenticeship in the exercise of political rights.

The whole French policy of the educational colonisation of tropical Africa, a policy that aims at creating "an advancing Africa," postulates a vast programme of popular education through the school, side by side with the school, beyond it and after it. The task is enormous, almost superhuman, if it is to be accomplished in a few decades. We are only at the beginning of things. The schools of French West Africa have less than 100,000 pupils, though this is already a remarkable achievement when we consider the need for selecting and training staffs, for establishing centres of culture in the most diverse regions. Very little has been done in relation to the whole problem. If we take the proportion of the population of school age to the total population as 1:10, there are in French West Africa 1,500,000 children of school-age: about 350,000 a year. Assuming the average school period to be three years, we might therefore provide for 10% of the total. In any event it leaves a big margin; the effort required is considerable. Unless spread over several generations and based upon the developing resources of the country, this effort is beyond the power of tropical Africa and requires the aid of the mother country.

Well, there is the problem. What is the solution? What view are we to take of Fundamental Education in French West Africa? The obstacles are many. First there was the need of accustoming the country to the idea of schools. Not long ago there were certain Tuareg tribes and a certain district inhabited by the Fellatas, in which the school was an object of fear, an alien element. Children, especially small girls, are needed for work in the home or fields. Until twenty years ago Sudanese chiefs did not send their own children to school, but only their servants' children. The recruiting of pupils for the schools was an act of the administration, an order from above. Since then, however, much progress has been made, particularly in Senegal and the coastal areas of the South. There the villagers are building schools with their own hands or with their own money; no sooner opened, they become overcrowded and on all sides arises the demand for schools, a demand that may be naive, confident or even imperious.

What form of school really meets the needs of the people? That brings us to the question of the use of French or of the vernacular for popular teaching. This is really a theoretical and political question rather than a practical one, since French official policy has remained consistently faithful to teaching in French.

Nevertheless, there are strong objections to the practice. If mass education is to reach grown-up people and girls, the task becomes impossible. It would call for thousands of non-existent teachers, thousands of schools and hundreds of millions in money. It would be a dangerous enterprise, open to serious criticism. In a few years or months you would undertake to impart to hundreds of thousands of schoolchildren instruction in a foreign language; a formal, bookish instruction out of touch with the environment and practical life, and the results of which for the great majority of those who remain in their village and home will be useless and ephemeral. Popular teaching must be in the mother tongue; the latter alone allows of a concrete and positive education having that social and moral value which is the African's first requirement.

The answers to these arguments are many. To begin with, the choice is political. France has deliberately pursued her educational policy by means of the French language, the official language of administration and teaching. On the part of France, this is no doubt one aspect of moral conquest, the stamp of spiritual rule; but it is also a symbol of emancipation, a gift of her culture and her medium of expression, a freedom of the city, as it were, granting access to French cultural life. It is a policy of equality between the races, of close association with the colonised peoples, just as conversion to Christianity is not an act of religious imperialism, but a sharing of the Truth and the Faith among equals. More than that, this policy of French schools accords with the wishes of the population in tropical Africa, the wishes not only of the "evolved" and the school-children themselves, but even of their families and the older folk. It is the French school they want; teaching in the native tongue is looked upon as an obstacle to progress and emancipation.

Secondly, modern-language teaching, teaching in French, is a necessity imposed by the facts. Tropical Africa does not, like Indo-China and North Africa, possess a powerful civilisation, inspiring culture, religious beliefs, customs and everyday life. On the contrary, tropical Africa, though far from uncultivated, is the home of cultures that are embryonic, incomplete and without unity. It is, as we have said, a linguistic chaos. In French West Africa alone more than 120 different languages are spoken. Some of these are confined to small areas and are threatened with extinction by expanding languages. Others intermingle without any distinctive frontier or domain of their own. In Lower Dahomey, which is hardly larger than a French department, the number of languages is astonishing. These different peoples with their many tongues require a unifying link, a language for their expression, a federating ideal. Some African languages like Haussa, Peuhl, Bambara, Wolof, are of course widely spoken and could serve as a "lingua franca." But if there must be an auxiliary tongue, a major language for current use, in fact a language for teaching, that language must be French, because of its general character, the progress it has made and its political and cultural value. Schools are not ethnographical museums. Moreover, Africans are naturally bilingual. The expansion and use of French by the Africans as a live and current tongue are no chimera. Latin America, the West Indies and Central America furnish us with notable examples in this field.

It is said that the French school is not indigenous, that it tears up roots, goes its way and builds nothing. Experience contradicts such statements. In the first place French teachers and, after them, African teachers have worked out the teaching of

French by the direct method, with speedy and notable results. Every attempt is made to avoid a purely bookish method, which exercises only the memory and provides an over-learned vocabulary, resulting in parrot-learning, the use of an academic and inflated speech, sometimes without the ability to write the language at all. French is taught pictorially, by practical examples, "learning by doing," a teaching of French by the use of objects, gestures, based on life and the environment, a "utility" French, a method of communication, a language that is talked and understood. "Pidgin" French has long disappeared in tropical Africa, and so has that verbosity of speech which has amused so many critics. After a few years at school Negroes are perfectly capable of speaking a correct, clear and serviceable French.

In addition, the French school is more than a purely formal school of books and language; it is a positive school making a definite effort to educate the people. All African schools, besides teaching the French language and the three R's, also teach ethics, a study of the locality and district, the care of children. The popular village school, a thrilling experiment fifteen years old, is a school for a new kind of hygiene, local agriculture, domestic economy and, to girls, life. In it, in their own environment, the natives learn and live in French. It is an African school translated into French, it is the focus, the centre of practice and experiment for everything that needs doing in the village or the locality to improve conditions of life. In it the children learn the French tongue, how to manage a small estate, cultivate a garden, plant an orchard, lay out a plantation. In addition to manual labour, the school buildings are kept in repair, furnished and decorated; the school accustoms its pupils to new forms of cultivation and new methods of feeding suitable for imitation by others; there they learn to tend animals, keep poultry and also to know and study the country, its legends and customs. Games are organised, there may be a cinema, possibly a radio set; the school organises palavers for the older folks; fêtes and school meals are held in common; the school is the store-house for all the educational material needed by the village and district for young and old alike. Such a school, multiplied by hundreds, is in need of qualified teachers, educated men devoted to their task, Africans who love their country and are zealous for its education and transformation. Their training is given them in training colleges, in the first place at the Ponty College, the principal school in French West Africa, and also in rural training colleges like that at Katibugu in the Sudan, at Dabu on the Ivory Coast, and at the Girls' Training College of Rufisque.

Nor does the French school neglect the study of the country and of the environment or contact with the facts of social life. Africa is the subject taught; French—in its elementary forms, of course—is the instrument, the key that opens the door upon life and the outside world. Language-teaching goes along with factual instruction, general teaching goes side by side with practical education, and the elements of a simple culture are acquired at the same time as the habits and customs of a new life. Nothing in this education is directed against the environment, nothing prevents the local tongue from playing its part in the whole scheme or from being taught in regions where it is alive and lasting, where it involves a true culture, or where it can rapidly create a popular education and a movement against illiteracy and ignorance. For the teaching of adults or when holding educational palavers for the instruction of a whole village by the modern means of wireless and the cinema, it is the local language to which recourse must be had. It is thus that the way must be prepared and the French popular school be maintained in order to establish a Fundamental Education.

That, then is what is being done in French Tropical Africa. The foundations are laid, the doctrine is agreed upon, aims and purposes are clear, but the work is still in its beginnings. Its instruments are now being trained in the training colleges and other modern institutes of higher education. But in order to accomplish this enormous educational task, to bring the school to all the villages of the African bush, to attack ignorance and illiteracy from every quarter, to convert the whole country and increase the number of schoolchildren from 120,000 to 1,000,000 and also attack the problem of adult and female education, there is need of more training colleges, more teachers. Enthu-

siasm must be kindled, a big educational movement set on foot
and support found for teachers by an appeal to all of good will
to join in the crusade for voluntary education. The French
Government realises the importance of the problem and the
tremendous effort needed to solve it. Plans are laid to expand
elementary education, ten-year plans, twenty-year plans. Out of
its overseas funds the home country will contribute to African
education and to the building of training colleges for teachers.
It will take its part in the teaching and will bear the initial
cost. The French colonisation of tropical Africa is a great educational work, and this work, the outlines of which already exist,
will be carried out by collaboration between the mother-country
and the African peoples.

As to South Africa (Hellman and Whyte 1, pp. 1-22) the
story is as follows:

UNION OF SOUTH AFRICA. An evaluation of South
Africa's educational system and of the complex problems con-
fronting it must be set within the framework of the totality of
the South African situation.

Population. The population of the Union when the last complete census was taken in 1936 comprised ten million people,
forming what has been defined as a "racial caste society".

The $2\frac{1}{4}$ million Europeans . . . are the dominant minority
enjoying almost exclusive political and military control, and
very marked economic, educational, and social privileges. Next
in this scale come the Asiatics, numbering some $\frac{1}{4}$ million people, the bulk of whom were originally brought to South Africa
in the latter half of the nineteenth century as indentured labourers to work on the sugar-cane fields of Natal. The vast majority of Indians live in Natal, and although necessarily affected
by contact with Western civilisation, they retain much of their
original cultural and social heritage. The Cape Coloured or
Coloured group of $\frac{3}{4}$ million, located chiefly in the Cape Province, are of mixed ancestry, mingling the strains of early colo-
nists, European sailors, Malay slaves, Hottentots, and other
groups. The Coloured have no distinctive language of their

own, but speak one or both of the official South African languages—English and Afrikaans.

Ranking lowest in the racial hierarchy are the 6½ million Bantu, generally referred to as "Natives" or, more rarely as "Africans", who form the majority of the population. Before the advent of the white man, the Bantu-speaking tribes of South Africa had attained a reasonable equilibrium with their environment. Theirs was a subsistence economy based on cattle-raising and primitive agriculture. The impact of Western civilisation has convulsed their culture and their economy but the reaction has not been uniform. To-day, the Bantu are a people in transition, ranging from comparatively unaffected tribal units in the Reserves, which are areas of land set aside for exclusive Native occupation, through farm labourers on European farms, to urban Natives with their own diversification of culture, education and occupation, varying from . . . mineworker or municipal labourer to teacher and trade union organiser. Roughly one-half of the total Native population lives in the Reserves, which will, when certain additional land has been acquired (to the purchase of which the Government has committed itself), amount to some 13 per cent of the total area of the Union's 472,550 square miles. Some two million live on crown lands or on European farms as labour tenants or farm labourers. Approximately one-fifth are in urban areas. But it must be borne in mind that South African economy is based largely on a migratory labour system and that accordingly these three groups are not static, but in a constant process of flux. In certain Reserves, up to 60 per cent of the able-bodied males are found to be outside the Reserves engaged on some wage-earning activity. This population instability and the effects of frequently changing environmental influences add further complications to an already complex situation. . . .

As in other countries, so too in South Africa, the tendency towards urbanisation has been assuming increasing proportions. . . . At the last census, 65 per cent of the European group were living in urban areas, 66 per cent of the Asiatics, 54 per cent of the Coloureds, and 17 per cent of the Natives. . . .

As in other countries . . . there has been a growing tendency towards self-analysis and assessment of the economic realities and potentialities of the country. Because of the high standard of living enjoyed by a small section of the white population and because of the steady output of the country's chief export, gold, it was long possible for the Union's actual economic position to be obscured. But the country is now becoming increasingly aware of the fact that its national income . . . averages some £50 per annum per head of the population and is far below that of the other Dominions, ranking among the lowest in the world scale. Chiefly this is due to the tardiness of industrialisation, the fact that the country's natural resources (particularly base metals) have by no means been fully exploited and that its potential labour force has not been harnessed into full productivity. The Social and Economic Planning Council, a body set up by the Government during the war, put the matter succinctly when it said that "the Union is doomed to a losing competitive struggle against the mentally developed labour of the Western Countries, against the awakening Eastern races and even against other parts of Africa, unless the educational facilities for the Non-European are improved". Growing awareness of these basic economic realities will be of importance in determining the extent to which educational facilities will in the future be provided for the large, comparatively untrained and undeveloped, Non-European group.

Present State of School Education: European. Education in respect of European children aged 7 to 16 years inclusive, in all Provinces except Natal, where the age is 7 to 15 years, is compulsory unless the child has passed Standard VI (Standard VIII in the Transvaal). According to the last South African Year Book, published in 1941, 94 per cent of the European children attend the state public schools, which are the schools "which everybody attends whatever may be his rank or economic position".

Non-European. The position is completely different in regard to the Non-European group. Apart from Natal, where the attendance of Coloured children is compulsory, and the Cape, where a similar provision has recently been introduced for Coloured and Asiatic children and will gradually become operative as facilities become available, there is no compulsory education for Non-Europeans in South Africa. Furthermore, European education is mainly public or state education, i.e., administered and financed by the State, private or local enterprise playing a very diminutive role; while Non-European education is mainly state-aided education—i.e., it is partly supported and controlled by mission enterprise. The relative contribution of the State, therefore, for Non-European education is very small in comparison with that for European education. European and Non-European children do not attend the same schools. While segregation is difficult in other respects, in education it is complete. . . .

The early history of education for Non-Europeans, and particularly for Africans, is one of missionary endeavour. . . . It was only in 1941 that regulations defining the conditions for grants, which were very meagre, for "Mission Schools" were laid down. The Report further states "as in other parts of Africa, the history of Native education in the Orange Free State is practically synonymous with the history of the Missions". This was the general pattern in all four Provinces, and the public was well content to leave the responsibility for Native education to the Missions. . . .

The pressure for greater governmental responsibility has been cumulative, clamantly voiced by the Africans themselves and the liberal European element, and is now being increasingly supported by intelligent public opinion, which is coming to understand that industrial development demands an efficient and trained labour force.

There is a growing demand, particularly on the part of Africans, not only for greater governmental financial responsibility, but also governmental in place of the present mission control of education. The development of this attitude might possibly be termed "ingratitude", for it is abundantly clear that the Mission Societies have been the generating force in developing Native education. That their own primary purpose could not be promoted without literacy and that there was an external pressure directing this development is immaterial. It in no way lessens the great value of the Missions' crucial role in Native education. But acknowledgment of this debt to the Missions cannot be expected to obligate the future of Native education to Mission control. With the need for planned and rapid expansion, the Missions will find themselves increasingly unable to provide the necessary personnel. This is the natural course of development in all countries. In South Africa, too, the Government must eventually take over complete responsibility for Native education, while making grants to denominational schools.

A number of government schools have already been established. Amalgamated schools, undenominational in form, are showing considerable increase in a number of centres.

The Government's response to this pressure is reflected in the increasing amounts being made available for Native education. Formerly Native education was dependent for its finance on the S.A. Native Trust Fund, which received the bulk of its revenue from the Native general tax. This system was abolished in 1945 when the Union Government took over financial responsibility for Native education. Under the Act of Union in 1910, "education other than higher" was relegated to the Provinces, but . . . the Union Government has since taken over certain educational functions at that time not visualised and hence not allocated, such as technical industrial and vocational education, agricultural training, and child welfare. . . . The Provincial Councils are therefore the legislative authorities in regard to Native education. The administration is in the hands of the head of each provincial education department, who is assisted by a specialist officer with the title of Chief Inspector of Native Education. Each Province has an advisory board representative chiefly of the missions controlling the schools. In addition there has been set up since 1945, when the Act was passed defining the new financial provision, a Union Advisory Board on Native Education.

Whereas the Provinces have always made substantial contributions to European education, expenditure from their own resources on Native education has been negligible. The total expenditure on Native education by the Provinces—chiefly for inspection—amounted to £58,071 in 1939. Until a short time ago, when the financial relationship between Central and Provincial authorities was placed on a new basis, the Government contributing 50 per cent of all provincial expenditure on services, the Government paid a subsidy for each European child in average attendance. In this way, it paid for some 70 per cent of Provincial expenditure on European education. Subsidies were also paid for Coloured and Indian children, but obviously in the absence of compulsory education, these subsidies, even though they were on a per capita basis, could not be compared with those paid for European pupils. The subsidy for Coloured children was £5 5s. od. per annum, and, with the exception of the O.F.S., provincial expenditure exceeded this figure in other Provinces. With the new financial basis established between the Central Government and the Provinces, there is now no reason why the Provinces should not cover the whole field of Coloured and Asiatic education falling under their jurisdiction.

There has never been, nor is there now, a per capita subsidy basis for Native education grants. Assistance is given by the payment of teachers' salaries, certain grants for equipment, a number of maintenance grants for certain students, payment of rent in specified cases, etc. Hence, although there has been a marked increase in the total allocations for Native education, it bears no relationship to increased needs or demands. . . .

ENROLMENT OF NATIVE CHILDREN IN 1941

Standard	Number	Median Age
Sub-standards	146,000	—
Standard I	66,000	—
Standard II	45,000	13.15
Standard III	35,000	13.94
Standard IV	23,000	14.72
Standard V	16,000	15.54
Standard VI	11,000	16.52
Standard VII	3,500	17.19
Standard VIII	1,000	18.35
Standard IX	350	19.13
Standard X	200	19.39
Total	347,050	

Up-to-date figures relating to the number of school-age children for whom educational facilities are not available cannot be given until the census figures have been tabulated. The report of the Provincial Financial Resources Committee published in 1944 gives calculations regarding the number of Non-European school-age children of 7 to 14 years not in school. According to these estimates, 71 per cent of Bantu children (1,129,129) were not enrolled: 23.3% (14,175) of Coloured and Asiatic children were not enrolled in all Provinces excluding Natal; and in Natal 55 per cent (23,451) Asiatic children were not enrolled.

The Committee drew up a rough budget of the additional expenditure that would be involved if 90 per cent of Coloured and Asiatic and 80 per cent of Native children were to be given school facilities, allowing £10 p.a. for each Coloured and Asiatic child and £5 10s. od. for each Native child to cover a "reasonable cost of education". This additional expenditure, which makes allowance for teachers' salaries based on the existing median of salary scales, a teaching load of 30 pupils per teacher and an allowance of 5/- per annum for books, an allowance for medical inspection, and an allowance of £1 p.a. for cost of accommodation, would amount to a further seven million pounds. It seems clear that this budget errs on the side of conservatism and does not make sufficient provision for the payment of teachers' salaries on a scale which is commensurate with their responsibilities and will not therefore help to stem the present tendency of Native teachers to leave the teaching profession in order to obtain employment assuring them greater economic reward. . . .

The fact remains, however, that no plan for the future has been formulated by either government or provincial authorities. The estimates are framed each year in a manner that appears to be largely fortuitous. The four Provinces put in their estimates, each Province attempting to get the maximum possible increase in order to expand educational facilities. It is hoped that the Union Advisory Board on Native Education, only recently established, will act not only as a co-ordinating body but will serve as an instrument for the development of long-term national policy.

The position obtaining in regard to Non-European primary education has been dealt with at this length not because of any belief that primary education is the sole educational provision that should be made for a backward population, but in the conviction that an adequate system of primary education is the strategic base for future progress. Acknowledgment of this principle is implicit in many of the findings of the Report of the Committee on Adult Education (1945) and explicit in its recommendation "that, with a view to the success of the programme of adult education, provision be made for the school instruction of all children of school-age on the basis of a long-term policy as suggested by the Social and Economic Planning Council". It cannot be sufficiently stressed that the greatest single immediate cause of educational backwardness and illiteracy in the Union of South Africa is the lack of facilities for the primary education of Non-Europeans and the inadequacy of the present existing facilities. To some extent conditions arising out of the war were responsible for accentuating difficulties: building practically ceased during the war owing to shortage of man-power and materials, and a number of school-buildings, the plans for which have been passed, have not been erected. But the overriding reason for the lack of primary school provision for Non-Europeans is financial strangulation. Although to-day there is a growing public recognition that the white Trustees of the Non-European people must, if only in their own interests, make adequate financial provision for Non-European advance, in the past it was generally held that the Non-European must pay for his own services. This has now appeared impossible, and most sections of the European population are prepared, however grudgingly, to accept their financial responsibility in the matter. While this represents a considerable advance in attitude, it must be remembered that in a caste society, such as South Africa is, it is unlikely that the services provided for Non-Europeans will approximate in quality to those for Europeans, at least for many years. If the country were prepared to make the money available, the children would be in school, the teachers could be trained and the buildings erected. . . .

The Non-European population does not have to be begged to

go to school. It wants to go to school. . . . Education represents to most Africans the open sesame to the world of progress
and advancement. This is the basic attitude, and the long waiting lists at the majority of schools, the large attendances which
unregistered schools enjoy, the periodic instructions from the
Departments limiting attendance to not more than fifty children
per teacher, all testify to this large and unsatisfied desire for
education.

The number of school buildings provided by Africans in Native areas and financed by the voluntary imposition of a special
tribal levy is further testimony to the eager desire for schooling.
A frequent reason for the departure of Native farm labourers
from a European farm is the absence of schools and the desire
to live where schools are available for the children. Despite this
prevalent desire for education, a large number of parents have
not yet come to understand that school-attendance must be regular and continuous. Children drift back days and sometimes
weeks after term begins. They are absent from school on the
most trivial pretexts, such as trifling physical ailments, inclement
weather, or some domestic need. . . . African parents have still
to be taught that the Western system of formal education cannot function effectively on an intermittent basis.

But despite these difficulties the important point is that the
Bantu have a positive attitude towards education. It has an
element of faith which at times verges on the pathetic. On the
other hand, the rebuffs and shocks to which this faith has been
subjected must not be overlooked. These are the result both
of the quality of the schools and the instruction given in them,
and of the general economic structure of the country. Non-
European primary schools in existence are too often overcrowded, poorly built and inadequately equipped, and the teachers, themselves with an inadequate cultural and educational
background, must teach children whose home circumstances and
home life are inadequate for the form of education they desire.
Ideals and ambitions formed in school turn too often to frustration on contact with the realities of the outside world.

That a similar desire for education exists amongst the Indian
population of Natal is proved by the number of voluntary

schools established by the people themselves. The vast majority of Asiatic schools in Natal are not owned or built by the Government. . . .

Particularly in the urban areas is the school need great, and the longest waiting lists and most numerous refusals to would-be school-goers are found in those areas. There, too, the consequences of inadequate primary school facilities are most serious, for in the absence of schools and in view of the break-down of parental discipline and the necessity for the mother to work because of the low earning power of Natives, the child is forced on to the street and frequently develops undesirable tendencies which cannot be counteracted in later life. In the country, where tribal structure and discipline survive to a greater extent, the social consequences of non-school-going are not as marked as in the towns. But in the rural areas a new set of difficulties have to be overcome. The children are required to carry out a number of activities, such as herding, which keeps them out of the schools. Apart from certain Sotho tribes, the members of which reside in small hamlets or villages, the majority of rural Bantu live in small family units scattered over a wide area. Placement of schools to overcome these difficulties of distance will have to be extremely carefully planned if children are to be safeguarded from having to walk five miles or more to school. The introduction of compulsory education in the rural areas will eventually have to synchronise with a concerted effort to rehabilitate the Reserves, which will involve, together with a number of other measures, extensive fencing. This would release large numbers of youths at present occupied in herding.

It is of significance to note that although the number of Native children more than doubled in the fifteen years between 1925 and 1939, the number of children in Sub-standards A and B taken as a percentage of the total primary and secondary school enrolment decreased only from 68 to 60 per cent. The comparative European figure is 17 per cent. The percentage of educands in post-primary classes (i.e., above Standard VI) increased only from 1.79 to 2.24 per cent, which must be compared with the European figures, which rose from 14.3 to 19.4 per cent. The implication of these bald figures is that much of the education that is given is sheer waste and of no lasting or permanent value to the pupils. The majority of school-leavers leave before reaching Standard I, and even if they have at that stage, as so frequently occurs, spent several years in school, they cannot be said to have had any education. Even if they reach Standard III and leave school, many of them do not use the education received and so, in effect, lapse into illiteracy.

An investigation carried out in Johannesburg showed that while poverty was the greatest single cause of school-leaving, 25 per cent of Native children left school of their own accord, which is a direct indication of the lack of holding power of schools, a holding power which cannot be increased until both accommodation and tuition are made to approximate more closely to requisite standards of efficiency. . . .

In view of the great incidence of early school-leaving among Africans, the need for agencies which can exercise a healthy influence on the young boys and girls in the dangerous period between school-leaving and taking up employment is particularly marked. . . . Greater attention has, indeed, been paid of late to the recreational needs of Non-Europeans. . . .

But of no less, and probably greater, importance is the fact that the economy of the country has been so developed that there is very little correspondence between educational attainment and economic reward. South Africa is the country of the industrial colour bar. While this colour bar is legislatively operative only in the mining industry, it operates without the necessity of legislative sanction but through the force of customary usage in the overwhelming majority of the country's industries. This means that the great bulk of Non-Europeans is in effect restricted to unskilled occupational levels, while the skilled occupations are reserved for the white workers. The disparity between skilled and unskilled wages is very great, the unskilled wage in South Africa being 16 per cent of the skilled wage, as against 60 in Britain, 53 in Canada and 75 in Australia. The increase in industrialisation, particularly during the war years, has brought about some modification in industrial structure and an increasing number of Non-Europeans are said to have found occupations in semi-skilled or operative ranks. But in general, it is still true to say that for the vast majority, unskilled labour is the one occupation open to them, and this form of occupation does not differentiate between literate and illiterate, educated and uneducated.

One of the most pressing needs is to find occupational outlets for educated Non-European youths. Reference has repeatedly been made to the eager desire of Non-Europeans for education, and what is thought of as education is schooling, passing examinations and obtaining certificates. Families make heroic sacrifices to keep their children at school: older sisters and brothers grind at some occupation in order to finance the education of the younger children in the family. The number of young men who obtain a Junior Certificate (8 to 9 years' schooling after the sub-standards) or the matriculation certificate is increasing, and so, too, is the number of such young men who can find no occupational outlet.

In regard to technical training, cause and effect are so interrelated that it is impossible to separate them. On the one hand, there is the appalling inadequacy of technical training facilities. In the Cape, for instance, out of 218,000 Native pupils in various schools in 1943, 924 were in industrial schools. Total State expenditure on technical, industrial, and agricultural training for Natives in the whole country amounted to £23,552 in 1939. The Social and Economic Planning Council states that a bare 250 children are enrolled at the Capetown Technical College and that some 750 Native youths and 875 Native girls go to trade schools. On the other hand, there is no occupational outlet for the majority of Non-Europeans even if they are fully trained and skilled unless they set up their own enterprises to serve their own people. The Apprenticeship Act contains no explicit colour-bar clause, but the manner in which it has operated— through a system of Apprenticeship Committees composed of representatives of the employers and the white employees—has given no entry to Africans and has, according to such evidence as is available, increasingly tended to exclude Coloureds. It is claimed that less than 1% of Coloured youths who leave school have any hope of entering a skilled job through apprenticeship.

Despite the restricted work-opportunities open to educated and skilled Non-Europeans, the demand for additional instruction, whole or part time, is growing. . . . The Union Government has agreed to the training of Non-European veterinary assistants and has plans completed for the necessary establishment. Nursing provides an outlet for Non-Europeans not anxious to teach or enter domestic service. . . . It is hoped to open up opportunities for Non-Europeans as dentists and pharmacists and there is evidence that more Africans are turning to law.

There are demands for night-school vocational training which are nowhere satisfied. A specific demand of this nature is for instruction in motor car mechanics from the large body of African drivers of private and commercial cars and lorries. This group has been swelled by demobilised African soldiers who were largely trained and used as drivers in the Mechanical Transport units of the army. . . .

Illiteracy. But even if—by some miracle—formal education were over-night to become available to every school-age Non-European, it would not, although representing an immense step forward and an incalculable easing of the problems of the future, dispose of the problem of illiteracy. There are no reliable figures available to show the exact extent of illiteracy among the various Non-European groups. A survey of African residents in Johannesburg showed that approximately one half of the sample group were illiterate. As this is a study of a highly selective urban group, the assumption that the proportion of literacy is much higher than in the general population is justified. At a military camp in the Transkei it was found that out of 2,000 Native recruits, 10 per cent were able to read.

Bearing in mind the inadequacies of primary schooling and the great turnover in enrolment, it does not seem that the proportion of illiterates can be appreciably reduced unless radical alterations in the present system are effected. This applies particularly to Africans. The introduction of compulsory education for Coloured should lessen the illiteracy proportion among them as the system becomes operative. The Adult Education Committee states "if we were to fix literacy at the attainment of

Standard III, it would, among other things, be evident from this
to what extent the numbers of early school leavers and youths
not attending school add to the number of illiterates". As only
15% of Native school-goers reach Standard III, the fact that the
present educational structure is not adequate to solve the problem or even to ease the path of the future, requires no further
emphasis. . . .

Africans do not restrict their desire for education to their
children. There is abundant testimony to the demand of adult
Africans, particularly in urban areas, for literacy. In all the
Mine Compounds, there are groups of workers receiving instruction from their fellow-workers or Mission workers. These efforts are spontaneous and, surprisingly enough in view of the
Mining Industry's interests in promoting the health and recreation of its African workers, in no way organised by it. The
number of night schools in various urban centres has increased
considerably during recent years. There is as yet no organisation to stimulate the demand for or to initiate the establishment
of night schools, nor is there any connection between them, except in Natal where the education department supervises them.
In Durban, where the municipality subsidises to the extent of
£1,000 p.a., there are 80 night schools with an enrolment of
about 850. In the Transvaal, the Education Department assists
a few night schools with grants. Classes are organised by missions, private individuals, members of the Transvaal Teachers'
Association, and pupils of certain European high schools. Recently the Transvaal Teachers' Association set up a Federal Committee on Adult Education to co-ordinate these activities and to
extend night school facilities in the Witwatersrand area. It is
expected that soon, with financial help from the Union Education Department and other assistance, a strong co-ordinating
Committee for night school work will take over the function of
the Federal Committee.

At this stage, then, the problem in South Africa is not so
much to stimulate the demand for education either for children or for adults, but to devise ways and means of meeting
existing demands. But expansion by itself will not eliminate
the high proportion of what might be termed "educational

wastage" now being incurred. Increased provision of primary school facilities must go hand in hand with a radical alteration of present educational methods and approaches. . . .

It would be difficult . . . to adjudicate as between rival needs. There does, however, seem to be general agreement that the most clamant need is to introduce compulsory primary education for Non-Europeans in the urban areas if the growing generation in the towns is to be safeguarded from the dangers which at present threaten its development. Next in importance would probably rank the education of Natives both in Native areas and on European farms, specifically in regard to agriculture and health. The soil resources of the Union, at no time lavish, are deteriorating at an alarming rate due chiefly to primitive agricultural techniques and wasteful and reckless exploitation of the soil. A process no less costly in the final reckoning is what has been termed "human erosion" which is undermining the Union's population. As compulsory registration of births and deaths has not been introduced for Non-Europeans, vital statistics which would accurately reflect the position are lacking. But enough data have been accumulated to point to an alarming incidence of gastro-intestinal and deficiency diseases, a mounting tuberculosis rate, and an alarmingly and abnormally high infant mortality rate. . . .

There are a number of voluntary agencies at present dealing with one or other aspects of the broad field covered by adult education. The Red Cross Society and St. John's Ambulance Society, the Child Welfare Society, the Public Health Department, particularly where Health Centres have been established, the clinics established by certain local authorities, are all active in the field of health education. The Red Cross Society, in particular, has made significant contributions through its pamphlets published in as many as four different Native languages, its posters designed particularly to assist illiterates, its reference and lending library, and above all, its production of films. Two of these films, one dealing with venereal disease and the other with typhus, were especially arranged for Natives.

In other fields of adult education for Non-Europeans are agricultural societies, co-operatives, women's associations for the betterment of home life, boys' and girls' clubs, Wayfarers, Path-finders, sports clubs and leagues, art exhibitions, child welfare societies, cripple care committees, association for the blind, deaf and dumb, Y.M.C.A. work, churches, and missions which carry on a number of activities in both rural and urban areas. Those activities along with social welfare are subsidised by the government, but there is a great lack of co-ordination in the work. What has been significant in the past four years is the increasing willingness on the part of organisations established to benefit the lower class European to include in their work provision for Non-Europeans. Advances, too, have been made in the attitude of the government towards the Non-European peoples who are now brought within the scope of most, if not all, social welfare legislation. . . .

(The article here discusses the radio, the press and libraries.)

But no plan, no matter how excellently devised, can exist in a vacuum. Education is not an end in itself; it is a means to an end. The aim of education is to enable the individual to improve his skills and his knowledge and to widen the horizons of his interest in order to live a happier, fuller and more constructive life and to utilise to their maximum the potentialities which his particular society provides. To educate an individual to certain skills and then to deny him the opportunity of practising them: to widen his intellectual horizon to an enjoyment of a variety of cultural pursuits which are no longer available after the conclusion of the educative process: such education must of necessity breed frustration and seething resentment, if not open revolt.

In other words, a successful educational system can only be evolved once a society has decided basic questions: namely, what occupations its members are to follow and what shall be their social and political status. To the first question South Africa has as yet given no definite answer; to the second it has given an answer which is not acceptable to the Non-Europeans to whom it applies.

Hitherto it has been generally accepted that the great bulk of Africans shall be unskilled labourers. The theory is that they shall live in the Reserves, that the men shall periodically leave the Reserves to sell their labour, which is the only marketable commodity of which they can dispose, and that by a combination of money wages paid on the assumption that the family's subsistence is in part provided for by the products from the land, subsidised by the man's earnings outside the Reserves, a workable economy will be attained. This is the theory. The practice has already been broken down in part and is increasingly doing so. It is estimated that in certain areas, such as the Transkei with its population of 1¼ million Natives, one third of the population is landless. The process of urbanisation is becoming more marked, revealing itself particularly in the townward drift of women. But as yet the bulk of the population in this transition stage is a "part-time" population; part-time farmer and part-time industrial labourer, educated for neither occupation and lacking in the skills requisite for both.

An efficient educational system for South Africa can only be evolved once it has been decided to what extent the population is to be stabilised and to what extent a full-time Native peasantry and a permanent industrial labour force is to be developed. At present, primary education in town and country differs little in content. Africans themselves are vehemently opposed to any deviation from the European system and tend to regard only book-learning as education in the truest sense. Even the most enlightened and liberal educationists themselves have their hands tied by reason of the fact that they do not know what they are educating their pupils for. Are the Native youths attending a school in a remote Native area going to be agriculturists, or are they going to leave the area and work and live in a town. . . .

(A promising Farm School experiment in the Cape Province, Glen Grey district, is here briefly described.)

While adult education lags far behind primary education in the extent of the facilities provided, the perplexity as to purpose is a far lesser one. Adult education for Non-Europeans is a necessity not only for the benefit of the individuals concerned but in order to make possible the implementation of such progressive health and agricultural schemes as are being sponsored by state authorities. It is a truism to state "that the general health of the whole community can only be secured and maintained if the whole mass of the people has a real share in education and has some understanding of its meaning and purpose". This is particularly true of a segregationalist society like the South African one, where the less privileged racial groups tend to regard all government-sponsored measures with antagonism. This is the present situation in some of the Native areas —where the salvation of the land and of the people is endangered by hostility to measures intended for their advancement. Without the co-operation of the people, which cannot be secured while they are lacking in understanding, soil reclamation schemes will fail as surely as will health campaigns. Only coordinated efforts in which the educational apparatus is geared to the total project can halt deterioration of national and human resources and set the signal for future progress.

IV. ASIA

Continuing to the east, the immense areas and great populations of China and India claim immediate attention.

CHINA. Fundamentally democratic, with a deep reverence for scholarship, relatively homogeneous, without the continuous burdens of foreign domination, productive in philosophy and the arts, and creative of cultural forms understood, enjoyed, and followed by a vast population, the Chinese have yet only recently initiated a successful national attack on the tasks of Fundamental Education. Perhaps the language difficulty may be largely accountable; and there are other reasons to be sought in the political, economic, and social history of the country. There is now ample evidence, in any case, that China, as a Republic, has been setting about the problem with a new national determination.

The devoted and enthusiastic work of Mr. James Yen has been reported in the volume from which a quotation is given at the beginning of this Chapter. Many other workers, fired with religious or humanitarian zeal, have taken part in the vast endeavour to bring education to a total population of 450 millions.

The following statement is taken from an authoritative Chinese source:

Since the introduction of the modern educational system in China it has been the prime object of the National Government, especially since 1927, to push forward elementary education and to combat illiteracy. Several attempts were made to accomplish this long-desired result in limited periods of time. Progress in different provinces has differed according to local conditions, but unfortunately all such efforts were interrupted by the outbreak of the Sino-Japanese war in 1937.

Meanwhile, however, the National Government did not abandon its purpose to reform the system of local government in order to give it a democratic character. After a number of experiments the new Statute on local government was promulgated in the summer of 1939. Within this new system of local government education plays a very important part. The essence of the system is to give people the opportunity of self-government and the practice of democracy by election. The system is based on the old tradition of the family as the unit in the formation of society. As a rule, the primary unit is one family. About ten families form a Chia, ten Chias a Pao, ten Paos a Shiang (with a variation of between six to fifteen). Each family is counted on a basis of five persons.

It was intended to have the local educational system called "People's Education" (or Universal Education). One People's School was to be established in a Pao (roughly 100 families) and one Central People's School was to be established in a Shiang. This project was to be carried out in a period of five years for all the provinces, with the exception of Szechwan, where three years was the period.

In the first year all the existing schools were to be re-organised starting on the 1st August, 1940. In the first year each Shiang was to have a Central People's School and three Paos, on an average, were to have one People's School. During the second year three Paos were to have two People's Schools and during the third year each Pao was to have a People's School, with the exception of the Paos in the Shiang where the Central People's School existed.

Despite the difficult times, this project has been carried through very successfully in Free China. Taking the Province of Szechwan, prior to the introduction of this project in 1939, among the 4,640,301 children between 6 and 12 years old, only 1,490,639 were in school. In the year 1939 there were altogether, including kindergarten, elementary, primary, and elementary schools with higher grades, 25,984 schools, which is only 32.12% of the number planned. In the year 1944 the number of People's Schools and Central People's Schools reached 47,341. Among 4,689,378 children of school age 3,516,946 were already in school, an increase from 32.12% to 75%.

In this local reform, "People's Education" differs from former primary education in this respect, namely, that it includes adult education in the People's Schools and Central People's Schools. This adult education is carried out in separate schools or classes. Since the introduction of the new system each People's School has two divisions, one for children between the ages of six and twelve, the other for adults between the ages of fifteen and forty-five, subdivided for men and women. The usual period of the elementary courses for adults is four months, devoted to civics, Chinese, "elementary knowledge", mathematics and music; further advanced courses in Central People's Schools are given to adults who have finished the elementary courses. This advanced course of six months will emphasise vocational training. This part of the work has not advanced as fast as primary education because of the shortage of labour during the war and also the difficult economic condition of the people, which did not give them time to attend adults' classes. But it is very encouraging to see that the ordinary people realise the importance of education and are willing to contribute either in money or in building materials, such as bricks, tiles and timbers, for building a new school. Everywhere there has been enthusiastic support for "People's Education". The result is the rapid development of schools on the primary level, and there have been rapid increases in the middle schools in the same province.

The aim of this People's Education is to give one tenth of the population free elementary education and to liquidate illiteracy in the first period for about 35% of the population. As to the number of graduates who are attending secondary schools, about one out of a hundred reach this goal.

There were great difficulties in getting trained teachers for the rapidly growing number of schools, and the standard had to be somewhat reduced to meet the situation after the introduction of this reform; but the Normal Schools have increased in numbers and the educational expenditure has also increased. Taking, for example, the same Province of Szechwan, the educational expenditure in the provincial budget in the year 1939 was 8.37%, increasing to 14.44% in 1945. The expenditure in the budget of the district governments was between 31.90% and 39.89% of the total budget, without counting voluntary contributions in money and in kind, including building materials and rice for the teachers.

The People's School and Central People's School are the centres of the Pao and of country life; teachers are taking part in the administration of their respective Pao and Shiang and they exercise quite a marked influence on the political life of the community.

This is a fine accomplishment during China's eight-year-long struggle against Japanese aggression; and the rapid progress in education in general, and People's Education in particular, must be recognised as a remarkable achievement in modern China. In time to come, side by side with the practice of the self-governing system, it is essential that China as a modern State should develop in the right direction, while education and Fundamental Education are pursued along the best lines.

The heroic efforts of Chinese teachers and students during the war are well known, and the formal governmental effort is proceeding in the face of economic and political difficulties the course of which is anxiously followed by the world.

Language difficulties are acute in China, especially because of the form of the traditional expression of the language in writing and in print. These difficulties are of such a special kind that they will be dealt with more fully in a later section of this volume. The general nature of the problem in China exhibits very sharply also the difficulties which arise in a well established culture when Fundamental Education is undertaken with aims which diverge markedly from those that have been consciously or unconsciously set in the older tradition.

Concerning these latter difficulties, quotations are presented from a printed contribution submitted to the Editorial Committee (Hsu 1):

Education in contemporary China is a problem which belongs to . . . a society which is in a state of rapid change. . . . Here the problem involves not only cultural transition from the older to the younger generation but also the change from old to new standards for all, as well as the ability of the society to assimilate the products of the new standards . . . it is a situation in which family, school, and the society fail, at least temporarily, to conform to each others' standards.

In order to understand education in contemporary China, it is necessary to grasp its basic features in traditional China . . . that is, China before 1842, when Chinese society was free from significant western influences and was more or less a self-contained whole. In that China, informal education had three objects . . . livelihood . . . social adequacy . . . and ritual adequacy. . . . In traditional China formal education was a part of informal education. . . . A livelihood was to be made studying the classics and working to pass a number of successive examinations. Successful candidates would enjoy opportunities of becoming members of the official hierarchy. . . . Officialdom, which absorbed the more energetic elements of the society, was practically an industry under the circumstances. In relation to social adequacy . . . a learned person was expected to show greater adherence to classical rules in matters of filial piety, sex behaviour, etc. Theoretically, Chinese scholars were not supposed to take too much notice of the spiritual world. . . . Nevertheless, as most ritual matters were communal matters and all scholars were taught to be harmonious with the communities in which they lived . . . this theoretical difference was of no material consequence.

Since 1842 and especially after 1911, when China became a Republic and when all traditional institutions of education and examination were formally abolished, . . . Western influence became definitely more fashionable. . . . Informal education remained, however, the same as before for the vast majority of the Chinese. As a result formal education, as given in schools, and informal education, as given in homes and neighbourhoods, were often conflicting. . . . The abolition of the old imperial examination system, the fact that the new schools taught new subjects and were no longer under the control of the family . . . that more schools were established through government, missionary, and commercial efforts . . . that schools became more expensive . . . led to the loss by the *literati* as a group of some of their old prestige. . . . Also a series of social conflicts resulted.

One category of social conflict appears in connection with sanitation and health. School children are taught not to spit on the floor, to take baths regularly, to have injections when there is a cholera epidemic, etc. When they go home, they find the barrier of age-old habits, deeply intrenched in the minds of their parents and senior relatives, practically insurmountable.

The second category of social conflict . . . involves the question of sex mores. . . . There have been many tragedies in which a man's educational level and that of his wife were vastly different.

A third category of social conflict concerns family bonds. Parental authority is being broken more and more by a greater expression of exclusive intimacy between man and wife. . . . Many parents find this experience very bitter.

The fourth category of social conflict may be called unemployment among the educated. . . . Among Chinese literati there has never been any tradition of experience in organisation for active purposes. Non-official organisations even on a vast scale have always existed in the country but they were organised along established lines for the purposes of maintaining the *status quo*. . . . The application of most of the newly acquired techniques in such fields as agriculture, co-operatives, and industries requires . . . modern types of organisation. Furthermore, many educated persons in the new situation are finding themselves unable to take advantage of some of the newer opportunities because they involve a certain loss of the *literati* status. Also there is a vast difference in standards of living between the educated classes on the one hand, and the majority of the population on the other. Before the present war, the average salary of a university graduate, if he secured a job, would be about eight to ten times the salary of a waiter in a restaurant or of a shop assistant. . . . The vast majority of industrial and commercial establishments had needs but were unable to offer rewards which would be equivalent to the standard of living of the educated.

Another difficulty is a most fundamental one. That is the lack of industrial development in China as a whole. We may say that China is overpopulated or we may say that she is suffering from under-production.

Without considering these fundamental points, some enthusiastic reformers have started the so-called college-student-go-back-to-village movement. These people and others exhorted products of modern education to go back to their rural districts with the intention of improving the life and conditions of millions of farmers while, at the same time, they would have to live, more or less, under the same conditions that they were trying to improve. This movement has two drawbacks: The first is that, without some sort of religious or other type of fanaticism, it has never been possible, throughout the known years of human history, to get people who are used to a higher level of comfort and have been taught the necessity of such comfort voluntarily to give this up in favour of a life which is literally a fraction of their customary standard. The second drawback is more fundamental. These reformers have failed to recognise that reformation of rural conditions must be sustained by improvement of urban production, for the disastrous conditions of many Chinese villages are the result of forces beyond the control of local communities and their inhabitants.

A second contribution (Laubach 6, pages 1-8) draws upon the experience of a veteran teacher of Chinese illiterates. This contribution emphasises the importance for China, as for all other lands, of high speed printing presses producing cheap reading matter. It asserts that the attack on illiteracy "can become a mass movement only through a number of organisations, institutions, and individuals working simultaneously from different angles in order to bring pressure on the life of the people." It speaks of the fact that the financial support for education tends to be shifted from the central government to provincial governments and from them to municipalities, which "in some cases hold up the whole project for lack of funds." It speaks also of the danger of political interference when the enterprise is made entirely governmental.

After reporting on the favourable results of certain missionary activities, this contribution goes on to say, "two difficulties naturally arise in connection with projects sponsored by small groups, institutions, or individuals. . . . The first is that the wide range of experiments which . . . are necessary tend to become so wide that they cannot secure adequate results or lead to accurate findings. . . . The second is that those interested are so very largely persons who have . . . become devoted to a certain method . . . and are absolutely impervious to the value of other methods." There are at least a score of schemes in use in various parts of China for the attack on the linguistic problem and this circumstance "makes a mass movement on a large scale, almost an impossibility." It also obstructs the production of follow-up materials, "produced cheaply in adequate quantities."

The contribution ends by pointing out that the Chinese common people have a culture, quite regardless of literacy, which is "so developed that they can, in drama, needlework, ceramics, and architecture, display a form of art that preserves the traditions of the past and reveals initiative in the present. . . . The development of economic life should have its place, but not to the exclusion of the traditional culture-life, nor to the exclusion of the spiritual and moral life essential to a fully developed personality."

INDIA. In the sub-continent of India, Fundamental Education faces a task not less immense, in terms of the numbers concerned, than the task in China, hardly less difficult in the matter of language, and profoundly complicated by historic tensions and present political uncertainties. A comprehensive contribution on the situation in India (Chetsingh 1, pp. 8-11) is here presented in part. The portion of this statement which describes the situation largely in factual terms reads as follows:

Less than 15% of the people in India live in towns and cities as compared with 79% in England and Wales, 51% in the United States of America and 42% in France. In British India nearly 74% of the population is dependant on agricultural or pastoral pursuits. India's problem of mass education is therefore largely a rural problem. Of the total village population about 179,000,000 live in villages with less than 2,000 inhabitants. Nearly 70,000,000 people live in villages which have a population of less than 500 inhabitants. The Auxiliary Education Committee of the Indian Statutory Commission wrote as follows in 1929:

"Primary education in towns is comparatively easy to provide, organise and make efficient. Schools and staffs are larger, good teachers are easier to secure, and adequate supervision and inspection can be more easily provided. It is less difficult to cater for the needs of particular communities or classes. On the other hand, sites and proper 'elbow-room' for schools cost more."

In considering the financial aspects of employing trained teachers a Committee appointed by the Government of Bengal to consider the problem of primary and adult education wrote as follows in 1939, ten years later:

"Happily there are several factors inherent in the present situation which minimise considerably the amount required to allow an effective start.

"Although the total number of children of the ages 6-9 in the province approximates 5,500,000, many of these reside in places or under conditions which make difficult, if not impossible, their attendance at a school. It will only be economically possible to create schools where at least 25-30 children can be gathered from within a radius of at most 2 miles. The population of Bengal is scattered over a very wide area and many children even with a properly distributed system of schools will be unable to attend. Communications are bad and for many years to come transport of children from outlying areas to centralised schools will be out of the question. There will be a certain number of children, also, who for other reasons such as infirmities, or attendance at private schools, will not attend the ordinary publicly provided primary school. We estimate that 20 per cent of the children will not for the above reasons have to be provided for, and the necessary expense is correspondingly reduced. This brings the financial requirements down to 4 crores." (Lakh = 100,000 units; crore = 100 lakhs.)

The following will help us further to appreciate both the magnitude and the complexity of the problem:

In many provinces large areas have a population density of no less than 150 persons to the square mile. The following Table illustrates this point:

	Percentage of total area of province having a population of under 150 per square mile	Percentage of total population of province living in such areas
Baluchistan	100.0	100.0
N.W.F. Province	88.6	71.6
Coorg	86.0	77.9
Assam	73.1	30.0
Central Provinces	70.5	49.6
Bombay	60.4	29.0

It is interesting to note also the average area served by a boys' primary school. The figures were arrived at by the Indian Statutory Commission's Auxiliary Committee in 1929 and doubtless the average area served by a school has tended to shrink during the following years. Nevertheless, the fact that during the war years, 1939-1945, there was little expansion is so vital that in the main the figures continue to be an effective guide.

AVERAGE AREA SERVED BY BOYS' PRIMARY SCHOOL

	Sq. Miles
Madras	3.07
Bombay	10.05
Bengal	2.01
United Provinces	5.65
Punjab	16.89
Bihar and Orissa	3.03
Central Provinces	23.84
Assam	12.10
British India	6.73

It should be remembered that in the Punjab there is an exceptionally large number of middle vernacular schools which are really enlarged primary schools, and that in the Central Provinces and Assam there are large forest tracts which are very thinly populated.

A remarkable feature of educational administration and policy in India has been the narrowness of its aim in the field both of primary and adult education. Literacy and little else has been the criterion of success. For instance, even in that most progressive government educational document, the Report of the Central Advisory Board of Education on Post War Educational Development in India (popularly known as the Sargent Report) we read the following (in Chapter I):

"In 1936-37 there were 11,985,986 pupils on the registers of some school or other as compared with approximately 60,-000,000 children in the 5-14 age group. Of these children 5,188,601 were in Class I, 2,355,418 in Class II, 1,722,292 in Class III, 1,214,504 in Class IV and only 703,628 in Class V. The balance were in Middle Schools, including the middle sections of high schools. Figures for previous years record a similar falling off. This means that less than one out of every four children stayed long enough at school to reach the earliest stage, Class IV, at which permanent literacy is likely to be attained. *The result is that money spent on the others (nearly 80%) may be regarded as largely wasted.*" (Italics not in the original.)

One or two observations on this extract from the report of the most weighty official body of educational administrators are called for. They seem to think of literacy rather than in terms of the co-ordination of the child's powers of observation, thinking and action. They do not seem to attach much value to the training in social habits that a school gives. Modern parents and teachers know that other things being equal a child of six who has gone to some sort of *modern* infants' class and has barely secured an acquaintance with the first primer is on the whole better educated and more socialised than a child of the same age who has, under a coach, learnt to read fluently. The board go on to say: "There is only one way to stop this wastage and that is to make education compulsory. In addition to attendance officers who know their duty and courts which are ready to do theirs . . . etc., etc." Their minds are set on the view traditionally held in India that it takes four years in a primary school to attain literacy. Upon analysis it is found that the evidence of facts is different. In his painstaking study of the problem of literacy in India, Mr. R. V. Parulekar has established that three years schooling enables the Indian child to become a literate.

A second observation is that in reckoning "wastage" those who are responsible for the present school system in India tend to pronounce judgments condemnatory of the poor primary school teacher and the ignorant village parent and omit to take into consideration all the facts—of which their own administrative arrangements form the main part.

A reference to the Report of the Bengal Government Committee (1939) on Problems of Primary and Adult Education already referred to will illustrate my point. There were 90,000 teachers teaching in 65,000 primary schools in Bengal. Of these, 53,000 primary schools were only two-class schools.

From what has been said above it will be seen what a colossal task India has before her if she is to secure for her adolescent population alone the most potent tool of acquiring knowledge in the modern world—*the ability to read with comprehension and pleasure.*

The problem of "wastage" and "stagnation" has another aspect to which attention must be drawn. The schools must carry the blame for continuing to make a good many children spend at least two years in the I Class. In 1927, the percentage of failures in Bombay in Class I was 54; in 1937, it was 50. In the Philippines it was 23 in 1934, while in the Dutch East Indies in 1935 it was 19.

"The low percentage of literacy recorded by the population censuses," writes Mr. Parulekar in his *Literacy in India,* "is attributable to yet another cause which is that the high birth and death rates prevailing in this country take away nearly three fourths of the literate products of the schools, leaving only one fourth to add to the actual increase in the percentage of literacy from decade to decade. In dealing with the Indian literacy problem this fundamental fact is often ignored and conclusions are drawn belittling the results of the educational system. . . ."

The brief statement of facts above makes it clear that for any real advance in fundamental education in this country three things are indispensable. They are: (a) very much larger funds;

(b) better trained teachers; (c) a bolder and more equalitarian educational policy.

Concerning adult education in India this contributor writes, in part, (Chetsingh 1, pp. 17-18) as follows:

To most people in India, adult education signifies literacy. One of the weakest sections in the noble effort at creative educational thinking which the Sargent Report has given us is that which deals with adult education. We may recall what an official spokesman has said in summarising it:

"The number of adults to be made literate will be approximately 1,270 lakhs. (lakh = 100,000). It is proposed to make literate all these numbers within a period of 25 years, of which the first 5 years will have to be devoted to recruiting and training suitable teachers. During the period of 25 years, a number of persons will inevitably pass out of the 10-40 range, and the anticipated decrease will be about 365 lakhs. This leaves 905 lakh persons to be made literate. Assuming that one teacher can make 25 pupils literate in a course of instruction lasting for 100 hours, the total number of teachers required will be 36.2 lakhs. It is proposed to pay Rs. 1 per hour per teacher, and the total expenditure on teachers' salaries will amount to Rs. 36.2 crores. (Crore = 100 lakhs or 10 million.) To this must be added 15% to cover the expenditure on books, equipment, administration, etc. The total expenditure will therefore amount to Rs. 41.6 crores spread over 25 years. This is the cost of a well-organised literacy drive, and 10% of this should be added towards adult education. Thus the total on both literacy and education will amount to Rs. 59.7 crores (about £4 billion, 447 million). In the process of working out this scheme, liquidation of illiteracy will be so telescoped with the real adult education scheme, that funds budgeted for the latter purpose will be wholly spent on those who are already literate. The estimated total annual cost will be approximately Rs. 3 crores."

While the proposals vaguely refer to "adult education" they fail to give an indication of the larger conception of education which is needed. One misses in planning to-day evidence of preparation for creating the right type of machinery for work-

ing out what adult education proper will involve. Indeed most
plans show a fatal dependence on the primary school teacher as
the chief instrument of liquidating adult illiteracy. No adequate indication is given of either the programme of adult
education proper or of the agencies to be employed in working
out that programme in most of the plans which have seen the
light of day. I do not for a moment suggest that literacy is not
important. Its importance cannot be emphasised too much at
this stage of our country's development. Lenin once said: "The
liquidation of illiteracy is not a political problem; it is a
condition, without which it is impossible to speak of politics.
An illiterate man is outside of politics and before he can be
brought in he must be taught the alphabet. Without this there
can be no politics—only rumours, gossip, tales, superstitions."
India dare not disagree.

We must also tell ourselves firmly that no efforts at liquidating
illiteracy completely can succeed which ignore the motto which
a Chicago broadcast gave many years ago. The speaker said:
"Education and recreation, united they stand, divided they fall."

It needs to be said, and said forcibly, that concentration on
primary education and ill-prepared-for literacy drives cannot
give us a reading population—reading as distinct from the
ability to read. I am doubtful if it can even secure us literacy.
Sir Richard Livingstone, in discussing the way out of the educational problems of England, has said:

"Unless we establish a compulsory part-time continuation system which will carry on to 18, the education of the earlier years
of youth of the nation will still be largely wasted."

India must arrange for continuation-education as a part of
her adult education programme. Fear of heavy expenditure
should not deter us from facing this question squarely. A great
deal of money which is now spent on ineffective measures to
safeguard public health, to combat criminal or wasteful tendencies such as gambling, drink and petty crimes, would be saved if
we offered such facilities. The working of the Shop Employees
Act provides us with an illustration of the way social legislation
in India fails to achieve its real objects simply because there is
no complementary educational provision. Most shop employees

do not make good use of their "holidays." All they have available to them are poor-quality cinema shows, card games and other more questionable ways of spending their leisure. *Expenditure on early education will fail to produce the results we desire unless continuation education is made available.*

Charts based on official figures show very great quantitative gains in education in India since 1882; but both as to the extent of education and still more as to its quality and results, disturbing questions remain to be answered.

Two charts are here reproduced, drawn from the Eleventh Quinquennial Review of the Bureau of Education, India, Vol. 1 (1932-37).

In 1937, at the Wardha National Education Conference, a plan was drawn up for the approval of the National Congress. Three principles already adopted by the Congress were restated: "(1) free and compulsory education should be provided for seven years, on a nation-wide scale; (2) the medium of instruction must be the mother tongue; (3) throughout this period education should centre round some form of manual and productive work, and all other activities . . . should be integrally related to the central handicraft chosen with due regard to the environment of the child." To these three principles the Wardha Conference added a fourth: "(4) the Conference expects that this system of education will gradually be able to cover the remuneration of the teachers."

This "Wardha Scheme" and other educational proposals for India are still under discussion; there is a constant ferment of thought and many examples of promising action in Indian education. Special difficulties are not minimized in the reports at hand: the education of village women is held to be indispensable to progress; the totally inadequate pay of teachers is a bar to effective work; religious differences and caste distinctions add special difficulties; and the primitive

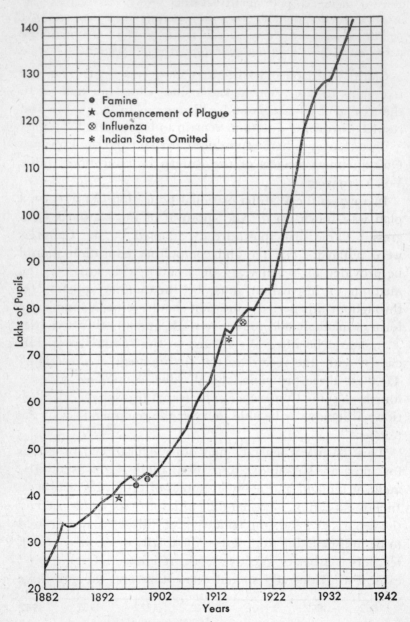

FIGURE 1
TOTAL NUMBER OF PUPILS UNDER INSTRUCTION IN INDIA

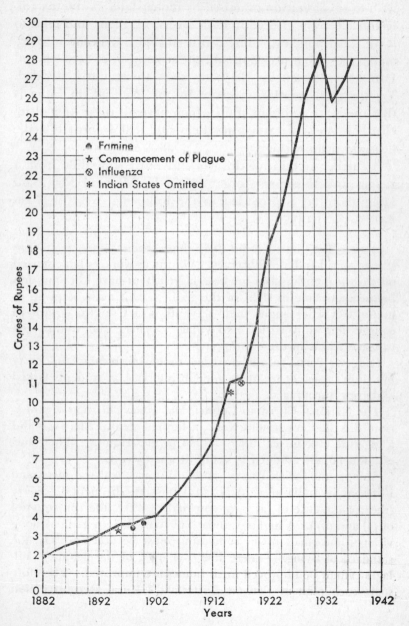

FIGURE 2
TOTAL EXPENDITURE ON EDUCATION IN INDIA

Famine
Commencement of Plague
Influenza
Indian States Omitted

Crores of Rupees

Years

and uneconomic methods of farming in the villages, together
with the exploitation practised by money lenders and tax collectors, keep the people in debt, overwork them, and tend to
leave them hopeless. The confused political situation over-
arches the whole situation and the separation of Moslem and
Hindu constituencies helps to keep the country divided.
Yet the total impression given by the material on India is
that there are forces in train which have all these difficulties
clearly in view, are attacking them, and will eventually make
headway against them.

A further account of the work in India (this time from a
report to a missionary organisation by Mr. and Mrs. Sam
Higginbottom) is provided in the following excerpts (Laubach 7, pp. 1-13):

During the last decade there have been many campaigns
started to rid India of illiteracy. Volunteer workers have started
off with real enthusiasm but to a large extent have lost ambition
before they came in sight of the goal. Credit must be given to
housewives who taught their servants, social service groups in
colleges and universities, and village teachers who volunteered
to teach adults in the evenings.

Congress Party volunteers tried to be spectacular and hasty
but didn't teach at frequent enough intervals, so students lapsed
and grew discouraged.

The National Christian Council and other Christian organisations did the most serious work in limited areas. The army did
a gigantic task in teaching soldiers in most camps. Their success was largely attained by using Roman script.

Among the chief causes of educational backwardness and
illiteracy in India are: (a) physical poverty, (b) mental poverty
(the consequence of (a)), (c) spiritual poverty (the consequence
of (a) and (b)). A higher standard of living is required. Among
villages and small towns something must be done to raise the
standard of living. (There live over 75% of the people.) Villages cannot be improved until homes are improved. Therefore
some such plan as Kenyon Butterfield's Rural Reconstruction

Centres to cater for eight or ten contiguous villages is a necessity.

The inferior social status of women and girls is one of the greatest bars to educational progress. Until the woman's status can be raised she suffers from an inferiority complex. She becomes hopeless because she has been taught that in this incarnation she cannot rise; she must wait for a subsequent one. The ignorant, illiterate, superstition-ridden woman, who lives by her fears and her doubts, whose world is peopled with gods and goddesses who wish to work her harm, can pass on to her children only what she herself believes and possesses. Many of these traditional ideas are not religion and can be overcome by the enlightenment of experience as education is received.

Therefore a drive for the education of village women is one of the indispensables of progress. The senior women keep the younger women bound to the home, therefore until some way is devised to get the grandmother and mother-in-law interested in getting the younger women and girls at work on small village industries sponsored by the rural social worker, which carry reading and writing as a requirement, there is little chance of getting improvements into the homes. Men can do little to overcome the traditions of the home without help from outside. This is a difficult task but should not be avoided because of its difficulty. A scheme for the education of women through the Village Centre Project was drawn up by the Home Economics Department of the Agricultural Institute at Allahabad for the Post War Economic Planning of the United Provinces, based on experience in such a centre. This was accepted and given prior claim to funds, but has been deferred due to the dislike of tackling such a large project and the great cost.

There are too few qualified women teachers in Indian villages to-day. The pay is too low to attract properly qualified teachers to work in the villages. Then there is the problem of the personal safety of the woman teacher or other social worker in the Indian village, one of the most difficult and baffling with which we have to contend. A single woman, unmarried or widowed, has great difficulty in protecting herself. So there should be two women workers put together to live in the same house and thus protect each other. One should be the school teacher, the other a social worker; known in the United States as the rural extension worker in Home Economics. Married women who have their husbands at work in the centre to protect them could teach in the average village. Also the wife would have her family and home to care for. Therefore her pay should be such as to enable her to have domestic servants to relieve her of some of the housekeeping so as to give her time for her teaching or social work.

The few women teachers for the Indian village are often not sufficiently educated and trained or properly paid. This also holds for a great majority of the men teachers. Few can live on their pay, so engage in other activities, not always helpful educationally. Far too many village teachers are teachers because of nepotism. It is a job on a public pay roll, a form of insurance, and sometimes the necessary qualifications for a teacher are lacking. Under such circumstances, the one-teacher village, where usually only the four primary classes are taught, is not likely to raise the literacy rate of India. Two thirds of the pupils who attend these schools have lapsed into illiteracy within five years of leaving school. (See Weir's report on village education in the U.P.) Another handicap is suitable literature for the child attending school and the adult who has learned to read and write.

Little literature is available for the village that relates it to our modern world or explains the changes that the railway, electricity, telephone and telegraph have brought about.

Suitable primers are needed and other readers adapted especially to the whole family if women are to be taught through readers; simple lessons in hygiene and home nursing; a better diet and better cooking; greater variety of food; beautification of the home in simple ways, such as how to make a mud fireplace with chimney; how to stencil artistic patterns on the walls instead of the crude hand and finger marks; how to put in small windows and where; how to make beds and bedding look attractive. Planned training of children instead of the capricious scolding and knocking about they usually get; with some ethical standards upheld. Some vegetable gardens can be useful within the small space in a courtyard. This also provides a use for the waste water. The value of a household patrine. How to overcome pests. Neighbourhood get-togethers on other occasions than weddings; games, exhibits, sing-songs, competitions. It seems easy to provide such literature but the fact is it is not yet available. If it were available there would be little market for it, because of the lack of purchasing power in the village. But without suitable literature in the hands of the villager, little progress can be made. This could be provided more easily were Roman script used as the army has used it during the war. Many of these things could be put into action—songs, plays, dramas, cinema, which the villager loves.

But even with Rural Reconstruction Centres, there must be a shift from farming on the present uneconomic scale to industry and the more highly paid service professions that would follow from the use of labour saving machinery. Agriculture must be mechanized in order to release adequate population for industry and auxiliary occupations. India must increase production per worker in order to provide funds to pay for the education (literary, mechanical and technical) which India must have in order to raise its standard of living. It is only out of the surplus of production per worker that the necessities and amenities of life can be provided and thus the standard of living raised. That is, education in the long run must be paid for by those who receive it. The present production per worker in India provides little surplus. Poverty is in direct proportion to the amount of hand labour used; the obverse is also true. The rise in the standard of living is in direct proportion to the amount of power controlled by each individual worker.

The average villager cannot yet see what gain or advantage there is in education either for himself or his children. They are afraid of their children becoming educated, because they may then look down upon their parents. The aim of Enoch Arden, to give his children a better bringing up than he had received, needs to be inculcated into the Indian villager. He asks, does it increase the income of the family? If his son is educated, does it mean he must leave home in order to make use of his education? If so he is lost to his family and village, which they do not like. As yet the village itself does not provide adequate scope for such of its members as become educated. And the average Indian student generally thinks one function of education should be to relieve him of physical toil and that he should not have to do manual labour; but the parents need the help of the child in the home or fields. It takes too long with the present scripts before a child is literate enough to read to the father or to save the father from loss of money due to his inability to read or keep accounts. This delay and inability to help his family with his literary attainments can be overcome by the more rapid pace of learning to read which the Roman script provides. But the villager will have to be shown before he will accept literary education. Another frequent difficulty has been the employment of teachers who insist secretly on being paid privately by parents for teaching children in Government schools. One often sees cases of the child being neglected or even tortured by the teacher until they either leave school or bring the desired "present" to the teacher. So a system of prizes to the teacher who had the greatest number of children pass examinations might be helpful. Poor parents cannot afford the frequent demands of the teachers in addition to the loss of the work of the child. So the child is kept at home. Also in many places children of untouchables are discriminated against, especially by the high caste teacher.

Again, lack of modern medicine reduces the vitality of the worker and thus reduces his production. The self-contained village can produce only a fraction of the desirable things for an abundant physical life. It may produce some things that can be more cheaply produced somewhere else, and may not be producing to capacity the things it is best fitted to produce but cannot consume and therefore must exchange. Hence the self-contained village standard of life is much lower than in a village that brings in what it needs and sends out its surplus of what it is best adapted to produce.

In the United Provinces village education received a set-back when it was turned over to the Local Boards and all supervision by the educational authorities taken off. School houses unfit for human habitation are often used, untrained and barely literate teachers are in charge, pay is usually inadequate. The teacher is sometimes an indigent relative of a member of the Board. Not enough of the Local Board's finance goes into village education, hence village education must be related to and supervised by a qualified body.

The Government should set up training schools with short courses as well as long courses and with refresher courses largely given in the field, as has been done in Mexico. Travelling inspectors with libraries, exhibits, demonstrations in motor vehicles and oxcarts; constant checks on and stimulation to inspectors as well as to teachers. A helpful supervisor should be so trained that he can inspire and teach the willing but poorly trained teacher. In any village, where any enlightened and up-to-date body maintains a school that seeks to meet the needs of the village, it is usually handicapped by incompetent inspectors who have little knowledge of modern education which provides work for the hands as well as the mind and the eye. The educational authorities now practice little of experimentation in education and try to squash any attempt to try new approaches. All through the Indian educational system, text-books are chosen years ahead; it is at least three years before a modern text-book can be used by students; thus most Indian education is years behind the new-found knowledge. Again far too much emphasis is placed on literary education and not enough on hand-work and skills; yet it is these latter that will be of value to the average pupil, few of whom will follow literary pursuits; most will engage in the ordinary work of supplying the physical needs of the village. In the last analysis village education must be frankly dollar education. It must pay for itself, it must pay the one who receives it. The way to make village education popular is to demonstrate that it is profitable. Let the cultural and aesthetic values wait on the economic.

The Laubach method had proved the most successful at the Allahabad Agricultural Institute where teachers as well as the Student Social Service League have used it for illiterate workers on the farm. These farm labourers in turn have helped their neighbours in the villages. Hindi was the language and Devnagri the character. Urdu with the Persian script is too difficult and takes too long for the ordinary adult illiterate to get much out of it. He becomes discouraged before he gets a working grasp. Roman script would shorten the time of the adult illiterate, but there is prejudice in India against anything smacking of being British. India is very much like some other places I know; the noble art of cutting off one's nose to spite one's face is very highly developed.

Dr. Laubach gave a demonstration of how to teach village women to read by using one of their common antiphonal songs. The verses of the song contain oft' repeated lines. There is so much repetition of the same words that before long several of the group of women could identify these words on the blackboard. Continuing this method the best women in the class got on well, but there was no suitable literature to continue the lessons. Petrol rationing limited the classes to one a week. The lapse in time between lessons soon discouraged us all.

Reformers in India cry to high heaven for free, compulsory, primary education. They forget that when they get this, they will have to tax themselves to pay for it. They fail to realise that any worth-while education costs somebody, it must be paid for, whether by parents or guardians, or by tax-raised money or a combination of these. But until the parents of the village child can afford to let their child go to school even though there are no fees, little progress can be made. In the average village home each child as it becomes old enough has work to do:— watching the live stock, gathering fuel, watching crops, driving off birds. The family cannot afford to dispense with this work. Therefore we come back to the problem of increased income for the parents.

The right incentive is the certainty that the villager will reap the reward for any extra toil he puts forth. At present he is generally robbed of this and so becomes discouraged and hopeless. I know of no government department that has dealings with the villager that does not regard him as fair game, to be preyed upon to the limit. The revenue, the police, the irrigation, the agricultural, the educational, the public health, the sanitary, the justice, through illegal exactions chiefly by petty officials, take unfair, unjust advantage of the villager. This contributes to his fatalism, which effectively cuts the nerve of all effort. Government has a Corruption Department; whether to find out and prevent corruption, or to further it, is not always clear. Of course there are honest, efficient officials in every department, but they are greatly outnumbered.

"A change of heart," to borrow Mr. Gandhi's phrase, is needed in India. As long as the majority of the high caste, educated Indian officials follow their present course, government can do little to help. I know of no village low caste who believes he can get justice in the courts against a high caste, or educated person. This leads to frustration and despair on the part of the common man in India to-day. Yes, government in India can do much, first of all clean house and control its own officers.

The Grant-in-Aid system for education in India has been of great value in extending education and maintaining and improving the standards. This gives to any individual or organised body, that will teach the prescribed courses, in buildings of an approved plan, with equipment laid down, and teachers with specific qualifications, a grant-in-aid up to one half of the cost of buildings and equipment and up to one half the running expenses of the school. Where government has availed itself of this policy, there has been more education and better quality education. But unfortunately government has had some narrow martinet type of officer who found it easier to start schools, government owned and managed. Such government-owned schools cost ten times the cost of an aided school. (See Meston's Report on an Educational Policy for India, Christian Literature Society, Madras.) According to Meston, with whom I agree, the Government should prescribe courses, lay down requirements for buildings, equipment and teachers. Its officers should spend their time in seeing that Government intentions are carried out. Government is at a great disadvantage compared to a private body in dealing with incompetent, lazy and unsatisfactory teachers. Once they are on a government payroll as government servants, it is almost impossible to remove them. Once a government servant and confirmed in his appointment, a teacher frequently loses all ambition to excel or to keep up in his subject. This is one reason for the inferior quality of education given in a government institution as compared to a well run non-government school or college. One of the best things for education in India would be for Government to revert to its own policy of grant-in-aid and get out of the educational business, leave it to more competent bodies.

Pay the teacher a living wage, encourage him to continue to study in his own line, and give increments for improvements. Get as inspectors, men and women, professionally capable but with a plus vision to urge on the slothful teacher, and further spur on the ambitions to succeed as a teacher. Encourage a spirit of enquiry in the teacher, let him try and test his ideas for improving the education he is engaged in.

There are qualified people in India who could prepare the needed literature but many of them cannot stand the expense of giving the time for writing and typing and other costs. These qualified men and women should be sought out and given grants-in-aid, according to the quality and quantity of work turned out.

Also the moving picture has great possibilities for removing illiteracy from Indian villages. Most of such schemes in India have failed because the one chosen for the work did not have his heart in it. Again too often the authorities baulk at the cost of doing the job properly, they want it to be done on the cheap and it will not work.

Any method of teaching that interests and inspires the pupil, and awakens his curiosity to such an extent that he continues to work when the teacher is not looking is justified. Teacher training does good in many cases. It also cramps the style of anyone with originality, the training teacher in India is often stilted and mechanical in his approach to the village school.

Mass education in India should aim at meeting all the needs of the individual: through better training for his vocation he should be taught that better health is a duty; that at least thirty per cent of the disease within a village is preventable, using means within his physical, mental and financial reach, i.e., malaria, dysentery, hookworm, cholera, etc. He should be taught the food requirements of his body to enable it to work efficiently. There is no place in the world where a greater variety of fruits and vegetables, tropical, sub-tropical and temperate, can be grown throughout the seasons than most parts of India.

The villager should be taught to stand up for his rights. One of the most discouraging things I know of in India is to try to help low caste village folk who have been forced to labour without pay, who have been beaten and had their bones broken. In several cases I have offered to provide a lawyer to take the case to court, but the villager begs me to desist, says all I do for him would lead to further oppression, extending to members of his family. The law is there to help him, but he has no confidence that it will protect him if he asserts his rights. Unfortunately, experience proves he is correct. The costliness of law, the perjury, the bribery of witnesses all go to discourage him.

To turn a primary school passed pupil adrift does not help to lift the educational level of the community. The Rural Reconstruction Centre might well have a vocational adviser, except that in India most vocations are determined by caste, but science and labour-saving machinery are bringing new occupations to India that can only secure the necessary labour by releasing enough workers from the caste callings.

It is fundamental to recognise the villagers as human beings, to let them have sympathy and understanding from above, to listen to their ideas and help them to carry them out.

SOUTH EAST ASIA. An extensive contribution from which excerpts are here given (Van Diffelen 1, pp. 1-5) concerns conditions in the Philippines, Siam, Indo-China, the States of Malacca and Singapore, and Indonesia:

With the exception—and that only in part—of the large Western cities, we see in these countries a very large number of genealogically and socially separate communities, rooted in thousands of more or less isolated centres, as independent units —almost complete in themselves—of religious, social, political and economic life. The place of the individual in these communities is determined by tradition, not by natural ability and in principle is capable of little or no alteration. The community and the land are bound by sacred ties. The exercise of the right of ownership is a social function, corresponding with duties towards society. Economically the community is a unit, which with its poorly developed division of labour is dependent upon a slow exchange of goods, while money changes hands only when a few articles are concerned which must be obtained from outside and for the few payments to the authorities in settlement of taxes. These communities live by the day, without the consciousness of or the care for to-morrow; they feel the measures of the authorities, destined gradually to convert the static community into a dynamic state, as an unwarranted interference with their lives; the school—as has frequently been proved—is surrounded by hostile feelings. The result is that, generally speaking, the community itself does not determine the nature of the education, as regards quality, quantity, or intensity.

A sound basis for primary education is the economic progress of the population, but such progress cannot be realised without primary education. This vicious circle can only be broken through by the combined action of a number of governmental measures in various spheres, by putting an end to the isolation of remote districts by constructing roads and railways, by spreading the gospel of hygiene, by agricultural and economic instruction and assistance, by helping to establish and develop co-operative societies, by regularising the credit system, by opening schools, etc.

In all the countries discussed here the authorities have broken through the vicious circle, to a greater or less extent, and a spontaneous "run" on the primary schools has taken place, though in many cases this movement is still local and though there are in each of the countries in question districts where the situation described above is the order of the day.

In the Philippines 1,400,000 children attended the primary schools in 1939 (population 16,000,000), in Indo-China 700,000 (population 23,000,000), in Siam 1,050,000 (population 14,400,-000), in Indonesia 2,000,000 (population 70,000,000).

From the school year 1934-35 till the school year 1938-39 the number of pupils in the primary schools in the Philippines increased fom 950,000 to 1,400,000. In Indo-China the increase in the whole school population in the last few years before the second World War amounted to 10% per annum; in 1919 the total number of pupils attending the various schools in Siam (not only the primary schools) was 160,000, while ten years later it was 610,000; in Singapore all the primary schools are full and it has become necessary to use some school buildings in two shifts.

In Indonesia this latter phenomenon is practically universal; nevertheless in 1939 nearly 50,000 children had to be turned away who wished to attend the first classes of the primary schools, because there was no room for them, while in the country as a whole the number of pupils of the primary schools from the school year 1933-34 till the school year 1938-39 rose from 1,400,000 to 2,000,000.

These figures show clearly that in the countries dealt with in this report the demand for education is beginning to develop on a large scale. Yet there are also districts in which, as a result of the gradual change-over from a barter to a money system, the development of industry and closer intercourse with strangers, and somewhat greater prosperity, the appreciation of the value of education has been aroused and in many cases has become very great but in which owing to a variety of causes this urge for education can only partly be met. Of all these causes, the economic factor plays the main part.

The labour value of a young lad or a young girl is so great even at an early age that attendance at school means a financial sacrifice for the family which, in the economic circumstances under which it lives, is not warranted. The result is that in districts where attendance at the primary schools is satisfactory or very good, only a small proportion of the pupils passes through all the classes; at six years of age, when they attend school for the first time, the children can still be spared from the production process of the family, but one or two years later they are taken away from school to play their part in that process.

In Indonesia in 1940, forty-two per cent of all the children of six years attended the first class of a primary school; not more

than twenty-four per cent of each year's group, however, finished
the whole three-year course in 1939. In the Philippines the
school population of the first and second grades is more than
double that of the third and fourth grades. In Indo-China the
number of pupils decreases from grade to grade by 50%, i.e.,
the number of pupils in all the first grades together is double
the total of all the second grades and four times that of the
third grade.

This falling off results in the education which is imparted in
the primary schools being acquired in its entirety by only a very
restricted number of pupils. It also makes it inopportune for
the authorities charged with education to increase the number
of grades of the primary school, now amounting to three (in a
few cases four) in Indonesia, four in the States of Malacca and
Singapore, four in the Philippines, three in Indo-China and four
in Siam.

It goes without saying that schools with a three or four year
course are really too short to combat illiteracy effectively, even
in the case of pupils who take the whole course, and that in the
long run a school with a six-year course will have to be the
minimum as the basis for fundamental education.

The great increase in the numbers of pupils attending the
primary schools has led to a concentric system of education being
built up in many of the countries discussed, whereby an attempt
is made to provide as far as possible a rounded-off programme in
each school year. This is particularly the case with the "cycle
élémentaire" in Indo-China. While the falling off at the primary school is very considerable, the number of pupils who have
passed through the primary school and who proceed to the
(three year) secondary schools (intermediate education) in the
Philippines, the (three year) "cycle élémentaire" in Indo-China,
the (four year) middle school in Malacca and the Straits and the
(two or three year) secondary school in Indonesia is much
smaller still. Thus in the Philippines the school population of
the secondary schools is 250,000 as compared with 1,400,000 at
the primary schools, in Siam 170,000 against 1,230,000, in Indonesia 270,000 against 2,000,000; thus in all three cases percentages between 13 and 18.

This contribution deals also with "school leavers" and their needs; adult illiteracy; the education of girls; the school curriculum; the language problem; the place of the school in the community; and the training and functions of teachers.

A more detailed study (Charton 3, pp. 1-9) of conditions in Indo-China completes our presentation of Fundamental Education in Asia.

INDO-CHINA. Of all the countries for which France is responsible, Indo-China is the one where popular education has achieved the greatest results and has acquired, as it were, freedom of the city, both in the Government's policy and in the eyes of the public. It has therefore obtained a firm and definite status and an original and national character which really make it a forerunner of Unesco's programme.

The position and the progress of fundamental education in Indo-China can be accounted for by the size of the population, the part played in the country by ancient civilisations that have guided its history and by the effects of French policy.

Indo-China is a territorial group, a union with a population of at least 24 millions. It consists of several countries, several nations combined since the Protectorate and the arrival of the French, in a Federation. First come the Annamites, who inhabit Tonking, Annam and Cochin-China, an Annamite border province colonised by Annamese rulers. There are some 17 to 18 million Annamites. Next comes the Cambodian group, a state with a king at its head. This group numbers 4 million people. Lao, on the higher reaches of the Mekong, is populated by Laoans, who are of the same family as the Siamese Thaïs and are a million strong. Lastly, on the Indo-Chinese central plateaus in Upper Tonking there are peoples of very diverse types, of Indonesian or Slav origin coming from China, who have been driven into the mountains and high table-lands by the expansion of other Indo-Chinese races. These are the Moïs, Thos, Thaïs, Meos and other ethnical minorities.

In this medley of populations, two ancient civilisations confront each other. On the one hand, we find the Chinese civilisation, which has left a very deep mark upon the Annamese population. It brought it Confucian ethics and ancestor-worship, the sense of law and the state, the mandarin and the scholar, Chinese characters and parables. In its habits, politics, and village life, old Annam is the heir of ancient Chinese civilisation. On the other hand, the Cambodians, descendants of the ancient Khmers, and the Laoans are still under the influence of Buddhism and Indian civilisation, which gave them their writing and their religion—the Buddhism of the "Little Vehicle"—their bonzes and pagodas, the rules of their social and personal life. In Cambodia and Lao, as in Viet-Nam and Cochin-China, we find elements of a nation and state; a complete but immobilised civilisation, conscious of its impotence in the face of modern life, but eager to be revitalised by the contact with the West.

Such civilisations have their own cultural and educational system. Traditional teaching is an institution greatly respected among the Annamese. In many villages a learned master teaches the children the most important Chinese characters, the elements of ethics and good manners. Reverence for the teacher and scholar is one of the main features of Annamese character. With the Cambodians, education remains religious. Children receive their religious and moral instruction from the bonzes in the pagodas. In the mountainous regions inhabited by the Moïs we meet with primitive conditions of life, out of contact with any organised or unified culture.

French policy worked upon this agglomeration of nations and peoples, this complex association of traditional and living, immobilised and static, civilisations, by creating an administrative and economic unity, by importing the cultural influences, political ideas and technical improvements of the West and by launching a campaign for modernising intellectual, economic and social life, which very soon satisfied the country's aspirations, especially amongst the Annamese educated classes and the old and new mandarin and business bourgeoisie. Hence the dual character of French policy in cultural and intellectual matters: on one hand, respect for the living civilisations of Indo-China, their culture and their language, and for national institutions and habits, as shown by the Protectorate's political regime, particularly in Annam and Cambodia; on the other hand, vigorous action to bring about the country's progress and development and its introduction to modern and Western life, by introducing the French language, creating schools and universities, forming new cadres and élites taught in Western schools. The opposition of these two tendencies and the reactions of the people themselves, who naturally cling to their national feeling and their traditional culture, but who are also eager for progress and instruction and anxious to assimilate modern culture and its technique, have led to a sort of compromise, a synthesis between the contribution of the West through the medium of French culture, and the spirit and tradition of Far-Eastern culture, which is not assimilated, but on the contrary assimilates and utilises French Western influences.

The solutions of the problem of fundamental education and popular teaching in Indo-China are due to this synthesis. To be sure, in the early stages of the French occupation of Indo-China, under the influence of the prevailing ideas in favour of assimilation and under the pressure of urban populations, who saw in the French school a means of attaining modern life and also offices and situations, the French Government established, above the traditional educational system which prevailed especially in Annam and Tonking, French or Franco-Annamese schools, where the teaching, freed of Chinese characters and the traditional organisation, assumed a modern and French aspect. The French schools led on to colleges and *lycées*. But it soon became apparent that popular education could not be based on direct opposition between the traditional and the French educational systems. Already in 1885, and more so in 1906, endeavours were made to broaden the scope of traditional education and to include in it the teaching of the Annamese tongue and local history and geography. It was soon found impossible, however, to introduce sufficient new life and modern elements into the rigidity of this school system to make it a popular educational force. The acquisition of knowledge represented by a few hundred Chinese characters was no answer to the call for a genuine popular education. On the other hand, to reduce the level of the French school to that of the village school would have been a fanciful, costly and materially impossible undertaking at variance with the facts of the situation.

However, the elements of a solution were at hand. The Annamese possess a language, the written form of which was fixed as far back as the 17th century by missionaries who came to preach the Gospel in Indo-China. This is "quoc-nghu," an original creation by Father Alexander of Rhodes. Quoc-nghu is Annamese transcribed in Latin characters. In the early days of the French occupation of Cochin-China, in the absence of educated men capable of teaching the Chinese characters, local schools were established where Annamese and its transcription into "quoc-nghu" were used. Quoc-nghu schools became more and more numerous. The experiment was conclusive. Henceforth, quoc-nghu became the expression of the national language, the means and instrument of teaching and of popular literature.

The 1917 educational code and the 1924 reforms fix the main lines of organised popular education in Indo-China. This organisation determined all progress and achievement in fundamental education until 1944. What are the general features of this system of popular education? In the first place, it is a system of teaching that aims at being really popular, a system that admits no limit or obstacle to school entry. The corollary of this definition of education has been accepted, and primary education is in principle recognised as being compulsory and free. The Emperor of Annam and the King of Cambodia have decreed the principle of compulsory education. In Cochin-China, where French law is in force, education has been compulsory since 1927. Children must attend school for at least three years. Compulsory attendance exists in 1,105 out of the 1,419 communes of Cochin-China. Inclined to become more and more compulsory, primary education, which the citizen considers his duty, is also free. In Indo-China, families pay no school-fees. Only private tuition has to be paid for. In fact, education is a heavy burden upon the regional and provincial finances, amounting to 13% of the budgets. To reduce this burden, the creation and upkeep of many rural schools are the responsibility of the local communities and villages. It soon became evident, however, that the local budget would also have to bear a share of the expenses of the district.

Elementary education in Indo-China is both a national and a regional undertaking. Instruction is given in the language of the region, that is, in quoc-nghu for the Annamite regions, in Cambodian and Laoan for Cambodia and Lao, and even in the ethnical minority tongues for the Moïs (Rhadés, Bahnars), the Thaïs and the Thos. As it is given in the mother tongue, it is not foreign to the life of the region, of which it recognises and teaches the traditional ethics and religion.

Elementary education is also modern. It is designed not only to combat illiteracy, but also includes in its syllabuses hygiene and physical training, geography and the usual branches of science. Finally, where there are teachers able to teach elementary French, such instruction is given as a preparation for supplementary and secondary education.

For elementary teaching in the mother tongue leads up to a second elementary stage comprising three years' study, which is conducted in the French language. Schools whose curriculum includes both stages, are known as full-course schools; in 1944 they numbered 545. The continuation stage is not of a markedly popular character; it is a selected course absorbing about 10% of the pupils receiving elementary instruction of the first stage.

Hence, a remarkable variety of types of elementary instruction is to be found in Indo-China. The different types of study are adapted to the tongues spoken in a given region, to its social conditions, its financial resources and its stage of development. The elementary school is modelled on the region and, where there are young Annamites, young Cambodians, young Laoans and young Moïs, there are Annamite, Cambodian, Laoan and Moïs schools. Similarly, the system of teaching varies with the type of school and the length of the school period. There are communal schools, rural schools, or rather village schools, whose main function is to combat ignorance, where the school period is short and teachers are untrained. There are "pioneer" schools with a modest curriculum, where the teaching is merely a preparation, an introduction to modern life. Finally, there are French schools with a full seven-year syllabus, which have been thrown open liberally to any Indo-Chinese who are capable, by reason of a practical knowledge of French, of benefiting from such instruction.

Three of these types of school are specially interesting and should be described in their original character: elementary schools, "pioneer" schools and the new kind of pagoda school.

The whole Indo-Chinese system of popular education is based on the elementary school with its three classes and three years of study. The language used is the mother tongue. A groundwork of modern language is, however, given, five or six hours a week being devoted to French wherever a qualified teacher can be found. The curricula are definitely and purposely Indo-Chinese. They are at the same time a beginning and a whole. Their essential object is to enable the child to read, write and count in his mother tongue. They aim at teaching him and making him practise the elementary rules of hygiene. They include the teaching and practice of the traditional ethical precepts: Confucian for the Annamites, Buddhist for the Cambodians. Finally, they teach the elements of geography, history, agriculture, and of the economy of the region. Some elementary schools have retained the optional teaching of the usual Chinese characters. Instruction is given by an Indo-Chinese teacher, sometimes merely an assistant, who is supposed to have been trained in a teachers' college. The curriculum ends with an elementary examination, the Indo-Chinese Elementary School Certificate. 63,048 candidates passed this examination in 1944.

The schools known as "pioneer study" schools, which differ in type in Annam, in Tonking and in the Moïs regions, are much simpler, more elastic, but also rougher and cheaper. In Central Annam, for example, there are regions inhabited by Moïs speaking different dialects, refugee communities isolated in a modern country, whose racial characteristics can be preserved with the help of the school. The Rhadés of Ban Methuat are an example. A school has been established to meet their needs, and they are also taught French by the direct method—this is the only language which can put them in touch with modern life without subjecting them to Annamite influence. In these sparsely populated regions free boarding schools are established; these schools have a simplified curriculum mainly devoted to manual work, practical agriculture and an initiation into the modern way of life. These schools are a means of salvation for the racial minorities of Indo-China.

Another kind of popular school is the communal school of Tonking and the village school which is its complement. The village itself is responsible for the school, including teacher and building. The curriculum is simplified; it aims at giving the child as early as possible the elementary knowledge necessary to raise him above the illiterate level. In Tonking the campaign against illiteracy resulted in two years in the establishment of more than 1,300 schools. Moreover, this form of village school is provisional, and, as soon as it can be changed into an elementary school with two or three classes, the work already done will be consolidated and quick schooling will develop into lasting and solid schooling.

Lastly, there is a new kind of pagoda school, established first in Cambodia and then in Lao. As we have seen, the Cambodians down to the lowest strata of the population, are imbued with the intensely religious spirit of Buddhism. The pagodas, which are to be seen everywhere, are at once a feature of the landscape and a centre of life and education; the bonzes in their yellow robes are still the priests and teachers of Cambodia. In this religious atmosphere, the official elementary school could have little influence on the common people. It remained for a long time the school of a minority, a preparation for secondary education and for official posts. The idea of the new kind of pagoda school arose in these conditions; it combines the traditional and religious education of the bonzes with the essential requirements of a basic education. The main feature of this type of school is that it will be run by the bonzes. Nothing will be done without them. The bonzes will be responsible for the greater part of popular and elementary teaching. The school will thus remain faithful to tradition, but will endow that tradition with its new spirit. The bonzes who become teachers are trained for their profession in "schools of instruction," a kind of training college where they finish their education and learn how to teach. Instruction is given entirely in the mother tongue, Khmer. It is essentially simple and practical, and is limited to writing, reading and arithmetic. The pagoda school takes children from the rice-fields and returns them to the rice-fields, furnishing them after two or three years with a new equipment for life and work. The school remains faithful to the pagoda, however; the morning is still devoted to religious exercises. The new kind of pagoda school may spread widely in Cambodia, and afterwards in Cochin-China and Lao.

In 1944 Cambodia had 1,028 new-type pagoda schools. The teaching in them has attained a level which allows 65% of the pupils to gain the elementary school certificate. Nor has the pagoda school been confined within its strict limits, for in Cambodia as throughout Indo-China there is urgent need of a wider and fuller modern and elementary education. Plans are laid for uniting the pagoda school with the official elementary school, the object being to provide in the pagoda school a preparatory teaching which will be carried farther in the popular schools.

In order to build and vitalise these different school establishments, they have had to be provided with the mainsprings of their activity—schoolbooks and teachers. There is no concealing the inadequacy of this material and the difficult problems connected with teachers and their training, education, and payment. Here we are up against budgetary and financial facts. Nevertheless, the results achieved emphasise the magnitude of the efforts made. The French administration has undertaken to provide the popular schools with the necessary school classics. School editions include books on all educational subjects, books on ethics, readers, arithmetic books, textbooks for object lessons, geography, history, hygiene and agriculture. More than 25 manuals have been published in the Annamite language and others in Cambodian, Lao, Tho, Rhadé, Bahnar, these latter for the Moïs regions. Further textbooks have been published for teaching French and for the use of teachers. School equipment has been supplemented by publication of maps and mural charts. These efforts of official publishers have been supported and extended by private initiative. Schoolbooks have been issued at low prices and sold for a few pence with astonishingly successful results. They are used not only in schools but also by grown-ups and are an indispensable weapon in the campaign against illiteracy. During 1944, 10,000,000 copies of different schoolbooks were published and put into use.

One of the main problems of education is the question of teachers. The very conception of the teacher's function has sometimes been difficult to define. The training colleges established in Indo-China have failed to furnish the necessary quotas. Moreover, it is been necessary to look for a district or village teacher who belongs to the same environment as those whom he has to educate. Only this type of rural and regional training college can prepare teachers who are not only suited to the district and live in the village itself, but are also capable of ensuring proper development of the local population. All the same, Indo-China in 1944 employed in its different schools more than 19,000 elementary teachers, all of them Indo-Chinese.

The spread of popular education in Indo-China applies to all parts of the country. It has been aided by private teaching, by local initiative, by groups like the association for the spread of "quoc-nghu," by adult courses and also by means of an ever-increasing volume of popular literature. In 1944 there were in Indo-China 5,400 schools of various types, and elementary education comprised 854,792 pupils, of whom 100,630 were girls. These general figures represent already a fairly high percentage of the school population, which should amount to 40%, if we reckon three years as the normal school period. It may also be noted that the distribution of schools varies greatly with the region; it is comparatively thick in the Annamite districts, where the population is densest, where education is compulsory and where economic development is rapid, that is to say, in the deltas of Cochin-China and Tonking, in the rich Annamite plains and along the Cambodian Mekong. On the other hand, Upper Tonking, the Annamite plateaus, the coast of Southern Annam and Lao still contain areas with a sparse distribution of schools.

Such was the state of popular education in Indo-China under

French administration in 1944. The work is well launched, its methods have been tested and its material means decided upon. What a national and modern popular school should be has been definitely laid down. There are, of course, large gaps to be filled: the school age must be raised and zones of illiteracy must be reduced; more girls must be sent to school and there must be a system of collective adult education. This will all be work for the Indo-Chinese themselves, who throughout have been associated in the responsibilities of popular education. In Annam and Cambodia a native administration, under the control of the Minister of National Education, has for a long time been in charge of elementary teaching. The new responsibilities will lie, within the Indo-Chinese Federation, with local authorities whom 20 years of experience have prepared for this arduous task.

To the uninformed western mind it may seem as if the task of Fundamental Education in the immense reaches of the Asiatic continent and among the diverse peoples is nearly hopeless. But the accomplishments here recorded and the plans reported belie such a pessimistic attitude. Fundamental Education is just beginning to be tried. Those who know it best have most faith in it.

V. THE MIDDLE EAST

In this area, where the political and economic situation is varied and confusing, the material at hand is incomplete yet in certain respects very enlightening.

EGYPT. The full story of modern educational effort in Egypt would go back to Napoleon's invasion of the country, and the background would extend, of course, to the rise of Mohammed in the 7th century and on into ancient times. Since our presentation can do no justice to historic development in any of the areas on which we touch in this account, we must be content with the statement that there were strong influences after 1882 which tended toward a sharp separation of the native (village) schools from the primary and secondary schools for the more privileged classes —a bar to Fundamental Education which is always hard to overcome. Since 1925 Egyptian nationalism and educational reform have been parts of one general movement. The difficulties due to over-population, small land holdings, lack of industrialisation, disease, and peasant apathy are reported (Kabbani 1) to be appalling; yet they are being attacked in various ways by national leaders.

Notes from the source just named add certain interesting details concerning the present situation.

In 1925 a scheme of compulsory education was elaborated, and a programme drawn up to get all children into elementary schools by 1948. Great impetus for some time—in 1925 alone about 700 schools were established. But in the thirties the programme lagged, chiefly because of political instability and financial difficulties.

At present there are schools for about 1¼ million children from seven to twelve years of age, approximately half of whom are girls.

Reconsideration of educational philosophy and policy since 1939. Principle of one school for all children up to the age of 12 has been accepted. Curricula of the elementary schools have been gradually brought up to the level of those of primary schools. Fees were abolished in the modern primary schools in 1943.

This year a new programme for educational expansion has been laid down and approved by the Supreme Council of Education, aiming at getting enough schools for all children from 6 to 12 within the next 20 years. Problems of buildings, training of teachers, and finance, have been fully considered.

Further, the new philosophy of education looks upon the primary or elementary school not merely as a place for instruction, but as a social agency to improve the life of the masses from all points of view.

Physical education and health improvement receive great attention. The schools now give a substantial daily meal to the children at the expense of the State, and adequate medical service is provided for the children.

In the villages experimentation in community centres is being carried on.

Efforts are not confined to children. Adult education has received a great impetus recently. A systematic campaign is developing against illiteracy. Evening classes for illiterates are spreading rapidly, giving instruction in health, in addition to the three R's. A law has been passed making attendance at these classes compulsory for adults of both sexes, and enforcing upon big landowners and employers the duty of providing the necessary instruction, or paying the costs to the State, which itself organizes it.

A People's University has been established, providing courses in a large range of fields at different levels, suited to the need of various groups of individuals who desire to attend them.

A strikingly concrete example of what Fundamental Education means under certain conditions appears in an article to which we have been referred by a correspondent. It was written by Edwin Muller for *The Rotarian* and condensed in *The Reader's Digest* for July 1946, under the title "Allah helps those . . ." The article shows what patience, tact, and sympathy are required if the mistrust of the very poorest and most ignorant village people are to be overcome. It may be commended to anyone who would like to read a realistic if somewhat highly dramatized account of what can be accomplished by skill and insight in lifting a community ridden by disease and poverty to the level of constructive self-improvement.

IRAQ.   A contribution general in character and hence not specifically suited for inclusion in the present chapter, may be cited as giving certain insights into the difficulties of fundamental education among peoples "largely the inhabitants of great deserts" (Salman 1, *passim*). The fact that many nations of the Middle East have been subject to repeated conquests is instanced as a cause of educational backwardness, as is also the fact that they live a wandering and isolated life, lacking easy communication, absorbed "in the struggle for bare physical existence"; and that the weaker and poorer classes are easily exploited by the richer and more powerful. "Feudalism . . . is the most effective element in the backwardness of the Middle East Nations" . . . and "highly centralised governments with strong bureaucracies [tend] to levy taxes mainly to pay innumerable civil servants." The degeneration of Christianity and Islam into dogmatism is also said to be detrimental to democratic educational achievement. Although these factors in the problem are not unfamiliar under other circumstances, this contribution assigns to them the major place in Fundamental Education in the desert nations of the Middle East.

From the section on Rural Education and Welfare of the Scientific Advisory Mission Report (by H. B. Allen, Director of Education, Near East Foundation), September, 1944, we present the following excerpts on basic factors in Fundamental Education in the Middle East.

The gradual development of the rural masses of the Middle East through schools of agricultural instruction, home betterment and health education is obviously a difficult task. Progress is bound to be exceedingly slow. But there are signs of awakening and in every area thoughtful students of the question and responsible leaders are facing the challenge. Directly affecting any comprehensive programme of improvement are several basic factors. Three that are considered to be fundamental in most sections of the Middle East are mentioned here.

First of all, before there can be much hope of real progress those who are responsible for the affairs of a nation must be able to appreciate the relationship of the rural factor to the total economy of the state. Extensive areas of the Middle East are suffering industrially as well as socially from the lack of such understanding. A country which is predominantly agricultural and which derives a high proportion of its national income from the productions of its rural workers cannot afford to neglect such a valuable asset. On the contrary, every action of the government should represent a policy which definitely includes that of protecting and developing this great national resource.

Such a policy would be reflected in the choice of the officials who are to administer governmental affairs; in adopting forms of taxation that do not tend to dry up the wealth of the country at its source; in the budgeting of all moneys that are annually appropriated for the well-being and general advancement of the people. In other words, the first requisite in any effective programme of village improvement in the Middle East is for the state to become thoroughly rural conscious. In practically every country of this area the make-up of the population and the main source of wealth justify this point of view.

Another item that directly affects this whole problem is the system of land tenure which prevails throughout a large part of that region. There must be a radical change in this system before there can be much hope of social or economic improvement. It is futile to expect educational progress, agricultural improvement or a higher level of living, so long as the ancient feudal system is permitted to remain. The very security of a nation and of every individual citizen within the commonwealth, however well entrenched he may consider himself to be, is seriously threatened by this long outmoded form of land tenure. Middle East countries which could profitably give serious consideration to this important matter need not be designated by name. The intelligent leaders in such areas, including many of the landlords themselves, are well aware of the serious handicap which this form of land tenure imposes on all social progress. They are seeking a method which will insure an orderly change. Just how such a reform is to be effected is not within the scope of this report to discuss.

Still another factor that frequently limits progress over wide stretches of the Middle East is that of water. The area properly farmed by one individual can be no larger and the yields no greater than the amount of water permits. No amount of education or improved management can have any considerable effect where water is seriously limited. Several of the countries covered by this survey once supported populations which were many times greater than the numbers found to-day, and they appear to have maintained standards of living that were actually better sometimes than prevail at present. One of the reasons is water. A number of these regions, for instance Iran, Iraq, parts of Syria and Arabia, have ancient but well-proven systems of supplying water that are highly effective when properly maintained. But in many places maintenance has slipped and the waters have decreased. One of the several important causes of this is the fact that the feudal system is no longer able, under present-day conditions, to cope with this situation.

Competent engineers have informed the writer that the water supplies of many of these areas can be tremendously increased through measures that are entirely within local means. One of these measures, they point out, is the restoration and proper maintenance of these old underground channels; even the utilisation of this method, with certain improvements, for the watering of new districts. Supplying this basic element in maximum quantity is to-day a primary responsibility, not of the wealthy land-owning group, but of the government. In the Middle East water for purposes of production has come to be a public utility. In many areas of this region water determines how far the nation is to go in educating and uplifting its people.

We of the West should not attempt to impose our form of government or our way of life on the East; nor should we measure their standards of living by our chosen yardsticks. In fact, there are certain realms in which the slow-plodding peasant or the freedom-loving nomad has much to offer to the hurried Westerner. At the same time we believe, and they know when they have an opportunity to express themselves freely, that a degree of literacy is the right of every man and the beginning of general enlightenment; that the tilling of one's own soil is a powerful motivating force; that widespread suffering from preventable disease is not an inseparable part of human existence. It should be the combined responsibility of the more privileged powers of the world, during the next era of peace, to give unfailing support to these basic concepts. If this can be done there is definite hope of achieving some of the goals that are suggested in this report.

VI. U.S.S.R.

This chapter has dealt in turn with sample areas on three continents—Africa, the American Hemisphere, Asia—and in the Middle East. We now turn to an account of Fundamental Education in a single nation, one of the Great Powers of our time. The full story of what has been done to lift the immense and varied population of the U.S.S.R. from illiteracy to active and literate participation in a great, revolutionary, social experiment commands the admiring attention of scholars and statesmen throughout the world. We cannot do full justice to that story here. In outline, however, we may set forth the main features of the amazing accomplishments of the Russian State in Fundamental Education. Our quotations (King 1, pp. 1-18) admittedly touch mainly the externals of what was attempted, although its spirit and aims are also brought into prominence. The methods employed, here briefly indicated, will be taken into account in a later section of this document.

The world is fortunate in that the Soviet Union provides a rich field of experience in dealing with problems of fundamental education. We are no longer working in the dark. Many questions of social anthropology have been successfully solved, while many problems in educational psychology for primitive or backward peoples are on the way to solution.

Soviet educationists had to deal with every type of illiterate community. There were tribes that had not yet emerged from primitive devil-worship. There were peoples who had boasted civilisation in ancient days but whom historic circumstances such as invasions and conquests had reduced to almost total illiteracy and destitution, and there were peoples, small sections of whom were highly educated, while the masses were illiterate. There was the problem of the position of women among Mohammedan nations. There was the problem of the small national groups of distinct nationality numbering sometimes less than 2,000, such as those found in the Russian North or in the mountainous Daghestan region. Thus Soviet experience in fundamental education can be said to be all-embracing.

The policy of the Tsars may be summed up under the term 'russification'. As the empire expanded and embraced new areas, officials were sent to carry out this policy. Education in the national or native language was prohibited; though the question hardly arose, as no schools were provided. As popular education anywhere was held to conflict with the interests of the Tsarist autocracy, there was certainly no intention of providing schools for such peoples as the Kirghiz or Kazakhs. Language was therefore not a problem that emerged for attention. The non-Russian peoples without a written alphabet were left to remain in that state, in spite of the fact that they numbered, even if one excludes small national groups, well over a hundred nations.

Missionaries opened a few schools in the far north where teaching was in Russian, while in the southern Asiatic provinces there were some medrasseh, where Imams and Mullahs taught children to recite long extracts from the Koran in an alien tongue.

The background for this educational void was extreme poverty and wretchedness, religious superstitions and customs having their origin far back in history, and isolation of villages or hamlets owing to lack of roads and other means of communication. The native peoples were used as sources of cheap labour, for the exploitation of the local rich. Not only did they have to provide labour, but the Tsarist government augmented its income considerably by levying taxes on the wretched people.

The first World War greatly impoverished the country and the chaos resulting from it was seriously aggravated by the civil war, supported by foreign intervention and by widespread famine. Thus at the time the Bolsheviks assumed power their government was not in a position to spend much time over the preliminary study and preparation required for solution of the problem of education for its backward and primitive peoples.

Because some aspects of the problem were urgent and bore a relation to the ultimate success of the new government, it was tackled as soon as conditions made the first attempts feasible.

The problem which faced the Bolshevik Government, and conditioned the approach and methods used, may be reduced simply to the statement "Building Socialism in Russia". Its implications, however, were far-reaching. The Bolshevik Government could not build socialism in a poverty-stricken country, and they could not develop the country's economy without widespread industrialisation and without a change in the methods of agriculture. This in its turn could not be achieved without education, both technical and cultural, of all the workers. It was not sufficient to obtain the support of the people because they were poor and had nothing to lose by the change. Support had also to come from a reasoned conviction that what was being offered would in the end be good. The mind must be brought to support the emotions. This again leads inevitably to education.

These immediate practical considerations had as their foundation the politico-moral faith of the Bolsheviks, that all peoples, irrespective of race, creed, nationality, or stage of development had equal rights as human beings to all that life could offer. They argued that the existing inequality of peoples was due to environmental factors which, acting on the individual throughout generations and sometimes centuries, had produced a lower mentality; that this lower mentality was *not* a stable or permanent characteristic.

Different environmental factors would produce different characteristics and if this environment were consciously and deliberately planned and modern techniques applied, the process of raising the mental level would be accelerated, and in a comparatively short period glaring and apparently fundamental differences between highly developed communities and backward and even primitive peoples would disappear. These theories received little support from anthropologists outside Russia, but this did not deter Soviet educationists and Soviet political thinkers. The Bolsheviks were convinced that the effort must be made to put their principles into immediate practice.

For the Soviet Government education of the primitive and backward people was indivisible from the whole political task, the building of a socialist state. They could not tolerate the existence of industrially undeveloped areas to serve either as markets for the highly industrialised nations or as sources of cheap raw materials or cheap labour. They were convinced that if education were to succeed among primitive and backward peoples it must lead to an obvious improvement both in their standard of living and in their status as citizens, and that in the reasonably near future the lands inhabited by these people must become as advanced economically, in so far as size and geography permitted, as the Russian lands. The feeling of dependence with its consequent feeling of inferiority must disappear, to be replaced by a voluntary co-operation of free peoples which would only come about when these peoples were in very deed masters of their fate. These principles formed the outline within which the pattern of Fundamental Education was to take shape in that vast territory.

All principles, whether educational or political, were subject to the stringencies of the immediate situation. It was not till some years after the revolution, between 1920 and 1924, according to the establishment of the Soviet regime in the particular state, that a serious attack was made on illiteracy among the backward peoples. In the Federated Russian Republic the campaign for literacy among the Russians began almost with the revolution. One of the greatest obstacles in the early period was the absence of a written language among so many of the people. Numbers of ethnographers and ethnologists were sent to the different regions. For many of these the first task was to learn the native language before they could even proceed with recommendations for an alphabet.

As an example of the complexity and difficulty of the task one may cite the peoples inhabiting the Russian north—the tundra and taiga, which covers about 40% of Soviet territory. In that region, in addition to such large nations as the Yakuts, there were listed in 1926, 26 nationalities speaking distinct languages, with different customs, none of whom had a written alphabet.

Missionaries had produced a dictionary and translations of the scriptures, using Russian characters, for such peoples as the Goldi, the Lopari and the Voguls.

The whole 26 nationalities numbered that year no more than 135,237 people, the population of the nationalities ranging from 38,804 for the Evenki (Tungussi) inhabiting the taiga belt or Asiatic U.S.S.R., from the Yenisei in the west to the Okhotsk sea in the east, to 229 for the Tubi (Soyoty), a mongolised tribe living in Buryat Mongolia. To add to the educational difficulties, nearly all these peoples were nomads (some still are).

To the purely linguistic difficulties were added political difficulties when the question of education of these primitive peoples was first broached. Both in the Archangel Province and in the Urals "a number of comrades infected with great-power chauvinism suggested a very simple solution to the (language) problem; to strengthen and develop penetration of the Russian language which will eliminate the problem of nationality in the North and with it the problem of creating alphabets. In the autonomous territories and republics of the major nationalities, as Komi, Yakutsk, Buryato-Mongolia, a form of local chauvinism was found which demanded the Komisation of Samoyeds, the Yakutisation or Buryatisation of the Tungussi."

This attitude was met with in other parts of the Union, too. It was fiercely combated by all those who followed Lenin closely, who had from the very beginning opposed any kind of Russification, and *ipso facto* of the domination of any larger group over a smaller one, and who were convinced that education must first be given in the native tongue. "In a socialist country there are not and there cannot be peoples of inferior status, this irrespective of their level of social development. To every nationality in the U.S.S.R. is given the right to use its own language and its own written form for the purpose of raising its national culture."

The research into native languages which had been carried on for the northern peoples in a somewhat unsystematic fashion, was organised centrally in 1926 when a Northern Faculty was opened in the Leningrad Eastern Institute. The status and the quality of this research was further improved after 1930 when the Northern Faculty was transferred into an independent Institute for the peoples of the north.

In the school year 1926/27 it was already possible to carry on education in the native Tunguss language, while in 1930 it was carried on in the native language of all the other peoples. In the first stage it was possible to give education in the native tongue for the Northern Peoples only in classes 1 and 2, owing to the lack of teachers with a knowledge of the native language. As these increased, the native language replaced Russian as a medium of learning until to-day it is used throughout the period covering secondary education. This includes the pedagogic schools for teacher training. In the universities most subjects are taken in Russian while the native language is a compulsory subject.

To sum up the problem of language, the principle of education in the native language, which the Russians consider fundamental, was applied from the beginning. It involved the organisation of a number of special institutes for the study of the different languages. It involved study of the native language on the spot and it involved finance to make possible printing and publication. Finally, it was found essential to have a centralised body for the whole Union to guide all the varied research on languages being carried on by the different republics. This step was recommended by the Conference on the Cultural Development of Native Languages held in April 1935. The Institute of Language and Thought of the Academy of Sciences has now disappeared. To-day research is being carried on in national institutes in the different union and autonomous republics.

The problem of language was not purely an educational one in the Soviet Union. Any attempt to give education in an alien language, however simplified, to a people that was conscious of its own nationality would have classed the Soviet Government with the Tsarist Government and made the road to socialism infinitely more difficult. The offering of education in their native tongue, with often the actual creation of a written language for a people, was a powerful weapon in the Bolshevik armoury. That was certainly a consideration, though second to their political conviction of the inherent right of peoples to learning and living fully through their native language.

Soviet theory is, however, integrated both with reality as it is and with the reality that it is hoped to achieve. The attempt on the part of a few to consider every dialect worthy of development into a language failed. There are something like two hundred languages and dialects spoken in the Soviet Union and education is carried on in ninety languages. A language had to show some evidence of a culture, however far back and simple, some evidence that it would grow into a creative tool, that it was capable of expressing thought processes. Thus for small groups linguistically or ethnically akin, where there was no marked boundary of separation, a common language was arrived at.

The question will doubtless be put, does not this insistence on different languages prevent the unity of which the world is so greatly in need? Is, for example, Bashkiria likely to feel unfriendly to Oirotia on any pretext, because the one speaks Bashkir and the other Oirot? Would it not have made for greater unity in the U.S.S.R. if all education had been in Russian? These questions tend to ignore the fact that language in itself is neither a cohesive nor a dissolving agent, that a common language follows rather than precedes common interests. The barriers to unity are to be found in attitudes and outlooks arising from a different historical development and from conflicting economic interests and in modern times from different ideologies. Let us suppose (a not unlikely premise) a German fascist and an English communist who both spoke Esperanto or Basic English. No one would suggest that the common language would unite them. One has only to think of the bitter hostility of the anti-fascist Frenchman to the Vichyite, or of the anti-Nazi Germans who fought the Nazis, their own flesh and blood, to realise that a common language, greatly as it may aid understanding, will not of itself bring unity.

Russian is compulsory in all non-Russian schools as the first foreign language. All the different nations can at conferences and congresses speak one language, at least in theory if not yet fully in practice. Under the Tsars, Russian was the official language in all administration and in all forms of government. Yet under the Tsars the Russian Empire was not united, while under the Soviets the same peoples covering the same territory are united, as was made obvious during the war.

There is always a danger of unity leading to uniformity just as there is danger of diversity leading to disintegration. The Russian experience is valuable where it shows how they have encouraged the development of the particular individuality of a nation so that it falls into the pattern of the whole and by its own individual contribution enriches the whole.

When local chauvinism and hostility to the Soviets ceased to be a danger, then attention was directed to the past history of the different republics and territories. Research into their culture, literature, art, crafts, music was set on foot by the Soviet authorities. Peoples were encouraged to feel a pride in whatever was worthy in their history. Their literature was translated into Russian. Different nations each had and continue to have their ten days arts festival in Moscow, when their native plays, operas and ballets are staged and performed by their own people, when their arts and crafts are exhibited to the world.

Later still, serious research was begun into the folklore of the different peoples, into their ancient music and dances. National costumes are encouraged, particularly for festive occasions. Their modern architecture still expresses native idiom. There is no attempt, however, to keep them "arty-crafty". There is an exchange of art and artists. The best Russian theatre companies and musicians tour the capitals and settlements of other republics. They not only perform, they also teach and advise. So far, therefore, the Soviet Union has succeeded in avoiding both the disintegrating effects of a multitude of tongues, and the dangers of uniformity. The other aspect of language, as a precision instrument for thought and intercourse, has had some attention but not sufficient. As is to be expected in so short a period of development, the word as word has still great power, it is still insufficiently challenged, but the word has opened the door to the proper conception of thinking and to the understanding of the idea.

In Russia proper, in the Ukraine, in Belorussia, there was an army of young teachers, who made lists of illiterates, produced cut-out alphabets and even text books, and organised play-rooms for the children while mothers were being taught. They helped the adults in carrying out a vast propaganda for literacy among their people, who often included their own parents and nearly always their grandparents. The opposition to education here arose from inertia, from an objection to changing one's habits and often from scepticism about its value. Though it took time, this opposition presented no such serious difficulties as were met with among the illiterate Mohammedan peoples, or among primitive peoples with their ancient customs and habits and their primitive religion.

Here the approach was quite different. It was essential to obtain the confidence of some of the native inhabitants, who would themselves spread the idea of the desirability of education. These had to be people who would also be attracted by the Soviet way of life. This ruled out the rich beys, the Mullahs and the Imams for the Muslim peoples, and the Shahmans for the peoples of the Soviet North, all of whom were opposed to education for the common herdsman, or silk-weaver, or hunter, and all of whom were opposed to Soviet ideas.

The iconoclastic approach was ruled out as being negative. There was no attack in the first stage on their taboos or religious customs.

An added complication was the attitude to women. There were the religious customs in the East that forbade women to go unveiled or to mix with men apart from their husbands, that forbade a woman to sing or dance in public, unless she was a prostitute; the belief that women had no souls, and so on. There was the economic factor. For practical purposes married women provided a source of unpaid labour and service to the family, a very weighty factor with Mohammedan husbands.

It required a very careful approach to the women, and centres for women only were organised in the first place. Co-operative societies for women only were organised in Uzbekistan. Out of them grew a Central Asiatic Co-operative school for women in Tashkent. The co-operatives played a great role in the emancipation of the women of the Soviet East, and the emancipated women joined the army of educators.

It was easier to get at the women than at the men for though they went in awe of their husbands and their men folk generally, they loved their children and were prepared to take the consequences if a child's life or health were saved by their action.

All this pointed to a clinic or health station as the centre from which educational work was to radiate. Well-trained young Russian women with an excellent knowledge of the language were sent down to selected areas to start the work. They met with bitter opposition, particularly from the section of the male population which feared the loss of the almost enslaved women. They were known in Russian as Kultarmeitsi—soldiers of the education army and they took the risks of soldiers. Many of them paid with their lives—they would be found murdered in the street or their home. Native women were threatened with all kinds of horrors. Sometimes a native woman, discovered attending the clinic or classes, was caught, murdered, and her body cut up in pieces and sent in a basket to her aûl as a warning to others.

While Russian women worked among the women, and sick babies restored to health gave courage to many who hesitated, Russian men worked among the poorest men, who had nothing to lose by listening to the new words. Side by side with classes in literacy went on classes in the organisation of Soviets for local government, and teaching of the strength that would come from unity. Then when the local Soviets were strong enough to benefit by the support of the Russian authorities, very severe punishment was meted out to those found guilty of violence to the natives or the Russians in the discharge of their duty. As soon as conditions permitted, co-operatives or collectives were organised with considerable aid from the Russians. In the native Soviets and in the collectives the importance of education was emphasised in practice. Printed circulars and instructions were issued by a Region Soviet to local Soviets. At first they had to be read by a Russian. Then came the day when the native chairman, hitherto illiterate, read the instructions himself to his people. That was a great day. The news spread that Mahmud Ali could read the words on paper sent to him from a long way off, and it had its effect on others. The day typewriters in the native language arrived was another historic occasion.

For the women the health centres were the literacy centres. From these, quite early, grew courses for the training of native teachers to work both with adults and children, for whom schools were opened as soon as the native teachers had become proficient in the elements of the three R's.

Simultaneously with the spread of education the standard of living for the poor masses began to improve. Thus for the mass of the people education was linked from the beginning with a better life.

Such were the first steps in the campaign for the abolition of illiteracy in the Asian territories, the emphasis all the time being on the new way of life.

It had been accepted in the beginning as a fundamental principle that the technical level both in industry and agriculture of the most backward people must be raised to that of the most advanced. It was part of the Soviet politico-sociology that the economy of every people must be developed to the utmost limits, as the only basis on which their society could be built. They argued that there must be a very close correlation between education and the encompassing of wider perspectives, that education must lead to a wider and deeper economic development, which in its turn would lead to a wider and deeper cultural development.

This was the underlying principle of the education carried on among the child population too, for among the backward peoples as among the Russian masses in Tsarist days, the young began their economic contribution to the family very early, and it had to be proved to them that education would be of practical benefit.

Every effort was made not to lower the educational standard for the schools attended by these children. Schools in the Far North or in remote Asian villages were expected to cover the same syllabuses as those in Moscow or Leningrad or Kiev, but they were given an additional year in which to complete the normal four-year course and their school day was an hour longer.

By 1932, when the First Five-year Plan had been carried out, the general reorganisation of education included the development of secondary schools (8—18 years) in the capitals of the different national territories and in district centres. This was a great step in advance. Henceforth there would be increasing facilities for secondary education in their own national territory, less and less would it be necessary to take a long journey, sometimes lasting a month, to sit in a school in Moscow or Leningrad or Kiev. This step had great publicity value among native peoples, and was an incentive to greater interest and greater efforts locally on behalf of education. Side by side with the secondary schools, technical schools, at first polytechnical in character and later monotechnical, were opened in the Far North, schools which trained skilled cadres of young workers for reindeer breeding, for fishing and hunting, for the breeding of fur-bearing animals and for the work of running local Soviets and local co-operatives. Later, as agriculture spread north, they were trained in agriculture.

Here again there was no concession to backwardness. The common standard was demanded. While the syllabuses allowed for variations due to local needs, the essentials were the same for all schools in the Soviet Union. The secondary schools in Igarka, a Soviet-built port in the Far North, or in Ulan-Ude in Buryat-Mongolia, had their science laboratories equipped as well as the schools in Moscow. Native pride made great contributions. By a decree published in 1939 *all* children in Soviet schools on reaching the age 11-12 were to begin learning a European foreign language—English, French, German—and had not the war intervened there is every probability that the decree would have been implemented.

It was difficult enough to find teachers to eliminate illiteracy among the Russians or Ukrainians, states which boasted centres of scholarship and learning long before the revolution. When it came to places like Buryat-Mongolia, Turkmenistan, Kirghizia or the Far North of Yakutsk, the task seemed insuperable. As already mentioned, for the Slav-speaking peoples it was possible to interest the children. Quite literally anyone who himself or herself could read or write was pressed into the fight for literacy. But for the other regions the number of people who knew any of the native language was absurdly insignificant, and besides they were foreigners. The first task was to train Russians and where possible natives, who could train teachers. In the first stage it was an obligation on a Party member to take up the fight for the enlightenment of the millions living in darkness. Special institutes were set up for the training of native teachers. The first students who came to the Institute of the Peoples of the North were illiterate young men and women ranging from 15 to 25—Evenki, Chukchi, Goldi and others. After 1938 they were not accepted unless they had completed secondary education (8—15).

It was a step that held many risks, to bring these really primitive people to live in Leningrad, but they were in excellent hands. Much of the education at first had to be education in European habits, such as sleeping in a bed. The psychological approach to all primitive or backward peoples was the same, a study of the origins of their customs and practices. Where the origin was fear, first of the unknown and then of the individual who made himself the intermediary between the unknown, as the Shahman or witch doctor, a very carefully planned attack on these customs and habits was launched *after* the confidence of the students had been won. The same applied to the custom of selling children into marriage or the wearing of the parandyha, which had an economic origin, but was equally a hindrance to progress. Customs which in their origin had a positive value were treated with care and the effort was made to transform them or sublimate them so that they served the growth and development under the new Soviet conditions. The case of the Ingushetians may be cited. As late as 1927 their children went to school in their clans (family), sat in clans irrespective of ages, would have nothing to do with the children of another clan, would not sit on the same bench. Living in clans was still deeply rooted, and clan hostility even to vengeance showed itself in school. Speaking on national and international culture Krupskaya pointed out that this could not be regarded as an altogether harmful feature. A careful observation of the children's life showed that side by side with the clan characteristic each child has a definite inner discipline which was developed by this very clan stage. "It is important that the clan isolation should disappear. The children should be provided as much as possible with common vivid experiences, so that their clan aloofness and hate should disappear. In common tasks and common occupations we must find elements that will draw the children together. At the same time we must make use of their habit of inner discipline created by the clan life, for quite a new purpose, for the creation of a new kind of self-government."

The Soviet Union has not yet wiped out illiteracy over its whole territory. There are still thousands attending the Adult Primary School, the equivalent of the seven to eleven years' grade for children, because their literacy has not gone beyond simple reading and writing. Even before 1941, the universal compulsory education for seven years—7 to 14—was not put into effect one hundred per cent. In the school year 1939/40, serious truancy was reported in a number of towns. The universities do not everywhere attain the high academic standard of Moscow or Leningrad. The vast amount of research that is being done is not of a uniformly high level. Inefficiency and lack of interest is still to be found in places. But when one has allowed all this, there remains an achievement staggering in its immensity and profoundly inspiring.

Surrounded by a hostile world, in a country that had been completely disintegrated by war and civil war, lacking in the beginning money, equipment, and trained personnel, it succeeded within twenty-three years (1917-1940) in reducing illiteracy in some areas to about 5%. Only in Kazakhstan, that vast land of shifting sands, was illiteracy among the people over fifty as high as 30%. The Soviet Union never stopped at achieving literacy. Step by step, always seeking the right methods, it led the primitive and backward nations onward, four year school, seven year school, ten year school, and technical school, then technical institute and university, with research facilities, and then branches of the Union Academy of Sciences, until the final

height was reached for a number of the more advanced republics, in the form of native Academies of Science, such as the
Armenian or Georgian Academy of Science. A few figures, for
one republic only, will give point to the claims of achievement.
In Kirghizia in 1914, there were 70 elementary (2 to 3 year)
schools with 4,000 pupils, education being carried on in Russian. There was no Kirghiz alphabet. In 1941, there were 2,-
159 schools with 328,000 pupils. Prior to 1917, out of the whole
Kirghizian population, only four people could boast a secondary
education. Already in 1934, out of 4,200 teachers, 2,159 were
Kirghizians, who had received secondary education. In 1930,
124 titles, reaching 1,341,000 books, were published in the native
Kirghizian and Dungan languages. In 1936, 40 Kirghizian newspapers and magazines with a circulation of 34,000 were published. There were no theatres in pre-revolutionary Kirghizia.
To-day, there are 17 theatres, 9 of which play in the Kirghiz
language and 2 in Uzbek, the rest in Russian. The first research
institute set up was in 1929, the Institute of Regional Lore.
By 1941, Kirghizia had nearly seventy research institutes and
experimental stations. In 1943, the Kirghizian Branch of the
U.S.S.R. Academy of Sciences was opened, and it is certainly no
wild prophecy if one predicts that the Branch will in a few years
become a fully-fledged Academy of Sciences. A similar tale can
be told for Kazakhstan, Uzbekistan, Turkmenistan, and the
others.

Two questions may be put now. One, are these peoples particularly gifted that they can take such educational strides and,
two, what does all this educational achievement mean to the
individual, to his community and to the world? The answer to
the first is simple. If we take the Russians who carried out this
Fundamental Education, they are no more intellectually gifted
than the English or the French or any of the other civilised nations. As for the people who had to be educated, they are as
varied as the people who to-day form the areas of illiteracy in
the world. Some of them belonged to peoples that had had very
high ancient civilisation and may be compared to the illiterates
in China, in India and in Arabian lands. Others were on a
level, though living under a different climate, with many of the

African tribes. The problem that faced the young Soviet Union is very similar to that which Unesco is considering.

Much more is involved in the reply to the second question. It has freed the individual from the grip of irrational fears. That does not necessarily mean he has become an atheist. A great proportion of the people in any nationality worships a God in church or chapel, in a mosque or synagogue, in spite of the fact that all education is secular. Having been freed from irrational fears, he has been able to take advantage of all the provision for creative self-expression, particularly in the case of women. He is developing an intellectual curiosity, and is learning to experience the delight of intellectual achievement. Aristotle and Plato are appreciated by the native student in his departments of philosophy or history. Homer and Sophocles and Aeschylus are understood (in translation) by the student in the Faculty of Arts.

He is learning how to rule, beginning simply in his local Soviet and rising to the presidency of his Republic. And in learning to rule he is learning to be disciplined. To-day all local government and administration is in the hands of the people of the locality, and the central government for his people in the hands of those they elect. The whole of the economy of a nationality that is of national importance is in the hands of that nationality. Only such enterprises as are of All-Union significance will be run by men and women appointed by an All-Union authority.

By 1940, shortage still existed, but poverty, i.e., near-destitution, had disappeared; for everyone the incidence of disease had been greatly reduced, while some diseases had almost disappeared. Through development, the individual has made considerable contribution to raising the standard of life for his whole community and through his community to raising that of the whole Union. He has to-day a great feeling of brotherhood for all mankind. The Russians, who have always possessed this characteristic, and for whom the word Bratzi—brothers—as a form of address dates far back, have carefully nurtured this feeling among the different nationalities. Because of this strong feeling of brotherhood he does not tolerate traitors to mankind.

He is ready to pay tribute to greatness and achievement anywhere, in the past or the present, and he is eager to learn from others and to share his achievement. I, who know the Soviet peoples very well, say this quite deliberately and carefully, in spite of impressions being spread to the contrary. He has still a long way to go but he knows how to travel.

The Soviet way is not necessarily the right way in every detail for other parts of the world. That is not important. What is important is that Fundamental Education can be successful and can bring great benefit to mankind provided we set out on the path with no reservations about the capacity of backward peoples and set no limitations to their development, provided there is a united will to achieve the purpose.

A Concluding Statement

In seeking to give concrete instances of the realities of Fundamental Education in action, the Editorial Committee is conscious that the samples given may produce an impression of confusion and of a variety of circumstances almost impossible to bring into a unified world perspective. It is our hope that the later chapters of this volume will serve in some measure to correct this impression of prevailing difficulty and complexity of circumstances. Fundamental Education is undeniably a world movement. In spite of local and national differences, it may be attacked by co-operative action on a world scale. The insistent requirements are exchange of experiences, analysis and sifting of plans, and the enlistment of a devoted and intelligent personnel at all levels.

I know no safe depository of the ultimate powers of society but the people themselves; and if we think them not enlightened enough to exercise their control with a wholesome direction, the remedy is not to take it from them, but to inform their discretion through education.

From a letter written by
THOMAS JEFFERSON
in 1820.

CHAPTER III

GENERAL CONSIDERATIONS

The Place of This Chapter in the Document as a Whole

The preceding chapter touches all, or nearly all, of the problems and issues which challenge thought and action in Fundamental Education. In Chapter II, however, these challenging questions have been set forth in the special terms of particular areas. The Editorial Committee thought it desirable to deal in this succeeding chapter with the tasks of fundamental education considered in more general terms. Description, statistics and argument over specific policies in well-defined situations here give way to analysis and to conclusions of a broader character.

It should not be supposed, however, that the contributors to the present chapter speak as "armchair philosophers". All have had contacts which entitle them to discuss questions which are general, not because they have been formulated by meditation or conjecture, but because they have arisen repeatedly in experience—and in experience which these contributors themselves have had.

This recurrence of problems is of special interest in connection with fundamental education. It marks the common character of the enterprise and emphasises the fact that it is a general human task, which can be viewed to some purpose in a world-wide perspective. The distinguishing differences of circumstance from nation to nation, from one colonial area to another, or between nation and colony, or in terms of the advancement of the peoples concerned—these differences will largely determine the course of immediate action, which must be primarily and mainly local. But the underlying conceptions of the nature of the work, the reasons for thinking it important, the approach that is most likely, all things considered, to be successful, and especially the possible assistance which can be rendered by Unesco—these are all elements of Fundamental Education seen as a world-wide problem, and in this sense as a problem to which intellectual analysis can be profitably applied.

It may be difficult to draw the line between an analytical treatment of fundamental education in its entirety and a treatment of any one of several issues of major policy or of a very basic question of method. Some of the contributions included in Chapter IV are so penetrating in their analysis that they might well have been included in the present chapter. It seemed best, however, to move from description in Chapter II, through analysis in this chapter, to policy and method in Chapter IV. This arrangement has produced in the minds of the Editorial Committee and its co-workers, and we hope it will leave with the readers of this volume, an ever-deepening impression that Fundamental Education is in truth a world movement, that it may be made a factor in human progress, that it calls for the best effort of the best minds and the stoutest hearts, and that it must be the constant concern of all who seek a lasting peace for the world and a happier and worthier life for mankind.

I. FUNDAMENTAL EDUCATION DEFINED

We begin with excerpts from an article (Charton 4, pp. 1-5) which deals with the general character and place of Fundamental Education in the total development of civilised life in our world.

We must first define the meaning of Fundamental Education. It is a basic education, the education of the mass of the people.

This concept needs defining extensively and comprehensively. On the one hand basic education is addressed to the largest possible number of persons, without limitation, differentiation, or discrimination. From this point of view it is opposed to any system of teaching founded upon the existence of privileged minorities, religious or social castes, or upon the desire to build up a scholar class having a monopoly of knowledge. It is thus one of the components of democracy and an essential instrument for establishing a democratic life in nations. Fundamental Education is therefore essentially popular and universal.

Furthermore, basic education must be defined according to its content and its purpose. It is teaching of the people for the people, for the people's needs and aspirations. The primary purpose of basic education will be to combat ignorance and illiteracy and to spread elementary knowledge and the means of acquiring it. Hence the fundamental importance of teaching the three "R's", reading, writing and arithmetic; this teaching is a necessary implement for all further instruction. Fundamental education, however, must have a content that is real and not purely formal; it must aim at improving the life of the nation, influencing the natural and social environment and imparting knowledge of the world. From this point of view basic education will be of incomparable social value, a force working for progress and evolution, even radical transformation.

What is the position of the different countries of the world from the viewpoint of popular education? This must be established by enquiry. Although the whole problem concerns all countries in the world, even the mightiest, it has a special importance in countries where illiterates form the majority, either because the country has no educational system of its own or because education is a recent phenomenon in those countries or, again, because the traditional system of education caters only for a minority or, lastly, because these systems are closed, limited by tradition or religion and incapable of granting to the peoples concerned access to the life of the world in general.

Although the question of illiteracy and popular education arises even in western and European countries, notably in Central Europe and the Balkans, the number of illiterates is largest

in countries whose civilisation has hitherto been static and traditional, in backward countries, where the great majority of
adults and children alike remain illiterate and the problem of
popular education presents itself in all its complexity and
urgency.   These countries may roughly be divided into four
zones.

First, a Far Eastern Zone, countries with an important and
ancient civilisation, where the problem is to modernise and extend popular education.

Second, the zone comprising the Middle East and Islamic
countries, where we meet with a religious civilisation, which
dominates the people and completely encloses them, but which
is open to penetration by popular teaching both through the
example of Europe and, from within, through movements of
Moslem reform.

Third, the zone of tropical Africa, where popular education
is a condition for obtaining access to the simplest forms of
civilisation and is also an essential factor in improving the life
of the people.   To this zone belong certain peoples of the Far
East, Indonesia and Central Asia, who cannot be classified
among the great religious and moral civilisations of Islam and
Asia.

Fourth, and last, come the countries of Latin America and
the West Indies, where the popular school is a new factor in
introducing the people to modern life, but where the people
themselves are awake to fundamental education and want it.

Thus we see that a large part of mankind is left untouched
by evolution through the advancement of human knowledge or
submits to it passively.   In all the cases concerned, illiteracy is
more than an ignorance of fundamental and elementary knowledge required by all who receive school education; we are dealing here not only with millions of individuals who cannot read
or write, but with societies and communities, which are, as a
whole, uncultivated or encased within rigid and ineffective forms
of traditional education.   They are "closed" societies, large areas
in which human beings are cut off from general communication
with the rest of the world.   But developments in the economic
life of the world, and still more, political developments brought

about by World Wars, cannot be arrested on the threshold of these countries; they work and penetrate in all directions, into every aspect of the traditional life, with the result that responsibility for a popular education that will discipline and organise these movements rests upon all mankind and upon their governments.

Accordingly, we are able to define the characteristics of basic education as applied to the big human zones we have considered, to state the conditions that must govern it, the obstacles it will meet with, and after that we shall be able to pose and classify the problems involved, while seeking the data for their study and solution.

To begin with, popular education in these areas is a complete novelty. In the groups we are concerned with, the movement towards mass education is only twenty years old. In Russia, popular culture is one of the most active movements in the whole of the Soviet Union. In China, the campaign against illiteracy has recorded its first successes and aroused its first enthusiasm since the time of Sun Yat Sen and especially in the last few years. Latin America adopted the popular school little more than twenty years ago. Lastly, it is only during the twenties and thirties of this century that the French and British laid the foundations for the education of African peoples. The inauguration of fundamental education will therefore be a real intellectual and spiritual revolution.

Another feature of basic education, popular and elementary, is the mass effort it calls for, and will continue to call for. We are dealing with peoples, hundreds of thousands of individuals, children and grown-ups, among whom the number of cultivated and educated persons is only a tiny minority, and among whom the proportion of illiterates exceeds 75% or is even more than 90%, where teaching is mainly confined to children and to the latest generation.

This fact is a measure of the urgent need for popular education. If the process of evolution is not to be extended over many generations, and if we wish to effect a rapid transformation, the problem must be attacked by concentrating simultaneously upon successive generations, and within a limited time.

This is a movement with almost no precedent in the past.

Popular basic education, however, must comply with conditions that are embodied deep in the life of peoples and that reflect their creeds, needs and aspirations. In the first place, popular education must be conceived on a national basis. A certain degree of education among the people is one of the surest criteria of the existence and consciousness of a nation. The most popular culture must respect and maintain national traditions, and teaching must not result in "denationalising the masses". Here, however, serious problems arise. In the case of non-national populations, where nationalities are reduced to tribes, there may be a question of access to a more advanced community, to an "adopting" nation, and this may even be the wish of the people themselves. This is the position in French tropical Africa. On the other hand, mass education, if regarded as a training, a matter of propaganda and collectivisation, may be the source and occasion of racial conflicts and lead the way to education for war. Both in Europe and the Far East, examples of this alarming kind of education are too recent to be disregarded. Such, then, are the political problems involved in the question of popular education.

Another feature of basic education is that it must rest upon the social, human and economic environment which it has to transform. In new countries, backward or poorly educated countries, as well as in countries with an ancient civilisation which have hitherto been shut up within themselves, there is a close inter-dependence between economic and social development and education. Economic and social progress is not only a consequence but also a condition of general education. In a backward, static country, there is a risk that education may operate in a void and cause confusion by being applied to no real purpose. Popular education must be progressive, positive, an introduction to a new kind of life. It must be responsible for the whole progress of the whole country.

A process of the same order occurs in intellectual and moral life. Even in illiterate areas, certain forms of ancient education have preserved much force. This is *a fortiori* the case in countries with an old and religious civilisation, countries in which religion is the main teacher of men. Islam, Confucianism and Buddhism possess a living moral force, which popular education must take into account. On the other hand, the new school, if it is to establish peace and awake the consciousness of peoples, needs a new form, a modern soul, an outlook upon the world, all of which are inherent in its definition. The spiritual and moral value of basic education depends, therefore, upon a successful synthesis between traditional forces and ideas and the modern progressive movement through the schools. This is a fundamental problem, the solutions for which may be studied in the light of experiments carried out in the Far East and tropical Africa.

Lastly, basic education, by the very fact that it is a novelty, a kind of intellectual revolution, a movement that seeks to sweep along with it the whole of the national life, must be as thorough-going and as continuous as possible. There would be serious drawbacks in educating special groups and communities within a society and an environment which were to remain otherwise unchanged. There would also be a danger in leaving these educated groups to themselves without providing them with the wherewithal necessary to put their capacity for teaching into operation. Too rapid instruction runs the risk of proving a 'flash in the pan' that quickly disappears. Hence the importance of educating adults and young girls, and of continuing education after school age; hence, too, the great importance of finding practical solutions to these problems.

II. FUNDAMENTAL EDUCATION AND CULTURAL VALUES

Our second article (Mead 1, pp. 1-17) is written from the standpoint of the social anthropologist.

Problems of Policy. When an international body looks at the question of education on a world scale, it will inevitably have to answer questions of policy which will determine all its future recommendations, even those which seem comparatively minor and technical. I shall therefore sketch in first what seem to me to be these largest policy questions, and then indicate those aspects of procedure most likely to implement a conscientious course.

The cultures of the world may be conveniently arranged in a double hierarchical system: the high cultures of the Occident and its dependent areas of less developed civilisation; and the high cultures of the Orient, and its dependent areas, with the Middle East standing somewhat between these two, looking both ways. When such a schematization is made, we are immediately faced with the question of whether this double hierarchy is to be dissolved into a single hierarchy. This might be accomplished in one of two possible ways: (1) by granting world preeminence to modern scientific industrial civilisation with its concurrent social institutions of political democracy (and its possible outcomes in various forms of totalitarian collectivism, some atavistic, some progressive), with its emphasis upon the importance of the individual life and upon this world as the only arena in which man can realise his highest purposes; or (2) by proceeding slowly enough so that the great cultures of the Orient may have an opportunity to contribute to the world view [1] so that some of their values which complement, counterpoint, and to a degree negate and cancel out the dominant motifs of occidental civilisation, may be incorporated in the world ideal which is finally developed. The persistent attempt during the last three years to include China as a world power in all decisions of world importance has been a structural step towards the realisation of (2); and it will be by such steps that (2) rather than (1) becomes effective—if it does so.

There are a variety of ways in which this provision for (2) may be made, which include: (a) the inclusion of China or India on all high policy committees, (b) the inclusion of an oriental language in all *original* drafts of important documents, (c) the delegation of educational problems within the areas of influence of great oriental and near-eastern powers to those powers, rather than the construction of world-wide recommendations, which at this stage of history, will almost inevitably contain an over-

[1] See Frank, L. K., World Order and Cultural Diversity, *Free World*, Vol. III, No. 1, pp. 83-86. June, 1942.

whelmingly western stamp. Whether (c) will be taken will depend in great measure on the extent to which China, India, Japan, the Netherlands Indies, and the powers of the Arab League are granted strong enough representation at a high policy level. If so, they will be able to demand and get control over the education of their own areas of natural political and cultural influence; if not, they will either lack the representation and power to do this; or even having it, will be represented by individuals whose education is overwhelmingly occidental and who will themselves elect occidental educational forms rather than forms which would evolve more directly from their own traditional cultures.

It may be plausibly argued, I believe, that nativistic movements, such as the American Indian ghost dance, the revival of Celtic languages, the return to Norse Gods, are expensive drags on the progress of human culture. Any cultural tradition which has grown so weak that it can be revived only by measures which can be classed as nativistic—revivals, prophets, cults of various sorts—should possibly be permitted to die. If this position is taken,—and an examination of the cost to civilisation, for example, of the revival of medieval languages, which cut down the communications developing through more widely understood languages, provides much evidence to support it—then the great oriental powers, if they fail to defend and promote systems of education based upon their own traditions, might in a sense be said to offer proof that the trend towards a unicultural world is worth following. It will be important, however, to be sure that sufficient play has been given to the statesmen and scholars of the East and Near East who did not go to Oxford or Harvard or Leipzig or Amsterdam or Paris or Moscow for their educations and who, if given a hand in the planning, would inevitably retain many of the values which plans dictated wholly by occidental standards would eliminate. Probably the only sure guarantee of such inclusions of non-westernised thinkers will be the purposeful establishment of sub-commissions which can work entirely with contributors who are unfamiliar with occidental languages and values, and then arrange for the work of these sub-commissions to be translated fully into the committees which work on a world scale, through the necessary mediations of Easterners who speak western languages or Westerners who speak eastern languages. There must be, of course, full recognition that in translation something will be lost of the cultural uniqueness of the recommendations; but the part which is retained will be the part which is most subject to successful communication through translation, and therefore most viable in that one world in which the languages used in the translations are playing a dominant role.

There are arguments against the idea of letting any civilisation die out. We know from the study of comparative cultures that each civilisation, no matter how great and how complex, only touches a very few points on the possible scale of human values, and while defining some problems with great clarity, is inevitably myopic to all the rest. The historical conditions which have permitted the civilisations of the world to develop in isolation over thousands of years, combined with the shifting circumstances incident to conquest, migration and trade, present us in the 20th century with a world which is still highly diversified and in possession of a large number of different and important cultural developments, involving different visions, different questions about man and his fate, and different social techniques for reaching their different goals. We have no way of knowing whether, if once the entire human race is subjected to the influence of one civilisation, diversities of comparable coherence will ever develop again. The degree of monotony which characterised many human institutions which we have every reason to believe developed independently one from another, does not give any very great hope that civilisation, once reduced to comparative uniformity, will spawn again a series of sub-civilisations of anything like the richness and diversity which we find in the world to-day. Add to this that the new world civilisation, if such a uniformity be attained at the present time, will be based upon the scientific view of the world, in which the direct observation of phenomena will be the guiding principle, and it seems even less likely that we will find a trend towards diversification.

These considerations being admitted, it might almost be argued that we cannot afford to sacrifice a single historically developed civilisation, no matter how small, no matter how modest its role has been through accidents of size, of population, of geographical position, or amount of natural resources, and that the first task of a world-planning cultural agency must be to cherish each of these civilisations, and to devise means, no matter how artificial, to preserve these differences at least long enough so that their contributions to world culture may make it potentially far richer and more diversified than it would otherwise be. This multi-cultural position at its logical extreme, would fight for the continued cultivation of the cultures of the Samoan, the Banyankole, the Greenland Eskimo, the Kaingang of Brazil, the inhabitants of the Isle of Man, and of course look with favour on the current attempts to make Welsh, Erse, Hebrew, etc., languages fitted for modern scientific use.

In either case, whether we argue, as this paper does, that it is artificial and probably unwise and, in any event highly unacceptable to the dominant sections of the present world, to try to preserve all existing cultures so that each may make a contribution, or whether one accepts the argument in their favour, it must still be recognised that a world culture is something yet to be achieved. The superficial imprint upon the whole world of occidental technology and occidental values will not be a world culture, for it involves too great a discrepancy between the traditional values (of both Occident and Orient) and a recently attained very thin layer of modern rationalistic scientific tradition. Two processes will have to go on concurrently, (1) the revision of occidental culture in such a way that the scientific tradition becomes not merely a technology of an assertive society but a tradition in which human values are given increasing recognition, and (2) the development of strategies through which the leading *ideas* of the scientific approach to the world—as contrasted with the simple technologies—may become genuinely blended with cultures other than the top layers of western Europe and Asia. Japan is a striking example of the successful transplanting of applied and even pure science—if narrowly enough conceived—where no real alteration in the feudal form of the culture was effected. In the development of a world culture, principal emphasis will have to be placed on the recognition of the need for criteria for social evaluation, on incorporating in any scientifically based world culture of the future the habit of subjecting its own institutions to continuous criticism and revision.

In this controversy it is possible to take the position of an umpire, a prophet, or a traffic director at an intersection which is regarded as important, to try to say which view is correct, which is most likely to win, or what the next step must be. To take either of the first two positions, that of umpire or prophet, requires more knowledge than the anthropologist has at his disposal to-day. Planning in the absence of knowledge is perhaps the besetting sin of western society, only too willing to lay down a blue print and ignorantly distort men's lives. When knowledge is as inadequate as ours to-day, the only possible course which will not be a betrayal of the future is to try to take a direction which is consonant with the highest aspirations of the group whose judgment is most likely to predominate, and to be sure, if possible, that that step does not bind the future to more than a continued fidelity to the highest aspirations of later generations.

If we then examine what are the aspirations in the world leaders who will be charting the course of such United Nations organisations as Unesco, we will find certain relevant values which, upon examination, will be seen to make a pattern out of which a policy may be formed. These may be indicated under the following heads: (1) A belief in enlightenment and education such that all plans made must be phrased as an increase in enlightenment and education; (2) a belief in the importance of the individual life such that the argument that any course which will advance the health, nutrition, safety, and general well-being of the individual will be an adequate sanction for its adoption; (3) a belief that change is good and is on the whole to be identified with progress, progress itself to be defined by (1) and (2). If these three premises are examined in detail they will be found to conflict actually with the established attitudes of all orthodoxies, political, economic, and religious, but they may nevertheless be recognised as so overwhelmingly important in the world to-day that all the exponents of orthodoxy and the status quo will have to phrase their apologetics in these terms and by that very lip-service end up by giving other service also.

If we consider further the implications of these three beliefs, we find that they commit the world to the rapid diffusion among those peoples who do not have them at present of the skills and techniques and ideas of the peoples who consider their civilisation to be higher. The high cultures of East and West share here the following identifications of a "higher" civilisation: a "world religion," as compared to some traditional cult which is tribally limited; literacy; access to one of the great literatures of the world; an economic system based on a full use of the instruments of money and credit; mechanisation which permits the substitution of other sources of power for human power (this last "good" is occidental in origin, of course, but so widely acclaimed and coveted in the East as to be worthy of this position); ability to integrate large numbers of people within a single political system within which violence is relatively rarer than between such groups. To this list must be added the special values of the Occident and the Orient.[2]

For the Orient, we would have to list such values as the integration of the individual life with that of the family, and the goal of psychological integration of the individual within himself. For the Occident, the most conspicuous values—when looked at from the standpoint of purposeful diffusion—are: health, all those comforts and luxuries usually included under the phrase "a high standard of living" and—with varying emphases in different cultures—forms of socio-economic mobility which are variously identified as freedom, political democracy and economic democracy, depending upon the particular ideology of the given occidental culture. Additionally, the western conceptions of nationalism, and of minority rights, combined with such conceptions as representation, quorums, vetos, initiative, referendum, recall, etc., together add up to an ethic which insists that you must listen to any group which is once defined as being part of your largest group of political allegiance, just *because* they disagree with you. This is defined as the proper

[2] When no mention is made of the Near East it is assumed that its midway position is subsumed under the discussion of East and West.

treatment of minorities in western Europe and as "the importance of unanimity" by the Soviet Union; but however phrased,
it means that that part of a group who differ from the rest have
rights which must be respected. If this belief is consistently
maintained, then cultures which will, if given a voice, insist on
values very different from our own will nevertheless he given
such a voice. Once China and India are recognised as part
of any planning group, their plans become to a degree operative, and this is so however the minority position is
phrased.

If, then, any world planning group pursues goals (1), (2) and
(3), is faithful to the idea of minority rights, and includes
oriental and near-eastern cultures, we may expect some blending
of the specific goals of East and West, as well as a very determined diffusion of all the values which in common they hold to
be the special responsibility of the higher civilisations.

Now, as the minority position will give an opportunity for the
inclusion of Eastern values, at least in terms of blockages and
negations of pace and tempo, so also it absolutely assures that
certain dearly held Western values will be implemented. Perhaps the most significant of these—as it affects the course of
world education because of its refusal to sacrifice one generation
for another—is the belief in the importance of the individual
life. Under this belief any planned slowing down of social
change becomes unethical, because one is denying to the living
something they might have now, simply so that another generation may have the hypothetical advantages implicit in slower
cultural change. This very simple refusal, rendered most important in those systems of ethics in which a belief in the
compensations of the after life has become almost or quite non-
existent, has very profound consequences. It means that the
Occidental powers, especially those of North America and Western Europe, in terms of their own highest ethic, will refuse any
programme of such gradualness that the present generation may
be said to be condemned to ignorance, or poor nutritional status,
or poor health, or a lower degree of political participation, in
the interests of these same values for a future generation. Any
educational programme which suggested limited literacy—say

for the sons of chiefs or for two or three chosen individuals from each native village—would be roundly attacked, and would be impossible to defend in the legislative bodies of Western Europe. Any agricultural programme which proceeded so gradually that the full possible rewards now were given up in the interest of a future sounder economy, or any health programme which suggested that it was unwise to lower the death rate before the birth rate began to fall, would be equally doomed. However far from a majority of the peoples of the world the number of people may be who hold that human lives must be assayed in terms of length, physical vigour and enjoyment of this world's goods and this world's opportunities—that section of the world includes the leaders of thought in the United States and the British Commonwealth, and in its separate versions, the Soviet Union, as well as most of the rest of Western Europe.

We may therefore safely say that as long as a world-planning group is proceeding at present according to its recognised highest aspirations and even if adequate representation be given on it to the great oriental and near eastern cultures, it will nevertheless tend to insist on the following values: (1) an educational system which will make as much of the higher culture as possible accessible to the largest number of members of the less advanced cultures, in the shortest possible time. This will not, however, usually include a demand for teaching literacy to those who are already adult. That demand will come not from those who plan for others, but from individual countries who are planning for themselves, and who are motivated by a desire to compete successfully with other more "advanced" countries. It will be important, however, to so frame recommendations for minimum standards to be recommended for a less literate nation that it leaves scope for and does not offend these internal aspirations. (2) An educational system which will make the individuals who benefit by it world mobile, potentially able to live and function in the most complex type of community which the world offers to-day. (3) An educational system which includes a high value put upon the means of attaining health and longevity.

Problems of Implementation. Having defined, as best we can, the trend which seems at the moment to be the best available, the anthropologist is on surer ground in discussing the means by which this set of values can be implemented. If the goals are to be literacy, access to world cultures as rapidly as possible, and horizontal and vertical mobility from the jungle to the metropolis, then certain definite steps can be recommended.

If full literacy is to be attained, there are several primary requirements: (a) the child who is learning to read must become literate in his mother tongue.[3] Where the mother tongue is spoken by only a few hundred people and the expense of producing texts would be disproportionate, an earlier but prerequisite step will be teaching the women, as well as the men of the tribe or village, to speak the lingua franca which is used over a wide enough area to justify the preparation of texts. As literacy in other than the mother tongue is hardly ever adequate, delay in this procedure can be justified even against the current ethic of haste. (b) Once literate in his mother tongue, he must be inducted as rapidly as possible into full literacy in some language which already has a full literature. There will be no time, if the one-generation criterion is used, to stop and translate an adequate amount of reading material, which would have to include elaborate texts on technical subjects, into the local language, even if this were regarded as desirable. (c) Steps must simultaneously be taken to introduce a need to use reading and writing into the society, on the community level. This can be done in a variety of ways, by sending frequent small governmental administrative messages in writing, by requiring written reports, by diffusing desirable information only in written form, by encouraging the institution of letter-writing, or preparation of court complaints in writing. The particular devices used will have to be local, but only by making the use of reading and writing a necessary part of everyday life, for purposes of inescapable inter-personal relationships can literacy of the average population be maintained after it has originally

[3] For further discussion of the detailed relationship between mother tongue and literacy see: Mead, M., "Some Professional Problems of Education in Dependent Countries". *Journal of Negro History*, July, 1946.

been achieved. This will mean the introduction of such paraphernalia of civilisation as clocks, price notations, time-tables, road signs, the purposeful complication of a life which can be demonstrated to get on very well without any one of these. But if the local village is to be the nursery of world statesmen, in the sense that an American New England village, with its school, its town meeting and its local library, can be said to be such a nursery, and as was the case in China under the old examination system and possibly to-day, then the institutions of the city must be extended deep into the life of the village. The world educator may deplore, in spite of himself, the destruction of the web and woof of local culture which will inevitably follow, and possibly the local culture may, to a degree unguessed of, succeed in defeating him, but if literacy is his goal, he cannot falter.

In addition to this simple requirement that full literacy can only be attained in the mother tongue and should be followed by literacy in a world language (that is, a language in which the full cream of modern knowledge is already in print and which is spoken by a large enough number of people so that those who speak it can participate, speaking no other language themselves, in world conferences), there still remains the problem of incentive. The child must want to learn as well as be given conditions which will make his learning possible. It is in this matter of incentives that the more advanced cultures, seeking to educate, missionise and generally improve less advanced cultures, have most often fallen down. By assuming a motivation on the part of their pupils similar to their own, they have been able to appeal only to the deviant, the unplaced, the untypical, the quislings among them. The very ardour with which the deviant learned to read or pray or brush his teeth, has in turn jeopardised the smooth running of the programme. Over time, the zest with which the dispossessed members of a society embrace a new religion or a new political form, may be a strong social force, but we, by definition, have no time. Without time, it is unsafe to rely on the motivation of the deviant or the abused, as the route by which new learnings will be accepted by a society. Means must be found to involve the motivations of the majority and most importantly of those who typify best the ideals of the group. Where communities are aristocratic, the quickest route is through implicating the monarch or the aristocracy; where they are democratic, "natural leaders" have to be identified. But the implication of the present leader is dependent upon adapting the new knowledge to a set of motivations which are coherent with the culture which he typifies. So those who plan the educational system must furthermore be sufficiently oriented in any local situation to be able to select as leaders and teachers the natural leaders of the people.[4]

Although ideally both methods—the analysis of the culture from the standpoint of available incentives to new learning and contexts within which the new learning can be located, and the investigation of the society to find the opinion-moulders and authority-symbols to be mobilised if the educational programme is to be a success—should be employed, actually, either one may pinch-hit for the other. Where a sufficiently systematic study has been made of a culture, which covers a very large homogeneous population, it will be possible to take that study and plot out, not only the major areas where the incentive system will have to be examined and revamped, but also to indicate what sort of natural leadership is to be expected and how it may be identified. Conversely, where no systematic study of a culture is available, but local staffs—if not themselves deviants—happen to have a good working knowledge of the structure of power and influence in a given community, submitting educational plans to such typical individuals and permitting them to play an influential role in constructing the educational system, will provide a fair degree of insurance against serious cultural errors. Work-

[4] Studies by the Bureau of Agricultural Economics of the U.S. Department of Agriculture in the rural United States have developed methods of spotting such natural leaders in societies of our own general type. Experience among the interned Japanese in the United States during the war revealed how difficult it was, without professional field work, to distinguish the leaders who actually held the power because of the tendency to hide real power behind dummy power. There are now in existence a sufficient number of analyses of the social functioning of different sorts of societies, so that it would be possible to prepare a handbook of types of influence and leadership which might be encountered. This, while it would not be exhaustive, would cover a wide enough gamut so that the investigator would be able to look for the right sort of clues and distinguish the real sources of leadership when he found them.

ing along these lines will, of course, tend to conserve the basic themes, organisational forms, and styles of personal relationships characteristic of each culture. The fortunately complementary nature of these two methods of procedure—formal anthropological analysis and local political mapping—makes it possible for educational planning to utilise both existing and newly initiated anthropological studies and existing and newly initiated local political studies as spring-boards for planning.[5]

So, a detailed study of the culture is called for if an educational system is to be devised which will hold the attention and the allegiance of the people to be educated long enough for it to have any effect. The desired effects might be defined as an integrated acceptance of the implications of the three major goals:—enlightenment, the value of the individual, and the positive and constructive possibilities of change. At present occidental science appears aesthetically and intellectually sterile and frustrating to many Indians and Chinese thinkers, and under those circumstances the only incentives for accepting it are appetite for power and political advancement. A basic condition of acceptance would be a re-orientation within the culture which would make occidental scientific thought intrinsically rewarding.

When detailed attention is given to the incentive system of a society, as for instance to the overwhelming place which fear of failure and its resulting shame plays in Japanese society, or to an apprenticeship style such as was usual in Scottish villages where the school master had himself been a "lad o' parts" and in turn selected successive "lads o' parts" to be specially trained and sent on to the university, or to the Samoan emphasis upon remaining at or below, and never above the level of one's age

---

[5] Where this is done, every effort should be made to match two areas where the two methods were used. This might be done in two adjacent African tribes, for instance, when there was a good working anthropological study available for one, and a District Officer with years of experience of local political functioning, available for the other. It should be pointed out, however, that utilising either sort of information, the formal anthropological study, or the well informed map of the political network, is in itself a skilled task for which special training should be given. Individuals so trained could also utilise a third source of information, watching native teachers teach, and systematically analysing the detailed alterations which they make in incentives and in the formal cognitive structure within which they present knowledge to their students.

group, this attention will to some extent serve as a way of perpetuating that value system. Even though, in the light of the general direction described earlier in this memorandum, each distinctive culture is studied and used only to expedite and facilitate the learning of cultural attitudes which are different from it, and often antagonistic to it, so that the local culture is regarded purely instrumentally, nevertheless the effect of such respectful attention will be to a degree the preservation and reinforcement of at least certain elements in each local culture. This in turn will strengthen the local culture, otherwise in such great danger of total dissolution before the impact of world cultures, and possibly also exercise a selective effect in preserving those aspects of the local culture which are most viable in the wider emerging culture of the world.

Under the incentive system it is necessary to consider not only such obvious matters as attitudes towards reward and punishment, but also whether, for instance, the major expectation of the culture is that failure to do the wrong thing will prevent punishment (instrumental avoidance), or that failure to do the wrong thing will bring reward, or that no relationship to the future is possible except divination, or that the only way to conduct life is to proceed in such a way that one's last act becomes the trigger for the next learning.[6]

In addition to these contexts of learning, there are also such questions as which sanctions are most appropriate, fear, shame, pride, or guilt, and whether any one of these may be relied upon in an internalised or an externalised form. For example, the Balinese child learns, by simple contact with its mother's body, to share her fear of the unusual or the unexpected. Later in life, the desire to avoid this unpleasant sensation provides one of the strongest sanctions for action as well as for the avoidance of any action. Shame, the fear of disapproval or contempt from a group, was and still is a strong sanction among most American Indians, while pride, the fear of not deserving the approval and praise of a group, is a characteristic Polynesian sanction and important in the character formation of most aristocracies. Guilt,

---

[6] For a discussion of this concept of deutero-learning, see Bateson, G., in *Science, Philosophy and Religion.* Second Symposium, New York, 1942. pp. 81-97.

the anticipated loss of approval of a definite person, parent, or parent surrogate, is a less widespread sanction, although one which western European and American educators rather easily tend to assume as present.[7]

A knowledge of the system of rank and caste will also be essential, as one of the most difficult problems of introducing a new skill into a society is to convince the members of that society that such a skill is appropriate for them. Abundant illustrations of this difficulty can be found in the refusal of members of minority groups, or of women, or children below a certain age, to try to master some skill which has been defined as not within their range. The member of the more advanced culture who initially introduces a technique, whether it be writing or driving a car or operating a telegraph key or setting type or thinking in terms of hypotheses, is defined, practically inevitably as "not-I" by all the members of the less advanced society, even though they be of the same racial stock. He must not only bridge this first gap and get someone to make the initial act of identification upon which learning the skill or thinking the new way is based, but he must inevitably choose as his first pupil someone with whom the other members of the society will have a specific relationship of potential superiority, inferiority, social equality, or whatever. If he chooses a child, the skill may later be rejected as childish by all who are older; if he chooses an old man, the young may refuse to try it for the next twenty years; if he chooses a high caste, to attempt to copy may be regarded as presumption; if he chooses a low caste, all of higher caste may look down upon the activity; if he chooses a man, he may debar women from trying; and if he chooses a woman, he will almost certainly debar men from wanting to try. Only a cautious survey of the particular culture will show where it is wise to introduce the new skill or way of thought, with the additional difficulty that those who learn first must become teachers, as well as examples of the fact that a member of group X can learn to drive a motor car or solve differential equations.

While this discussion inevitably over-simplifies the problem,

[7] For a discussion of these various sanctions, see Mead, M., "Social Change and Cultural Surrogates", *Journal of Educational Sociology*, Vol. 14, No. 2, pp. 92-110. October, 1940.

it is probable that the exceedingly different speeds with which
different societies have responded to the new skills and ways of
thought made available to them by culture-contact are to be attributed in part at least to the fortuitous circumstances by which
the new method was introduced at a point of low or high potential diffusion.   In each case the educational planner will want to
regard the point of entry as a channel which will ultimately
touch the whole of the society and for such purposes sometimes
paradoxical choices are best; as for instance when a skill is taught
first to a high caste woman, high castes may accept it as an appropriate decoration of caste; while lower caste males may decide
that they can do what a woman can do, but in turn low caste
females may be persuaded to identify along sex lines and forget
the caste position, so that in the end, all castes and both sexes
can adopt the skill with maximum social facilitation.

We have, then, these necessary conditions, that new learning
must be introduced in terms of the emphases of the local culture, that it must be commended to the learners in terms of
sanctions which are familiar, and that it must be established as
the sort of thing which would be done by the sort of people
these people conceive themselves to be.   There remains, however, the question of the capacity to learn, and the varying ways
in which the new learning itself, in such matters as mathematics,
cause and effect relationships, exactness or reference, can best be
fitted into the existing cognitive structure, or *eidos* of the culture.   Whether we compare the experience of the missionary or
government school attempting to teach geometry to some primitive tribe, or the school achievement in different subjects of the
children of recent peasant immigrants from different parts of
Europe to the United States, we are equally struck by the way
in which certain cultural backgrounds provide a setting in which
languages are learned easily or with difficulty, in which hard and
fast exactness is a pleasure or a punishment, in which the laws
of rhetoric are more or less congenial than the laws of mechanics,
etc.   The individuals from any cultural background who tran-
scend the limitations of their own background and compete successfully with the most gifted from other groups, merely serve
to point the moral.   The observed abilities and disabilities are

to be related to culture and not to some inalienable hereditary characteristic which makes German children good draughtsmen, or Japanese children indefatiguable copyists, or Russian Jewish children good linguists. But the inabilities and the special preparedness for certain types of learning are inherent in every culture, and children reared in that culture have imbibed these limitations and potentialities in large measure long before they come to school. To set up an educational system which will make modern culture accessible to the children of Siam, the Philippines, and to the Javanese, it will be important to analyse the culture and language of each large group (and the cultural type of the smaller groups where individual analysis would be too expensive) from the specific point of view of how well prepared the members of that society will be to learn the kind of thing which we mean to teach them.

It will be possible here only to touch very briefly on certain outstanding problems in this field. The most conspicuous is perhaps the relationship between language and script. The nonliterate people, among who, however, a few priests and scribes are literate, will be prepared to understand ideas like *word,* or *sentence,* as well as an idea like *symbol,* to a degree that completely preliterate people will not. The problem therefore of *spreading* literacy *within* a society is extremely different from the problem of introducing literacy, and similarly the problem of teaching literacy in a standard or high form of a language is very different from the problem of teaching literacy in a world language completely different in structure and vocabulary from the mother tongue. All through the attempted solution of such problems as these, it should be borne in mind that there are certain log jams that have to be broken, after which later learning flows easily. It is such ideas as that a written sign can stand for a sound, that any given language is only one of the sets of systematic sounds by which the same phenomenal world can be referred to, or that numbers need not refer to objects which can be simultaneously seen while they are counted, that are difficult to learn. And back of these lie the even deeper difficulties, the belief that it is impossible to think things out, the reliance on authority which makes each man refer you to his more learned

neighbour until the final authority has no resource except meditation, or the state of mind of the Samoan who when his false
etymology is challenged remarks cheerfully, "Well if that isn't
the way it originated, it ought to have been."

Even very primitive peoples differ enormously in their capacity to use concepts of number, and it will be a very different
matter to teach arithmetic to a people who can count to a hundred thousand and a people who count to twenty and then say
an "uncountable number" were there. These sharp contrasts
are obvious, but a finer analysis will show underlying capacities
to handle concreteness or abstraction, inherent in the very syntax of the language, in the naming of the plants and animals,
in habits of adoption or change of foreign words, in ways of
resolving anomalies of kinship or law, all of which will contribute either to a readiness or an unreadiness for mathematics,
for direct controlled observations, and other forms of exact
thought.[8]

If, for example, we compare the way in which the tribes of
the Sepik basin in New Guinea and the tribes of aboriginal
Australia handle nature, we will find that the Australian aboriginal builds nature, and also all his social relationships, into a
logically inter-related closed system, within which it is always
possible to work out point-for-point equivalences, so that a trav-
eller to another tribe can immediately be placed in a network
of exactly defined relationships. In New Guinea, on the other
hand, both social organisation and classifications of flora and
fauna are open-ended, unsystematic, and inconclusive in structure. Such a difference as this, which the child learns as he is
told the name of a plant or the term for a grandparent's brother,
will make a great initial difference in the acceptance or non
acceptance of such an idea as that one thing cannot be in two
places at once, nor simultaneously A and not-A, which would

[8] If all the existing material were brought together with special emphasis
on those aspects of the higher cultures, and especially of modern scientific
culture, which had been most readily assimilated by particular less-advanced
cultures, and also by cultures which had developed to a very high level
previous to the introduction of western scientific thought (e.g., Japan), we
might have a very valuable set of leads on the short cuts by which members
of one culture can take on the cultural equipment of another, and the prices
they will have to pay.

be congenial to the Australian and uncongenial to the Sepik river native.

Examples could be multiplied. In discussing any matter with a Balinese it is always important to avoid the introduction of any element which is historically untrue into a hypothetical question. If one begins a question: "If Djero Balian Baroe had lived, would . . . .", the Balinese will simply answer, "But he didn't live, he died", and refuse to go on with the discussion. I am told that those who have worked with Japanese students of physics have found it very difficult to induce them to simplify their equations instead of including all the possible variables till the equation may cover several pages. Such an approach obviously contains both constructive and obstructive elements.

It is also probable that there are several different routes, themselves expressed in different cultural forms, by which different aspects of modern scientific civilisation can be mastered. If one compares, for example, the way in which a native of the Manus tribe of the Admiralty Islands [9] and a Balinese native of the Island of Bali,[10] learn to handle a motor-car or a motor-boat engine, there is a very marked contrast in the routes by which they both arrive at an unusually high degree of proficiency. The Manus child is brought up in a world where attention to the properties of matter is made a question of moral behaviour; to attribute to a canoe or a paddle attributes which they do not observably have is simply treated as lying, and lying is wrong. Moral responsibility, with heavy sanctions of parental disapproval, group shame and ghostly punishment, combined with physical accuracy and attentiveness, are so closely tied together, that the whole of the child's organised moral character is brought back to his interest in how machines work, and how tools are used. His survival, in the sense of being a morally approved person, depends upon his competent mastery of his environment. Each new machine which enters his experience is studied carefully, with an intense attention to the actual properties of its

[9] Mead, M. *Growing up in New Guinea*, New York, W. M. Morrow, 1930; and, "Investigation of the Thought of Primitive Children with special reference to Animism", Journal Roy. Anthro. Institute, 62, 162-190, 1932.

[10] Bateson, G. and Mead, M. *Balinese Character: A Photographic Analysis*. New York Academy of Sciences, 1942.

structure, and the Manus native was recognised by all the Europeans who came in contact with him in the early days as unusually adept at handling modern machinery and the conceptual
machinery of western civilisation.

The Balinese, who drives a motor-car with an ease which
makes it seem almost as if he were a part of the machine, is given
no such early training in responsible mastery of his environment. Where the Manus baby is taught to cling, and hold on,
no matter what happens, to his mother's neck while she climbs
up the perilous ladders to the high houses, or punts the canoe
about a treacherous lagoon, the Balinese baby is securely sus-
pended in a shawl which hangs under his mother's breast. Passive and relaxed, he can sway and sleep there, adjusting himself, not by effort and attention, but by relaxation, to her movements. When he is older, he is not told what to do and
rewarded if he does it, as is the Manus child, but his limp and
flaccid little hands—which seem as boneless as a monkey's in
their enormous relaxation—are simply pressed into the appropriate gesture or skill. In between learning by being literally
poured into the appropriate mould, he learns, as the Balinese
say, "with his eyes". Verbal descriptions only confuse him, effort
is supremely unapposite, he relaxes and absorbs the details of
an activity.

Neither Balinese nor Manus handle machinery in the destructive way which characterises many primitive and peasant peoples
who resort to shaking, banging, and verbal imprecations whenever anything goes wrong. The Manus look carefully to see
what has gone wrong, the Balinese drive with an ear so delicately
attuned to the sound of the motor that they never drive a machine to the point where serious difficulties occur.

If we consider for a moment the case of the Japanese who
succeeded in mastering such enormous areas of western scientific
civilisation in the course of 100 years, we find that the Japanese
combine, in their child-training,[11] some elements of both Manus
and Balinese training. The child is given a sense of responsibility, of its duty not to fail, which while more negative than

[11] Benedict, R. *Patterns of Japanese Culture*. Boston, Houghton Mifflin.
In Press.

the Manus who reward success and ignore failure, still lays the ground-work for careful intentness. But the Japanese child, like the Balinese child, is carried in a shawl, learns to make many relaxed adjustments to its mother's body and later is taught a great many things by having its compliant body bent into the appropriate positions. Here we find combined a degree of moral earnestness and capacity for taking infinite pains, with conscious effort, which is reminiscent of the Manus child but which would be meaningless to the Balinese. But like the Balinese, the relaxed infancy and habit of permitting his body to be bent into any desired position, has given the Japanese some capacity to identify with the skills which lie back of the products of other cultures which he wishes to copy. By analysis of Balinese successes in imitating the *style* of a foreign artist, we get a clue to the Japanese capacity to copy, not merely the finished object, but the style of its construction.

When one goes further and considers not only the capacity to drive a car or run a motor-boat, or build an exact replica of a foreign machine, but what will be the price which Manus, Balinese, and Japanese have paid and must pay, while exercising their peculiar types of receptivity and adaptability, we encounter problems we are unable to deal with at present. Certainly studies of Japanese history which include accounts of the painful assimilation of Chinese culture as well as the later spectacular assimilation of the technological aspects of western industrialised culture, suggest that Japan has paid a very heavy price—in human happiness—for her determination both to take from the outside world and yet retain a definite cultural integrity. If records are kept of the educational experiments which seek to facilitate the incorporation of modern scientific elements into primitive, peasant, and pre-scientific high cultures, we may begin to get clues as to where the more expensive strains are likely to arise and how these in turn may be obviated.

To this point, this memorandum has concerned itself with the problem of introducing to peoples who either lack high culture or possess a high culture based on different premises, either modern western culture, or the high cultures of the east, especially in their modern forms, which incorporate the techniques of scientific thought and of industrialisation. Throughout, it has been assumed that the people who were to be educated had cultures which were themselves homogeneous and intact, comparable to the culture of Japan in 1840, or the culture of Bali to-day. This has been done because the issues can be posed more sharply and some of the major recommendations outlined more clearly on this assumption of intactness.

Actually, however, the principal educational problem which faces the world to-day is not the task of bringing modern high civilisations to less advanced, but intact, cultures, but rather the task of educating millions who have been torn from their cultural moorings by unsystematic, sporadic and uncontrolled contact with parts of the higher cultures,—with the armies, the diseases, the tinned food, the missionary and public health endeavours, the slavers and recruiters, the prospectors and engineers, the propagandists and the business men, of the great societies. In many parts of the world the populations who should be the special concern of a concerted United Nations effort have been in partial contact with the West for hundreds of years. Their illiteracy is not the illiteracy of a primitive people who have never heard of writing, nor the humbly accepted ignorance of a peasant people who leave writing and such matters to the priests and scribes, but rather a wretched mixture of the two, in which whole populations, often of mixed cultural origins, live in a kind of no man's land between the effective enthusiasms of the really primitive and the uninformed but coherent status of the peasant. Many of these peoples—in Latin America, in the West Indies, in the East Indies, in parts of Africa—have passed through the period of either violent resistence or eager hopeful orientation to a new world, and sunk into an apathy which can only be matched by the apathy of the urban proletariat in a depressed area. The problem of setting up educational systems for them is strikingly different from the problem which we face when those who learn can meet the new knowledge on the firm basis of a sound cultural adjustment of their own.

But the millions of uprooted peoples of the world, their own kinship systems and local groups shattered by forced labour and arbitrary and intrusive forms of government and commerce, their value systems corrupted by trade tobacco and commercially-fished shells, their time perspective narrowed to the next meal or the next pay-day—these peoples have almost nothing except the toughness which goes with a selective high infant death-rate with which to accept a new form of education. Where the educational planning for the intact cultures should lean heavily upon anthropology and political knowledge of the local scene, upon careful analyses of language and thought patterns, educational planning for these broken and uprooted millions needs other sources of help,—the work of the child psychiatrist, of the social case worker, of the nursery school set up in concentration centres for evacuees and for war-traumatised children. All of these experiences are the laboratories out of which methods may be developed which will give to the children of the culturally disinherited sufficient emotional integration so that it will be possible for them to learn anything. The child from a Japanese home, strict and formal although many of its demands are, has the necessary character for hours of tiresome effort while it learns that the Chinese characters are after all not the way the Japanese write them but must be written differently. Equally the child from the English or Chinese or German home, in which both parents and grandparents share and accept the same value system and reward and punish and criticise and praise within the same set of premises, is ready to learn, even by methods which many psychologists would vote clumsy and circuitous. But the child whose parents both come from different culturally broken backgrounds, whose father drifts from one occupation to another, the union of whose parents is a temporary one, very often without blessing of state or church, who has been capriciously hungry and well fed, ill and frightened and baselessly elated, has no firm character on the basis of which to pursue learnings which are difficult and exacting. It has never been disciplined to attention, nor given enough consistent love to find the world a reassuring place. Reading may prove an unfathomable mystery to a child who has seen so much of life which was both frightening and unexplained.

For these millions of children—and their number has increased by many more millions owing to the damage wrought by war—the problem cannot be posed in terms of language, curricula, choice of teachers, sequence and tempo, but rather in terms of an educational system which must be directed towards reconstruction rather than instruction, therapy rather than the acquisition of knowledge. There is need here for a great amount of research, especially in the field of social organisation. From among these damaged and depressed populations, who can be chosen to teach? Is it possible that among the old, the grandparent generation, there may be some who are sufficiently in touch with the new ways of life, even though they have been battered and defeated by it, and also sufficiently with the old coherent ways, so that in their keeping small children, given space and light and cunningly devised toys which will let them learn to deal with their myriad unsystematised fears and hostilities, may regain their capacity to learn? Certain it is that education for these de-culturalised millions must be concentrated on special nursery education which will so integrate the children's disorganised personalities, that later, probably not at six, but perhaps by eight years of age, they will be ready to learn.

The changing, frayed, patternless character of their culture will give no systematic contours to their thought, either hospitable or inhospitable to the ideas of modern civilisation. Their time-perspective will still partake of that desperation which distrusts the appearance of the next meal. Their sense of the past has been informed by no loving narration of old events clustered about named places, they know neither local history nor world history, and what history they know, whether the death of Christ on the Cross, or the defeat of Napoleon by Wellington, or the Spanish Armada by the English, they tend to think happened yesterday. At the worst, they are so disorganised that they cannot learn at all. At best, they may have retained from their conflicting and contradictory experiences, a sort of flexibility which is not found among those who have grown up within a coherent and homogeneous culture. If these bruised personalities can be given emotional coherence and form—and experience with war-traumatized children shows this can be done—they may form a reservoir from which can be drawn a group exceptionally free to accept and create new patterns and new ways of thought. The sorts of flexibility, of willingness to tackle a new job, live in a new place, in a new way, which has been characteristic of Americans, can be laid to a process of deculturalisation which went on under conditions of optimism and physical betterment sufficient to leave the next generation with enough strength to face a world for which their ancestral past had provided them with no patterns.

In discussing these two types of educable populations, I have of course emphasised the two poles and failed to deal in detail with all the shades in between; with the problems of the immigrant group, lost in a new environment, as compared with the group who on their own home territory have nevertheless been so disrupted that they live as strangers under familiar physical conditions; with the groups where homogeneity of original background, or a hybridisation which is relatively stabilised, have led to a sort of low-level equilibrium, as compared with those groups where people of many different origins are actively intermarrying and interacting, and a number of homogeneous patterns are mutually destroying each other; with the groups who are tied down in the smallest details of choice of their daily bread to the pattern set by the planters or mine-owners for whom they work; with the roving bands of casual labourers who follow commercial agriculture from one locality to another, or the pitifully cheap labour of the oriental village which is brought into the sweated factories of recently industrialised cities to work for a few months and then die. There are many different ways of rendering people rootless, and there is not enough information for us to say surely whether we need therapies devised for each special type. Meanwhile, the tried therapies, of projective play, of controlled emotional expression, of supervised interpersonal relationships with other children, can be applied.

Because of the great emphasis which has been placed in most of the various United Nations discussions on the role which the United Nations must play in bringing to the disadvantaged areas of the world the advantages of civilisation, this memorandum has centred about educational planning, by those who have for those who have not, emphasising also, of course, the need of involving the leaders of the less advanced countries in the planning.

When these leaders are involved, however, they will need to be
protected against certain errors which were included in the education which many of them will have received at the hands of
the more advanced societies. Too often they will have learned to
despise the mother tongue of their own peoples, or at least to have
elevated one dialect or one language to a position vis-a-vis
French and English and to relegate the rest to a limbo where
the very word "vernacular" is now regarded as abusive. Recommendations that village schools be taught first in the language
in which the children are hushed to sleep and waked to play
will seem to them retrogressive. It will be necessary to stress
that the use of the mother tongue will give to the masses of their
people an access to the world language, *more* quickly, not less.
To be convincing, the advocates of such a course must be able
to speak without nativistic sentimentality in their voices, and
with a genuine ring of confidence in the rapidity of learning
which will be possible and desirable. Sometimes the relationship of leaders to masses will be complicated by race, caste, and
religious differences, and harshly and extravagantly mirror, in-
ternally, the discrimination to which the leaders themselves feel
they have been subjected. Plans which appear to favour those
who stand at the bottom of the ladder, on which the leaders have
a none-too-sure foothold, balanced as they are precariously
against members of more completely advanced cultures, will be
fought unless the whole ladder, and the resultant strengthening
of the foothold of the leaders, is kept in mind.

There is also a danger that those leaders who have been educated in the West may demand for their own countries the content of western education rather than the form.[12] Certain it is
that to put upon a people not only the burden of assimilating a
whole pattern of thought which is different from their own—the
burden of achieving literacy, and mathematics, scientific think-

[12] Considerable confusion has been introduced by the translation of the
official plans with respect to cultural groups within the Soviet Union, as
permitting local cultural *form* and socialist *content;* for the translation
obscures the fact that each people, as it participates in the national life,
comes to accept—in the sense in which I am using the word—the *form*
of thought of the wider group. In the sense in which I am using the word
content here it applies to the traditional classical literature and body of
historical allusion which has constituted such a large part of "education"
in the advanced civilisations of the past.

ing and a secularised approach to natural phenomena, freedom from caste and local ties, which will make it possible for them to work and live far from their birthplaces—but also the burden of learning the mythological references in Milton or Racine or Goethe, is too much. If the members of less advanced cultures are to catch up and work side by side in the world with members of cultures which have been literate longer, there must be something in their present disadvantageous position which can be turned into a virtue. For the members of homogeneous but not yet modernised societies, this virtue must be that they carry less baggage, less weight of scholarship and accumulated traditional stuff. For the deculturalised it must lie in their flexibility and ability to take on new imprints. Neither can stand the burden of a "classical education," western or eastern. We may be able to teach them to think well—in one generation—if we do not add the impossible task of asking them to assimilate other people's pasts.

It is in keeping with the philosophy stated at the beginning of this memorandum that the education of all should be postulated on the possibility of any one rising to the top. The village school should never be set up as a dead end, and while it should be much better adjusted to the needs of agricultural populations than have the schools of the past, it should also contain steps by which some individuals can go on and out. The educational systems which make it possible for frightened children of eleven and twelve, dismayed by strange examination systems, to take their feet off the educational ladder and turn finally and fatally into some by-path, simply perpetuate an educational philosophy which leads inevitably to the reinforcement of existing class structures or the formation of new class systems, with an inevitable waste of talents. In a plan such as is envisaged here, there must be no needless waste of talents through avoidable rigidities in the system.

But if these new educational systems are to function within a widening world pattern of enlightenment, certain changes will be necessary within the educational systems of the high cultures of East and West, also. Both East and West have based their university systems on single hierarchies with the classics and

achievements of their own past and contemporary tradition at
the peak. Unless this hierarchical system is broken down, and
the universities of the West teach something of the high culture
of the East, while the universities of the East, although incorporating much from the West, retain a part of their own tradition also, we will be perpetuating a hierarchical system of educational values in which it will be impossible for the late comer,
he who enters from a simpler or wholly different cultural past,
to participate on an equal basis. A systematic attempt to break
down these single hierarchical systems by the inclusion of the
peaks of other cultures' developments, will automatically bring
more of the world into the line of cultural inheritance.

Finally, if we are to direct our work toward a world in which
all stand side by side, without giving artificial advantages to
any, then the hierarchical distinctions between those who teach
the younger and those who teach the older, those who teach the
beginnings and those who teach the ends of subject matter
courses, must be obliterated. Once social recognition is ac-
corded to the non-verbal skills of the nursery school teacher who
reconstructs a child's personality, as well as to the geometry
teacher who teaches how to bisect an angle, or to the philosophy
professor who has all the philosophies of the past on the tip of
his tongue—then those societies in which the most interesting
teaching is still going on among the very young and in the
beginnings of subject-matters will not need to stand young and
ashamed, because they have as yet no institutions which give
Ph.D's. By a kind of ruthless logic, once we reject the idea of
education undemocratically graduated to occupational status—
two years of school for rubber-tree tappers, six for coal miners
or six for automobile workers, etc.—and say instead that we must
have an educational system which offers every child the opportunity to acquire the basis for complete mobility, both horizontal
(over the world) and vertical (up the socio-economic ladder) and
yet will make him a whole functioning human being at whatever point he chooses to stop, then all the other hierarchical
gradations of age and tradition, of one set of classics against
another, of the high school teacher against the elementary school
teacher, of the teacher of the liberal arts as against the teacher of

the manual arts, of those who study books as against those who observe phenomena—all must go. If they do not, the attempt to build a world educational plan, however noble in design, will fail, defeated by the half-heartedness of its designers.

III. THE OBJECTIVES OF FUNDAMENTAL EDUCATION

In our third article (Read 1, pp. 2-20) social analysis, informed by experience and observation in various lands and areas, is applied to the general situation in which Fundamental Education is commonly carried on—the situation of "backward" peoples.

Certain Basic Assumptions: The field which we are contemplating is so vast and so unlimited, and the implications of taking any action in it are so far-reaching, that unless we are clear about, and agreed on, our starting point and our objective, we shall go easily adrift and waste our efforts and the resources at our disposal. There are certain assumptions on Fundamental Education which we need to look at first, and out of them arise other implicit assumptions which are even more important for an international organisation to be acutely aware of at the outset.

(a) *The Menace of Ignorance*. What is suggested in the first place is "a campaign against ignorance." That assumes at once that there are vast numbers of people in the world who are ignorant, and that their ignorance is a menace to themselves and to the world at large. Ignorant of what? Are we thinking of them specifically as being illiterate, unaccustomed to the skills of reading and writing? Or are we chiefly concerned with their lack of knowledge of modern science, with all that it has to teach in health and agriculture? Or are we thinking of them as people who are unaware of *us,* that is, of people living in societies whose social and political or economic life is wholly different from theirs? These questions are not a mere quibble over words and their meanings. If we assume that people who are illiterate, unskilled in modern science, and unaware of other societies and ways of living, are ignorant—if that is the sense in which we are going to use this word—then we know what we are talking about and can go right ahead. In the next section of this article I am going to challenge the wisdom of taking this idea of ignorance as a starting point in an educational campaign among adults. In the meantime we have to recognise that this kind of ignorance is generally regarded as a menace to the health and happiness of the people who suffer from it, and less directly, perhaps, it affects the prosperity of the world as a whole. This is of course a "One World" outlook. The old laissez-faire attitude would leave people in their illiteracy, in their unhygienic ways of living and in their isolation, and would have justified that attitude on humanitarian and even on scientific grounds. It is perhaps important for us to realise how widespread among thoughtful people in every country is this new "One World" outlook. It has, however, as I shall show later on, many implications which are often only partly understood.

(b) The Menace of Backwardness. We have further to consider the special problems of "under-privileged groups," whether living in less developed nations or under the ægis of more advanced nations. No one will deny the existence of these groups, nor the fact that they constitute a menace to the unity and progress of mankind, in so far as they cause deep cleavages in society on the one hand, and are unable, on the other hand, to use to the full the resources of their country and lands and therefore to contribute adequately to their own needs and those of the world as a whole.

If we assume, however, that these groups are in this sense a menace, is it inherent in this assumption that we have to discover and attack the *causes* of this lack of privilege, whether they be geographical, economic, racial or socio-religious? And is it further assumed that fundamental education will necessarily, or eventually, remove those causes? This last seems to me a misleading, and certainly an unwarranted, assumption. An easygoing optimism might very well give assent to it, without examining its implications, but a responsible body like Unesco will have to beware of raising false hopes on the one hand, and on the other of embarking on projects without a thorough understanding of what is involved in them.

(c) A Minimum Level of Living. Reflecting on the approach

indicated by the Preparatory Commission, which was indeed foreshadowed by statements issued and action taken by the United Nations before and since the end of the war, it seems as if we must accept, or at least consider, two or three very fundamental assumptions before we attack this sprawling and necessarily ill-defined field of Fundamental Education.

The first is that there is a minimum level or standard of living, that is of food, health, education and amenities, below which no group of people should be "allowed" to exist in the world of to-day. In plain language, no groups of people must be "allowed'" to starve, or to perish from preventable diseases, or so to struggle for existence that their lives become brutish and on the animal plane, in a world where there is what is loosely described as 'plenty,' or at least where large numbers of privileged groups and 'advanced' nations live on a wholly different plane, and are prepared to take joint action to meet the needs of the underprivileged groups. If the United Nations accept this assumption, we, the people of the United Nations, accept the responsibility for thought and action along these lines.

The next two assumptions arise naturally out of this one. I have spoken of a *minimum* standard of living—a loose and unscientific expression which, however, can be very generally understood and accepted as I have just stated it. It is clear, nevertheless, that if we are going ahead with fundamental education, we have in mind that the under-privileged peoples should attain eventually a standard of living that is necessarily far ahead of the minimum as described. Here we meet immediately with much confusion of thought, which must be cleared up if we are to agree on adequate and clearly defined objectives.

(d) *A Suggested Aim.* I suggest that we assume in our concept of fundamental education that we are aiming at a standard of living, and a mode of living, for the present underprivileged groups, that approximates at least to some rural groups and to some peasant societies in Western Europe. This will be immediately challenged from all sides. "Why," it will be asked, "should African agricultural peoples aim at a European peasant standard of living, and what does that mean anyway?" This is no place to explain in detail what that means. But we have a responsibility, which we cannot evade, to decide on some yard-stick with which to mark out a goal and measure progress.

It can be assumed that people working in Unesco share certain common ideas about standards of living in rural areas, and that in facing the needs of the underprivileged groups, which are mainly rural, they at least start with a common understanding on the subject. I suggest that the common ideas are those of Western European peasants. It may seem on the face of it fantastic to compare standards of living in Central Africa with those in French Switzerland. If we look below the surface of the material surroundings, however, it may not seem quite so fantastic, and indeed there are many links which only a close study of the two societies can reveal.

The consequence of agreeing to this objective would be that the people of the United Nations, and in particular those of the 'advanced' nations, accept their responsibility with what one can only describe as a kind of "missionary zeal." It is obviously quite useless, and indeed nothing but hypocrisy, to give lip-service to the conviction that there *is* a minimum standard below which no group should drop, and that there *is* a goal to be attained represented roughly by European peasant society, and not to take thought and plan action to bring this about. It is the responsibility of Unesco to make this "campaign" a reality. But, to speak in agricultural terms, I think the people of the "advanced" nations have very little idea of what kind of plough they are putting their hands to, and what length of furrow they will find themselves ploughing in this vast field.

(*e*) *A Philosophic Basis*. All the foregoing paragraphs are based on assumptions still more fundamental than any we have discussed hitherto. One is obvious; that we take for granted a certain social and political philosophy that we can call for the moment "democratic." It is unfortunate that that word has been so bandied about that it is in danger of losing all meaning. However, for the moment we can assume at least a measure of common agreement about what we mean by 'democracy' as a social and political philosophy, and I shall be discussing some of the consequences of this in a later section.

The other fundamental assumption is that man is a spiritual

being, who needs more than food and medicine for his welfare, and that the underprivileged groups have spiritual needs and aspirations which cannot be satisfied by even vastly improved material conditions. If that conviction is not basic in our planning for Fundamental Education, then we shall fail the people whom we want to help. In the words of a recent Gold Coast report: "Any process of education which is not founded upon spiritual values may ultimately destroy human virtue." The Nazi near-success is the best comment on that statement.

Analysis of the Concept of Fundamental Education. Fundamental Education has been defined by the Preparatory Commission as a "campaign to raise educational standards both at the level of children and of adults." If we were considering a campaign in a territory and a society where there is little or no modern education, we should have to be aware at the outset of the very different approach needed to adults and to children. This does not mean that we cannot include both within the one concept. Indeed I think it is essential that we should approach the educational needs of any society as a whole, and not waste our efforts by dealing with isolated sections of it, in such a way that new ideas and new knowledge introduced to children in school are countered and perhaps vitiated by parental opposition and indifference. But the campaign, to use the original phrase, must involve distinctive planning, different personnel, or at least different methods of training personnel, and separate tactics, for adults and for children. We should also have different ways of assessing results, as education among adults and among children has obviously a very different time-schedule and time-lag. The results among adults can be seen more quickly than among children.

(a) *The Approach to Children's Education.* Let us take first the approach to children, because the basic ideas in this are common knowledge in what might be called the modern educational world of to-day.

Young children are eager for knowledge of every kind and ready to absorb it according to their capacity. As far as aptitude for school education is concerned, their ability at the outset is obviously untried. Some learn new knowledge and new skills quickly, others more slowly; and some are quick at applying their knowledge, others uninterested in application. The children's environment, especially their social setting, conditions to some extent their ability to learn and to use their knowledge, but only to a limited degree, because their interests and capacities, as well as their bodies, are growing and developing. Children also have an amazing capacity for living in two worlds, and where they can achieve this, the limitations of their environment are less hampering than they might otherwise become. They may, however, achieve this "double life," as so many children do, at the cost of something approaching a split personality, and this possibility, which is ultimately so cramping to a child's full development, is one of the most serious drawbacks of introducing modern education in a "backward" area through the channel of the schools alone.

Modern educational thought, though based it is true mainly upon "western" educational experience, emphasises the primary importance of concentrating on the growth and development of each individual child, giving him every chance to acquire knowledge and to use new skills to the full extent of his ability. His adjustment to his environment and the direction of his learning towards "a job" should be of secondary consideration. I make this statement deliberately, knowing that it will be challenged. Emphasis on the individual development of children in schools in "backward" areas raises a host of difficulties, social, economic, psychological. But we must grasp this nettle, and make up our minds on the subject, for we cannot have two educational philosophies, one for the privileged peoples, and one for the underprivileged.

That is perhaps too facile a way of speaking about a very intricate problem. One form in which it is often seen in "backward" areas is an "agricultural bias" in the schools, given with the double purpose of relating school education to the children's environment, and of keeping the children on the land when they have finished school, and preventing a drift to the towns. The first motive is wholly good, that of relating school work to the local environment. The second, viewed as an *educational* motive, is very questionable. There may be excellent economic and sociological reasons why boys should not drift to the towns and should follow their fathers as workers on the land. But that should not be accepted as a directive in educational planning without being examined from every point of view.

What we have perhaps been doing in the former paragraph is to lay down a warning against a misuse of that rather well-worn cliché, that children are a country's greatest asset. They may be, but they can never be treated, and should never be regarded, as assets in a mass fashion, like land or cattle or forests. It seems necessary in large-scale education plans everywhere to keep reiterating that school education should exist to give each child his or her chance of fuller development, intellectually, and also physically and spiritually.

This is a revolutionary idea in many of the "backward" areas. The aim in what for the moment we will call "primitive education" was to condition and train children to fit into their society, and to acquire such skills and attitudes as would make them eventually satisfactory adult members of that society. The objective of developing each individual child to his full capacity, and doing that by giving him a chance of learning knowledge and skills that are unknown to the rest of the society, is not only a revolutionary idea, but, if achieved, a revolutionary act. That is to say, education on "modern" lines for children in "backward" areas is at variance with the traditional methods of bringing up and training children, and, if persisted in, causes deep-rooted divisions in social and economic and political life. If this conclusion, which can be illustrated from many parts of the world, is accepted in all its implications, it forms a very strong argument for the dual approach envisaged in fundamental education.

(b) *The Approach to Adult Education.* We come now to what I have called "the very different approach needed towards adults" in planning educational campaigns which include them as well as children. To begin with, all adults have some experience of life. This is such a truism, that we had better be a little more explicit about what this actually means for educational planning in "backward" areas. It means for a young adult that he has vivid memories of his own childhood and adolescence just behind him, and of his efforts to acquire adult status by preparing for marriage and assuming some economic responsibility for a wife and household, or for contributing his due share to a joint household. If he is an older man he adds to this experience that of providing for and bringing up children, of assisting the needy older members of the family, and of taking some share in public affairs, whether social, political, legal or ceremonial.

If this is the normal background of any adult in a "backward" area, then we are surely right off the mark if we describe him as ignorant. He may be illiterate, he may know nothing of modern science, nor of the United Nations and their ways of living, but he obviously has knowledge within a certain range and the ability to acquire it. He has confidence in his knowledge and the use he makes of it, and confidence in his ability to learn from others and from his own experience, and from trial and error experiments. This confidence establishes his 'humanhood,' which is the nearest equivalent for an untranslatable Bantu word: *umuntu*.

Because the adult has confidence in the knowledge he has learned in traditional ways, he is correspondingly diffident about acquiring new and "foreign" skills and often sceptical about new and "foreign" knowledge. New skills such as reading, and new knowledge such as injecting cattle against tsetse or boiling drinking water to prevent infection, are right outside his ordinary range of knowledge, and he has no criteria by which to judge his ability to use the new skills, or the validity of the new information he is given. Those who have had experience of teaching adults to read are emphatic that the first step is to give them confidence in their ability to learn quickly. We have here an easily recognisable process of carrying over the confidence in the old knowledge and its value to a man, into the new sphere, where he has to make an effort to acquire new skills as yet unrelated to his customary way of living.

This customary way of living sets up another obstacle in the path of the adult. It matters little whether it is called conservatism, traditionalism, fatalism or even superstition—those are merely labels tacked on to the manifestations of a certain attitude of mind by an impatient person coming from outside into a "backward" area, who is surprised because the adults are not immediately interested in his plans for reforming them. The labels explain nothing in the attitude of the adults, nor the underlying causes for that attitude—and are best discarded. The basic fact in the situation is, that when people are mainly occupied in a struggle for existence, they keep to the old and tried ways. Such tried ways may not have been entirely successful, but by and large they have worked, and hence the confidence in them. With unerring logic an old African woman once said to me: "You Europeans think you have everything to teach us. If, as you say, we have been eating the wrong food all this time, cultivating our fields the wrong way, rearing our babies the wrong way—why we'd all be dead. But you see we are not."

The clue to understanding and overcoming this resistance to new ideas is to approach adults from a common human standpoint. No one *wants* to be hungry—it is a very painful experience. No one *wants* to be ill or *wants* his children to die. If ways can be found to prevent or remedy these admitted evils, on the ground that they have been successful with other human beings, then the unfortunate but all too common, "right or wrong" approach can be avoided. In general, too, most peoples are eager to improve their lot, and this is especially true when a 'backward' group has been in contact with a more advanced group, as is the case in almost every territory to-day where underprivileged groups are to be found.

It follows from all this that no one can expect to be successful in teaching adults unless he knows something about their society and ways of living, and respects their efforts at winning an existence from the soil, even though the people may be hungry and dirty and prone to disease in spite of all their struggles. This is an absolutely essential starting point for all adult education—and unfortunately extremely rarely found.

(c) *Types of "Backward" Areas.* In order to raise the educational standard of children and adults, the Preparatory Commission suggests that the campaign should provide them with knowledge relevant to their needs and to those of their country, as well as with the tools (such as reading) to extend their knowledge further. It will make discussion of this aspect of Fundamental Education more realistic if we recognise that in rural areas, to begin with, there are at least three distinct fields to which such plans should be applied. The first is the type of "backward" area where there are no schools for children and no education in the modern sense for adults. Such areas are only of limited extent to-day, but where they exist they present certain special problems of pioneering work. The second is a common type of area where there are scattered schools for children, by no means covering the whole child population, and where any attempts at adult education have been sporadic and unco-ordinated, and for the most part the adult section of the population is living still on traditional lines. This is probably the commonest type of rural area with which those planning for fundamental education will have to reckon. The fact that school education of a certain kind for some children has been started has a dominant influence in this situation, and it creates the kind of cleavage in the society, and in the lives of individuals, which has already been referred to. The third type of area is that in which school education, although rudimentary, has over a number of years produced adults who understand and appreciate certain aspects of modern education, though they may have forgotten much of what they learned and may not have applied their own school education to improvements in their standard of living. They at least wish their children to go to school and expect them to benefit from what they learn there.

The first kind of area calls for a pioneer approach; the second for a levelling up and integration of effort; and the third for a general move forward in which the people themselves should be prepared to play a large part. There is no opportunity within this article to do more than make these rather general statements about the three types of "backward" areas. I shall be referring to one or another of them in subsequent sections. It seems vital, however, that in all discussions we should recognise at least these three distinct fields, and consider their special needs as regards policy and method of approach.

(d) *Literacy and Economic Development.* Before we leave

this analysis of the concept of Fundamental Education there are two subjects of discussion which should be indicated, though they cannot be dealt with adequately here. Both refer mainly to the field of adult education, though they are not without a bearing on schools and their curriculum for children.

The first is the question of whether in adult education priority is to be given to literacy campaigns.

This is a very controversial question, and it must obviously be settled by experiment and practice in "backward" areas. Though it is of no value to decide such an issue on doctrinaire lines, it is at the moment being dealt with mainly by "hit or miss" methods, according to the whim or conviction of people on the spot. It is clear that evidence should be collected on this matter and the two opposing views examined in the light of the evidence.

Put crudely, the two views are:—(i) Teaching adults to read and write opens their minds and makes them receptive to new ideas about health and agriculture and ways of living. Also, when they have learned to read, they can be supplied with literature to extend their knowledge. As one experienced educationist put it: "A thousand books well distributed are far more effective in getting ideas across than one highly paid official." (ii) When the standards of living are so low, it is more important to teach people better agriculture and village hygiene than to take time teaching them to read. When they are better fed and in better health, then literacy campaigns can be started, but the most essential thing to begin with is practical demonstration of better methods of living.

In addition to this question of literacy, a second question is suggested by the large-scale plans for "development" which are now being considered in many "backward" areas. These plans envisage extension of communications, exploitation of mineral wealth and other resources, and greatly improved methods of agriculture. The question then immediately arises: what is to happen to the traditional subsistence farming of the underprivileged groups? Put more concretely, and in terms of Africa, isn't it impossible for hoe cultivation, based on the family as a unit of labour, to support improved standards of living and an educated people demanding various social amenities and services.

If it were accepted that the old cannot continue, that would mean two things. One is that planning for economic development would involve radical changes in the existing social-economic order. The second is that fundamental education would have to prepare people for these changes in every way possible. It would no longer be a question of patching up here and improving a little there, but of introducing in agricultural areas the same kind of drastic change as takes place when a nomadic tribe is settled on irrigated land, or when people living in densely settled rural areas emigrate to industrial and urban centres. Such far-reaching decisions in large-scale planning are not within the sphere of Unesco. But the concept of fundamental education is built on assisting men, women and children to be, not the passive victims of these large-scale plans, but intelligent co-operators in them.

The Starting Points for Fundamental Education. We have spent time so far, and given what might be considered an undue amount of space, in analysing the basic assumptions and the concept of Fundamental Education. One of the main difficulties, however, in an international organisation is that any national, even if he is not speaking or writing as a representative of his country, approaches a problem such as this from his own social and political and educational background. This is unavoidable and must be taken as a *chose donnée*. When we add to this the difficulties of language and the varying connotations which apparently common terms, such as school, have in each language and social-political setting, then a common basis of discussion is difficult to establish. It is for this reason I have tried to clear the ground in the opening sections of this article, endeavouring to get rid of clichés and well-worn terms, which conceal rather than reveal the ideas behind them. We are perhaps now assembled on a common ground, on which we can ask: where do we go from here? I propose in this section to give my own conclusions drawn from the previous analysis. I have called them, perhaps rather illogically, the starting points of Fundamental Education. As we are using the analogy of a campaign in which the advance is essentially on a broad front, perhaps this expression is not wholly illogical.

(a) *The Homes of the People*. We start, then, by declaring that fundamental education is primarily an affair for parents and their children. We begin, that is, with the basic social unit in every society, which is relatively the same the world over. Note that we do not begin with what the state, or the government, or any outside agency ought to do. We begin with the people who are most concerned about their children—that is, their parents. And what we are saying in effect is that fundamental education must be rooted in the homes of the people. The implications of this are very far-reaching. In the first place in the pioneer areas to which reference has been made, adult classes must be started if not ahead of, at least alongside of schools for children. Adults, if handled in the right way, will learn far more quickly than children, and will therefore be able to supplement in the homes what the children learn in school. And one must take 'learning' here to cover not only such skills as the three R's, but certain principles and practices affecting health and hygiene and the use of natural resources, such as the land. In any pioneer area teachers will be scarce, because they are normally the product of schools and it takes time to make them. Until enough teachers of the right calibre and training are forthcoming, parents and other adults can assist in the process of education at least in their own homes, if they are drawn in from the start. It would be idle to deny, on the other hand, that peasant people, occupied in a grim struggle for existence, have little time or energy at certain seasons of the year to give to either learning or teaching. This is, however, merely a challenge to careful planning, not a reason for abandoning the principle. It is much easier to set up a school for young children who have no economic responsibilities, and who can sit all day in a classroom with a teacher without anyone being the poorer for it. But in how many cases is such an effort wasted, because the purpose of the school is not understood, and the children are withdrawn as soon as they can assist in the family food-getting activities?

In the extensive areas of the world where some of the children go to school while their parents have been relatively untouched by modern education, there arise conflicts and maladjustments, not only in the family between parents and children, but in the society as a whole between youth and age. That may be no exclusive characteristic of "backward" areas, and if the malady is a common one, perhaps the remedy can also be widely applied. It is probably true to say that in a great number of countries, and in many different types of societies, the schools and the homes exert conflicting influences on the children. The psychological result is inevitably some retardation of the child's ability to learn, as well as a slowing down of his all-round development. It has an equally serious social effect; for the child, finding at home little sympathy with his newly-discovered life at school, gradually loses the sense of security which his home should give him, and there is no carry-over from the home in which he grew up to the one which he will eventually set up for himself. Such a break in the continuity of social institutions is harmful in any society. When it affects that basic social unit, the home and the family, it is casting adrift both parents and children in a society which offers little or no other form of security either social and economic. The malady calls for drastic treatment. Parents have got to be helped to "catch up," and there is perhaps a case to be made for some slowing down of school education until this has been achieved, if resources are limited in finance and personnel. Anyone who has studied this kind of social dislocation is aware of its serious consequences, and prepared to support active steps to remedy it.

When the stage is reached at which a proportion of parents have themselves been through the schools, a somewhat different approach is needed to the problem of "gearing in" home and school. The parents may have been at school in the days when the three R's formed the whole curriculum, and they may look with suspicion on any effort to widen the scope of school work, to include among other things various forms of handwork and dramatics. Adult education at this stage has an important contribution to make which I will refer to again in a later section. Here, however, we can emphasise the importance of associating the parents with the schools, either through Parents' Days, or

Parent-Teacher Associations, or through parent representation on school management boards and local education committees. Parents on such bodies may sometimes be obstructive to new ideas or to the spending of more money. But their co-operation must be sought and won if this alliance between home and school is going to be built up and extended at every stage.

(b) *Economic Development.* If the first starting point for fundamental education is the homes of a country, the second is its economic resources. When all that is possible has been said about the uses to be made of voluntary effort, the fact remains that the education of children and adults costs money—for buildings, equipment, salaries, books and libraries, and school welfare service. It is a well known fact that most of the less developed nations have poor educational facilities because their economic resources are inadequate. It follows from this that any advance in education in these less developed nations, or among underprivileged groups, must be linked with economic development. We have seen the significance of the fact that in many "backward" areas plans are being, or have been, made for "development." This term, as we suggested, covers a wide range of activities, including improved communications and water supplies, conservation of forests and anti-erosion measures, as well as the investigation and exploiting of mineral wealth, commercial crops, and secondary industries. Here we meet, within the territories which form our field, widely differing conditions according to whether the countries are small independent nations with few potential resources, large independent nations with underdeveloped areas, or countries under colonial powers or held in trusteeship.

We are concerned with this problem of economic development only insofar as it is related to, and makes possible, plans for fundamental education. One point is essential to grasp: neither can wait for the other. It would be relatively simple to say 'Educate the people and then let them develop their land'; or to say 'Let them first develop the country's resources and then pay for their education.' Both these are doctrinaire positions and untenable in the world to-day.

The impossibility of separating economic advance from educational advance was emphasised in 1945 by the Commission on Higher Education in British West Africa. Speaking of the relation of education to political, social and economic development, they said: "The standards of production generally of foodstuffs, economic crops, local industries and crafts, are all far too low. Any great increase in the wealth of the country is unlikely unless the people accept new technical knowledge, new methods of production, new incentives to produce more goods and increase their distribution . . . the schools and adult classes must awaken new incentives and point the way to new achievements."

There are two grounds on which this view may be challenged by some who know tropical areas. One is that a tropical climate, combined with poor diet, saps physical and mental energy, and it is therefore unlikely that any efforts to increase production will be successful beyond a certain point. The other is that in many tropical countries the incentives to acquire wealth by harder work in order to attain a higher standard of living are apparently lacking. This is brought out clearly in one section of a recent sociological study of village life in West China by Dr. H. T. Fei.[13]

But if inertia and lack of incentive are going to be accepted as permanent characteristics of a poor peasant society, then it will not be much good going on thinking about Fundamental Education. It will be the task of those who are engaged in this work to find a way through these formidable barriers to progress, and to keep clearly in view, what may often be an unpalatable truth, that the price of education and higher standards of living is harder work and better work by all concerned, which may still, we hope, be accompanied by some reward in a greater enjoyment of leisure. It is undoubtedly true that in many parts of Africa, if not elsewhere, the acquiring of some education acts as an incentive to further effort; and the correlation between educated parents and a higher standard of living in the homes is to be found almost everywhere.

Other aspects of economic development with which fundamental education is concerned can be found in the large-scale planning which is being considered. One form of relief for poor

13 *Earthbound China.* Fei Hsiao Tung.

and over-populated agricultural areas is to relate them to an industrial area through a recognised policy of labour migration; or, if conditions are suitable, to establish secondary industries in the territory itself. I propose to discuss this issue later on in the particular setting of certain African territories with which I am familiar. But though we have considered so far the development of fundamental education in peasant societies in rural areas, industrial workers in "backward" areas are mainly peasants uprooted from their villages, and plans for education must take account of the fact that in over-populated rural areas labour migration is most likely a necessity. The right kind of education must help the adults as well as the children to make a bridge between the village and the mining compound, between agriculture and industry, between living among friends and relatives and living among strangers.

Another aspect of large-scale planning has already been hinted at. It is the possibility, one might almost say the necessity, of envisaging radical changes in the social and economic life of the rural populations. This will involve substituting other methods of agriculture and of animal husbandry for those practised in the past when a subsistence economy was all that was needed. It may mean alteration in traditional forms of land tenure; or the shifting of large sections of the population to avoid prevalent pests, or to enable eroded land to recover its fertility.

If the face of the rural areas and of the villages is to be altered so drastically, the people will have to be prepared not only for the material changes but for their own adjustment to them. Such changes will inevitably bring peasant life in tropical areas much nearer to the conditions of peasant life in Europe, which we thought at the beginning of this article might be a goal to be aimed at. It sounded rather fantastic then. Perhaps it sounds more reasonable now in the light of what we have just been saying. There is a small book published by a medical officer in East Africa called "The Book of Civilisation," and on the cover is a picture of an African farmer with a neat little house and a small holding stocked with cattle, fowls, etc. Although it is unfortunate that small holdings and civilisation should be considered synonymous, it has proved a very successful way of "selling" both improved agricultural techniques and the ability to read.

(c) Living in the Modern World. As starting points for fundamental education we have considered first the homes of the people, and secondly their part in developing the resources of their country. The third starting point is the relation of these underprivileged people to the world at large. An experienced administrator, who had spent a lifetime in the Orient, summed up his work by saying, "We have failed in our job with these people. We have not taught them to take their place in the modern world." The span of fundamental education must therefore begin in the homes of the people, and reach through the arc of economic production to increase their country's wealth, to touch earth again by bringing the world's knowledge and the world's culture into their country, and by helping them to meet and adjust themselves to every kind of contact with the modern world.

There are two major ways in which the underprivileged people living in "backward" areas come into contact with the modern world. One has been in existence for a long time, through groups and individuals from more advanced territories living in these "backward" areas for purposes of administration, missionary work, commerce and industry. Such contacts have offered knowledge of different standards of living, opportunities of wage-earning employment, and incentives to work in order to approximate to these new standards. The reverse side of these contacts is a feeling of frustration at being the plaything of forces which are not understood, and resentment at restrictions based on colour and race. The other form of culture-contact is more personal and more limited, namely the exodus of scholars to centres of learning in more advanced countries, and since 1939 the experience of African and other soldiers on war service in countries far from their own homes.

It is therefore not unreal to speak of various forms of contact with the modern world experienced by people from "backward" areas. It seems clear that one of the tasks of Fundamental Education is to bring, through journals, books, visual aids, and radio, further knowledge of how other people live to men and women who have hitherto been limited in their outlook to their own neighbourhood. Allied with this kind of knowledge will be that of a more technical nature which will help them in the development of their resources, and make them aware of the relation of their own productive work to the world economy.

In the past the isolation of these "backward" areas was in one sense a protection for them. That isolation is breaking down, and they are perforce becoming part of the modern world, whether they wish it or not. Fundamental education must take this fact into account, and prepare both children and adults to take an intelligent share in the wider opportunities which are open to them. There is probably considerable difference of opinion about the urgency of this aspect of our task. No central organisation like Unesco can possibly set the pace. But Unesco can, and should, take account of social, economic and political forces which are propelling "backward" areas and their people into the stream of modern life, and should be ready with suggestions for helping them to make adjustments and to understand and control their own future.

Some Conclusions from Experience in British Africa. *(a) The Welding of African and British Cultures.* One of the leading questions which has to be answered about fundamental education in the British African territories is one which is of great importance in the international field, and also one about which misunderstanding can easily occur. No country which has colonial responsibilities in dependent territories can avoid putting its stamp on an invisible export like education. To what extent, therefore, is education at the fundamental level in these territories typically British? It is difficult to give a very precise answer. Modern schools and modern educational ideas have an almost international character to-day. But the "bush" schools of West Africa and the sporadic attempts at adult education, hardly fall within the realm of modern schools. In the "bush" schools African languages are used as the medium of instruc-

tion, African crafts are taught and practised, and increasingly
African stories and music form part of the children's curriculum.
In that sense this part of fundamental education is becoming
more and more African. Yet the educational philosophy which
lays stress on local initiative, on voluntary effort, on co-operation
between church and state and people in the organisation of education—all that is typically British.

In the field of adult education this is perhaps particularly
evident. The people of Britain, with the possible exception of
a small highly privileged class, believe in adult education of
every kind but of no one stereotyped pattern. The Workers'
Educational Association, the Churches, the Co-operative Societies, the Women's Institutes, the Trade Unions, the Young
Farmers Clubs—to mention only a few organisations—have all
made their distinctive contribution to adult education in Britain.
The educational philosophy which accepts and endorses these
voluntary spontaneous efforts is now beginning to leave its
mark on adult education in Africa, as it has on the "bush"
schools. And just as the Africans over a period of years have to
a large extent made the "bush" schools their own, so they will
in all probability do in time to the adult education movement.
There is an additional and distinctive feature in adult education in Britain, namely the connection with the universities,
about which proposals were made in the Report on Higher
Education in West Africa.

Characteristic, too, of the part played by the central government in Britain is the giving of expert help when asked for, and
of financial assistance, to voluntary efforts in adult education.
As that policy has been transferred to the African territories in
the field of primary school education, it is likely also to be
found in adult education.

This first conclusion, then, is that in spite of the inevitable
export of the educational ideas and philosophy of the metropolitan country into the colonial territories, the results in British
Africa have been on the whole a welding of the two cultures
and not a distinctive stamp. This applies to the field of fundamental education only, and hardly at all so far to the fields of
upper primary, secondary and higher education.

(b) Literacy and Village Betterment. The second conclusion is about the methods of approach in adult education. The Mass Education Report [14] laid particular stress on the value of "combined operations," that is, on associating literacy campaigns with village betterment schemes and improvements in health and agriculture. Although the evidence comes from scattered areas, and is as yet limited in quantity, it is clear that the method works from both ends. Literacy campaigns lead to demands for better villages. Better village campaigns lead to demands for fundamental education for children and adults. It should be stressed that the evidence is as yet not extensive, but one proof that the combined approach has been accepted lies in the development plans made in certain African territories, where this "combined operations" method is proposed.

(c) Needs of Women and Girls. The third conclusion is about a particular aspect of Fundamental Education which we have not so far touched on specifically—namely the education of women and girls. The grim fact has to be faced, that in spite of the existence of village schools over wide areas, and in spite of the beginnings of adult education movements, the economic standard of living and the health standards are deplorably low in the villages. This is partly due to the poverty of the people themselves, which has its roots in a number of factors. It is also due to the fact that women and girls have so far taken little part in educational advance. To most African peoples, being educated is an economic asset, and it has not yet been demonstrated to them in terms of hard cash that educating women and girls *pays.* The West African Higher Education Commission stated: "We are deeply concerned about the backwardness of women's education, especially since all improvements in the homes and in the bringing up of children will be delayed until a great drive is made to educate the women and girls. . . . The health and hygiene of the masses of the people in West Africa are largely in the hands of the women. While women and girls are uneducated, little or no progress can be made." This statement applies to all the African territories. Both in the schools and in

---

14 *Mass Education in African Society.* Colonial Office, No. 186, H.M.S.O.

adult education, special attention must be paid to the needs of women and girls, and special efforts made to draw them into any plans. Only if this is done can parents and their homes be the pillars of Fundamental Education. No sound structure can be built on one pillar. This may be easy to say, but it is in existing circumstances in British Africa extremely difficult to carry out. But as a principle it should be written large on all plans for development.

(d) The Demand for Literature. The fourth conclusion is again concerned with methods. It is the need for literature of every kind, and the importance of its distribution. From the first reading charts, to primers, to simple books of interest and information, to periodicals, to small village libraries and reading rooms—the conditions can best be described as a *famine* of reading material. A famine suggests that people are starved of what they need for living, and that is the situation wherever schools and adult classes have been started. This importance of reading material need not be stressed further here, except to mention its relevance to two aspects of Fundamental Education, both of which can be studied in published material. One is the need for easily accessible reading material on health and agriculture, on better homes, on current affairs.[15] The other is the relation of literature to language policy. This is far too big a subject to embark on here. It is, however, an outstanding example of two typical forms of co-operation. One is between the state and voluntary agencies, for on the various Language and Literature Bureaux and Committees are to be found members of the different government services, of missionary societies and churches, and of educated Africans. The other kind of co-operation is between the universities and Fundamental Education. For it is at the university level that African languages are being studied, and the groundwork of language policy is being laid down; and the giving of scholarships to Africans to study their own language with linguistic experts in the University of London is an indication of the importance attached to this aspect of Fundamental Education.

[15] *Africa Advancing*—Davis, Campbell and Wrong, pp. 181-195.

(e) The Use of Leisure. The fifth conclusion can be stated in the words of the West African Commission: "The schools, the youth services and adult education must make a contribution to the wise use of leisure. Many of the traditional forms of leisure-time activities, in which the people in the villages joined together, are in danger of dying out. To help young people to enjoy their leisure and to cultivate a strong sense of practical citizenship, some of the traditional forms of amusement should be fostered and developed, and new interests such as libraries, debating societies, women's institutes and scouting should be encouraged." The Mass Education Report had a section on Art, Music, Dancing and Drama which should be studied in this connection.[16] We have so far laid stress on the fight with poverty and the need for hard work as well as knowledge. Fundamental education, both at the children's and the adults' level, must also be concerned with forms of relaxation, recreation, and creative effort in the æsthetic sphere. These are common human needs, and never more important than when human beings are in the throes of a struggle for better living.

Commercialised amusements such as the cinema and the radio have undoubtedly an important recreative as well as educational part to play. But there are two great drawbacks to their widespread use in rural areas in Africa. One is obviously the prohibitive cost of these forms of amusement in poverty-stricken areas. The other is the inescapable fact that they are entirely passive forms of entertainment, and call for no creative response on the part of the audience. If African villagers are not going to turn into economic machines for producing food and other crops, they must have recreations which call out their undoubted skill in the æsthetic line.

(f) Need for Research. The last conclusion is perhaps the one which calls for the most, and the most immediate, attention. It is the need for research. In the field of Fundamental Education in the British African territories, research is wanted along many lines. The primary need is for a type of sociological research which will examine the changing societies in Africa

[16] Col. No. 186, p. 49 to 51.

and the external and internal influences which are changing them still further every day. No education of children and adults in backward areas can be built on any sound foundation, unless it is planned and carried out with a full knowledge of the social and economic conditions in which the people are living. In addition to sociological research, linguistic, educational and psychological research are all needed to establish sound approaches and methods. Both the Mass Education and the Higher Education reports have emphasised this need.

IV. A FURTHER DISCUSSION OF AIMS

The conclusions of the preceding article are re-inforced by the next contribution (Baez 1, pp. 1-7) which deals in general with the main aspects and objectives of Fundamental Education.

The purpose of Unesco as stated by its Constitution, is "to contribute to peace and security by promoting collaboration among the nations through education, science and culture. . . ." To attain this purpose in the most efficient way, Unesco must start by planning a sound programme, comprehensive in its scope, practical in its results, and feasible in its enforcement. To make any contribution at all to peace and security through education, science, and culture is certainly an easy goal which may be reached in many ways; but to reach the highest goal in the best possible way is something different. It is necessary to have a right general view of the prevailing conditions throughout the world, in order to focus upon the most important aspects of the present situation; and it is necessary, also, to know concretely what our aims are, in order to shape our knowledge to suit the problem and to try to solve it.

Two aspects might be considered as within the scope of Unesco, as the most important factors in building the universal good understanding and mutual respect necessary for a real and lasting peace. One is the great difference between the cultural levels of the most advanced peoples and the backward peoples; and the other is the misuse and the insufficient or inadequate use of education, science and culture, as a means of serving the cause of peace and better understanding. In other words, education, science and culture can help efficiently to build peace; but many millions of men and women are at present deprived of the possibility of using such means, and, on the other hand, education, science and culture have been wrongly used as weapons not for peace but against it.

Unesco's most important job must be the dissemination of culture, "for the sake of the dignity of man"; "to give fresh impulse to popular education by instituting collaboration among the nations to advance the ideal of equality of educational opportunity without regard to race, sex, or any distinctions, economical or social" and "by suggesting educational methods best suited to prepare the children of the world for the responsibilities of freedom."

It is very important to give the highest priority to raising the cultural level of backward peoples. As long as we are not resolutely decided to change the present situation, and, still worse, as long as there are people in leading positions who think that it is only natural and right to have mankind divided into far advanced peoples and backward peoples, into bright zones and dark zones, there cannot be a fruitful and lasting peace.

I do not mean, of course, that it is necessary to attain uniformity among the peoples, for I do not think that it is possible, nor even desirable, to attain uniformity among individuals. But I do think that it is necessary that all men and women should have at least a minimum of health, food and shelter, a minimum standard of living, and a minimum of education, affording everybody a chance to develop his individual potentialities.

The Allied Nations, after fighting together in the most dreadful of wars, and realising that our present civilisation and even our very existence were in danger, started to build a strong and lasting peace; and the first conference called to deal with such problems was one devoted to the study of the food situation all over the world. Nobody doubts that it is absolutely necessary that all human beings shall have a minimum of food, a minimum in quantity and in quality. Nobody thinks that all men and women all over the world should always eat the same foodstuffs, in the same quantity and prepared in the same dishes. We know, of course, that age, sex, kind of work, climate, habits, etc., must be duly considered and that the local possibilities as to production and distribution have to be taken into account. Notwithstanding, we know well that there is a minimum of food that everybody must have in order to live a positively healthy life.

But in order to live a fully human life, man must have something besides food. If he is to be able to get such food, then in order to enjoy life and to help others to live a human life, man must have some education. And if he is expected to go ahead and not to stay forever at the same spot, man must be duly prepared to help progress.

To the learned scientist it has been quite easy to establish accurately the minimum food requirements for men. It is not equally easy to establish the minimum requirements in education. As with food, education is not an end in itself, but a means to an end. We eat in order to get fuel to keep our bodily machinery going and to enable it to do some work; to repair and replace worn cells and tissues, to ensure the growth and the development of our body at certain ages, and to build a reserve for the purpose of keeping a good balance when occasionally the input goes below the output. We know that we must eat clean, wholesome, digestible and assimilable food, providing us with the right amount of every element we need to keep on living, healthy and fit. We can think of Fundamental Education, as the minimum of education that is necessary to enable everybody to keep on living, healthy and fit.

Man must learn to keep on living; he must be taught how to use his physical and intellectual energy to keep the earth yielding its fruits; how to use tools; how to use his brains, his hands and feet and his senses. He must be trained to live in society. He must learn how to teach his descendants.

Man must not only live, but he must live a positively healthy life. He must not only know how to prevent disease; he must know also how to develop all the potentialities embodied in his own individuality; he must know how to get and promote security; how to enjoy beauty, truth, goodness. He must develop his comprehension and his sensibility, his mind and his soul. He cannot live forever just on what he has been taught. He must be able to go farther, in the prosecution of the truth, in the creation of beauty, in fostering better ideals.

Finally, man must be taught the duties and the rights of a free man, in order to be able to fulfil such duties and exercise such rights.

Unesco must deal with Fundamental Education as the most important of the items in its programme. If we want to fight misunderstanding and miscomprehension, we must build good understanding and right comprehension. If we want to deter people from wrong dogmas and substitute for such dogmas a democratic ideal of equality, the peoples must be enabled to detect and abjure false science and false dogma. If we want human solidarity, human dignity and freedom to become the leading ideals of mankind, we must do our best, through education, to inculcate such ideals in every human mind.

If we consider Fundamental Education in these terms, we will immediately see that there is a need for basic education not only in the dark areas and among backward and illiterate people, but that it is necessary to enforce such basic education in the bright areas, and among the most advanced peoples also. For the brightness, the greatest advances, consist generally in the higher forms of literacy, technical knowledge, and specific training for a certain type of civilisation; but due consideration has not always been given to the very important matter of uprooting dogmas of the inequality of peoples, feelings of superiority, and imperialistic attitudes.

Fundamental Education is, then, to my understanding, the process of transmitting the minimum of knowledge, training and attitude that man needs to live, to enjoy positive health, to profit by the chances offered to him for higher education, and to be prepared to fulfil the duties and exercise the rights of a free citizen of the world.

Literacy is an indispensable requisite for Fundamental Education, and must be considered as a part of such an education. It may be actually possible, though very difficult indeed, to transmit some knowledge, training and attitude to an illiterate person, but it would be impossible for such a person to increase his knowledge and to improve his training and his attitude if somebody is not constantly acting upon him as a teacher. Nobody can reasonably pretend to higher education without being able to read and write.

Literacy alone must not be thought of as fundamental education. It is only a step, an indispensable step, on the path leading from ignorance to knowledge, from backwardness to progress, from barbarism to civilisation. In all peoples where illiteracy is still an important problem, literacy campaigns must receive immediate and adequate attention. Lowering the percentages of illiterate people must be the first goal, but immediate steps should be taken to give the new literate people something to read, and not merely something to read, but something that is useful, adequate and wholesome, according to the peculiarities of each people.

It is important that literacy campaigns shall take into consideration both children and adults. The mistake of trying to reach only the children, through new schools, is only too evident to anyone who has dealt seriously with educational problems. Literacy campaigns must probably deal mainly with adults. Nobody, of course, would think of forgetting children.

The planning and conducting of literacy campaigns is something that cannot be done in the same way for all the peoples. Due consideration must be given to the circumstances prevailing in each particular case. The goal is a single one, but the ways to reach that goal must be varied.

The same diversity must exist in the concrete purposes and methods of the aspects of fundamental education other than literacy. In some peoples a systematic minimum curriculum must be covered, while in dealing with other peoples perhaps it would only be necessary to deal with the subjects and apply the techniques generally included in the field of mass media.

V. BEYOND LITERACY

This chapter closes (Kandel 2, pp. 1-10) with a critical analysis of the idea that literacy alone is Fundamental Education and the related idea that only illiterate populations are involved in the problem.

It would be a serious mistake to approach the whole problem of Fundamental Education within the terms of reference of the present inquiry as though it was solely a problem of the liquidation of illiteracy. The problem is far broader and has far wider ramifications than that of training in ability to read and write. The basic issue is a consideration of the ultimate ends to be achieved. In this consideration other sections of the United Nations organisation are as much concerned as Unesco. The intellectual liberation of so-called backward peoples is a responsibility not only of Unesco but also of the Economic and Social Council, the Council on Human Rights, the International Health Organisation, the International Labour Organisation and the Trusteeship Council. It should be the task of Unesco in formulating plans for Fundamental Education to stress ways and means whereby all agencies involved in implementing Purpose 3 of Article 1 of the United Nations Charter may co-operate in the common effort. Purpose 3 of Article 1 is defined as follows:

"To achieve international co-operation in solving international problems of an economic, social, cultural or humanitarian character, and in promoting and encouraging respect for human rights and for fundamental freedoms for all without distinction as to race, sex, language or religion."

The examples of the success of certain techniques for teaching reading cannot be denied, but convincing evidence has not been produced on the lasting effects of such success in the life of either the individual or his community. The fundamental questions to be asked are: What did the neo-literates do with this newly acquired ability? In what ways was that ability directed to improving personal and community standards of living? What happens to that ability if the environment itself provides little or no opportunities for its use or even creates opportunities for its misuse?

These questions are not concerned only with the fundamental

education of backward and illiterate peoples; they are as much
the concern of educators in those countries which have had
compulsory elementary education for all for more than a century. Sir Richard Livingstone in the first paragraph of *The
Future of Education* did not speak for himself alone nor only
of England when he wrote:

> "Why are we an uneducated nation and how can we be-
> come an educated one? We have compulsory education,
> magnificent schools, an impressive array of teachers, and an
> enormous educational budget. Yet most of the passengers in
> a railway carriage will be reading the *Daily Mirror,* and the
> *News of the World* has a circulation of between three and
> four millions. The advertisements, cheap newspapers and
> films of a country are the best index of what appeals to the
> masses. What view will posterity form of our civilisation
> from these manifestations of its taste and intelligence?"

Nor is there any greater validity in the claim that the
acquisition of literacy is a guarantee of democracy. The most
rapid advances in the liquidation of illiteracy have been made
in recent years under forms of government which are far from
democratic, in order to control the spirit and soul of the individual by means of the printed word. And the nation that has
committed the greatest crimes against humanity has the highest
percentage of literacy in the world. Literacy is a two-edged
sword. The fundamental issue is not literacy, but literacy for
what?

In discussions of the education of backward peoples, there is
another false assumption that it must be different from that of
more advanced peoples. Of course it must be different, but that
difference is one of degree in cultural advancement and in
environmental factors, but not in the type of education to be
provided. It must be emphasized again that educational theory
has changed and that the approach to the education of the child
solely through literacy is being abandoned. This change is more
than a change from passive to active methods of education; it
involves also a change in the materials of instruction. Out of
the wealth of literature that is available on the subject it is only

necessary to cite the definition of the functions of the school in the last edition (1937) of the *Handbook of Suggestions for the Consideration of Teachers and Others Concerned with the Elementary School,* issued by the English Board of Education. Those functions are defined as follows:—

"(1) To provide the kind of environment which is best suited to individual and social development; (2) to stimulate healthy growth in this environment; (3) to enable the child to acquire the habits, skills, interests and attitudes of mind which it will need for leading a full and useful life; (4) to set standards of behaviour, effort and attainment by which they can measure their own conduct."

In discussing the new edition of the *Handbook of Suggestions,* Mr. Oliver Stanley, then President of the Board of Education, drew attention to the new order of subjects:

"The first thing they noticed was the clear statement that 'There has been a shift of emphasis in teaching from the subject to the child.' That meant two things; first, that the curriculum was to be dictated by the nature and capacities of the child, not by any preconceived code of regulations; and secondly, that the subjects in the curriculum had changed their order of importance. In 1918 the order was English, arithmetic, science and so on, with physical training dealt with last in two pages. To-day, health and physical training came first, followed by music and practical subjects and then by intellectual subjects, ending with mathematics. The order, in short, followed the organic development of the child—first, the physical; then the concrete; finally the abstract."

The principle underlying this change of order is not derived merely from the interests of the pupil but suggests that education starts in a particular environment, that it should be related to that environment, and that there should be a reciprocal relation between the school and the environment in which and for which education is provided. This means further that the school can flourish best if its activities are supported by the community and if it seeks through these activities to develop a social or community spirit. It was in this sense that German educational theory under the Weimar regime placed so much emphasis on *Heimatkunde* or study of the immediate environment of the pupils as the foundation of education. It was in this sense that educational theory and practice in Soviet Russia has attached so much importance to "socially useful activities" in the educative process. And finally, American theory has in recent years broadened from the child centred to the community-centred school.

One of the causes of the high percentage of illiteracy in many countries is not the lack of schools, but a curriculum which is not adapted either to the language or the environment of the pupils. To this cause among others can be attributed the sharp tapering off of attendance in many school systems and the swelling of the percentage of illiteracy through recidivism or lapse of literacy. Since what has been taught in schools is not related to the environment of the pupils, what is learned has neither meaning nor use for them or their parents. They may acquire literacy, but the spirit of education is lost.

There is another lesson in the principle which has been stated—that the best way of enlisting the interest and support of parents and other adults in the work of a school is to enable them to understand that what is done in the school is directed at the same time to the improvement of the community. In many areas, however, a tradition of literacy has already been established which tends to look upon education as a means of escape from the everyday tasks of a community. This has been particularly true in colonial dependencies where the reward for literacy has been some form of public employment. While this has been true of secondary education in large measure, it has also applied to the product of elementary schools.

The 19th century practice in bringing education to dependent or backward peoples was guided by the desire to "assimilate" them to the standards of education of the rulers or of the countries from which the educators themselves came. Since World War I, there has been a wholesome movement in the direction of "adaptation" to the cultural environment of the pupils to be educated. There has thus been a parallel movement in the theory of education in both backward and advanced countries. It is from this point of view that the statement was made earlier that the difference between the education of backward and of advanced peoples is one of degree rather than one of quality. The basic principle should be the same in any consideration of Fundamental Education; organisation and practice will inevitably differ. It is for this reason that the educational worker among primitive or backward peoples should have some training in anthropology or the co-operation of anthropologists, just as in the more advanced areas educational theory is relying increasingly upon the co-operation of sociologists or upon educational sociology. The success of new ventures in education depends upon the understanding and co-operation of a community as a whole. If this is not developed—and this means that the education of adults should proceed simultaneously with the education of children and youth—there will always be the danger of a rift between young and old. It is for this reason that parent-teacher committees or associations have been organised in many countries in order to acquaint parents with the meaning of an educational theory different from that which prevailed in their own school days.

Experiments in fundamental education directed to the improvement of standards of living have been made in many parts of the world—in village education and the Moga experiment in India; in a number of missionary schools in Africa and China; in the Near East in the education of displaced Greek children about 1924; in Mexico and in some backward areas in the United States. In addition to recent publications of the British Colonial Office Advisory Committee on Education, valuable contributions on Fundamental Education have been made in the surveys, conducted by the International Institute of Teachers' College, Columbia University, of education in Porto Rico, the Philippine Islands and Iraq, and in a number of dissertations—reports on missionary experiments in Africa and proposals for the reconstruction of education in Iraq and Egypt. A bibliography on the subject would no doubt be extensive, but a bibliography alone would not serve the present purpose. An evaluation of theory and practice and a study of the continued results of the experiments are greatly needed as a basis for the formulation of general principles of Fundamental Education. In this way a cross-fertilisation of ideas would be stimulated. Educators do not need to be reminded that it will always be necessary to adapt theory and practice to the local conditions.

The task of stimulating national government to provide adequate systems of education in their own areas is not a simple one. There is some truth in the statement that some groups in some nations fear lest education of the masses may threaten their own privileged positions. There are others who allege that their nations cannot afford the cost of an adequate system of education. It has been forgotten that the so-called advanced countries had to meet similar opposition in the last century. Cubberly, in his *Public Education in the United States,* devotes three chapters to the battles that had to be fought to establish adequate systems of popular education—the battle for compulsory education, the battle for taxation for education, and the battle for free education.

Many countries that now claim financial inability to support schools devote large sums to the maintenance of armed forces, sums which could be better devoted to constructive purposes. This is an aspect of the problem which illustrates how closely the work of Unesco must be associated with the work of the United Nations. In the proposals for the post-war reconstruction of education in some of the advanced countries a new note has been sounded—the recognition that education yields dividends. Thus in the first paragraph of the English Board of Education's White Paper on *Educational Reconstruction* (1943) appears the statement that

> In the youth of the nation we have our greatest national asset. Even on a basis of expediency we cannot afford not to develop this asset to the greatest advantage.

In one of the plans for the reconstruction of education in France, published in the *Bulletin du Ministère d'Education Nationale,* November 1944, it is declared that

> There is, in truth, no better investment of funds than that devoted to the instruction and education of children.

The National Education Association of the United States, in a pamphlet, *Proposals for Public Education in Postwar America* (1944) stated that

> One of the major problems confronting the American people is that of further conserving and developing our human resources through education.

Finally the Educational Institute, the largest teachers' organisation in New Zealand, stressed the same point in its proposals for educational reconstruction (1943) when it urged that

> The greatest wealth of New Zealand, or of any other country, lies in the children. But, like minerals hidden in the earth, till it is developed, that wealth is only potential. To develop that wealth thoroughly requires education in its broadest, richest and fullest measures.

In all plans for educational reconstruction—India and Australia can be added to those already mentioned—the cost of education is faced frankly and unhesitatingly, despite the effects of war upon national resources. The New Zealand Education Institute's statement on the subject is as relevant to backward as to advanced areas:

> This report is drawing to a close, and those who have read so far will possibly have in mind a question mark—a question mark that has gradually been increasing in size as they read— *What of the cost of such a system?* Can we afford such changes and improvements? That question can be answered by another, *Dare we not afford them?*

A study of the rise and development of public systems of education in the nineteenth century and an analysis of the new trends in the proposals for the post-war reconstruction of education which have appeared should give great encouragement to those concerned with the problem of Fundamental Education. They would find in both the study and analysis a confirmation of the statement made earlier that the problem is one of degree rather than one of the type of education to be provided. The important advance that has been made is that attempts are now

being made to answer the question, Literacy for what? in place
of the earlier expectation that the dissemination of literacy
alone, of the three R's in other words, would help to solve the
social, economic and political problems of the day.

Fundamental Education as a Universal Cause

The four essays which constitute this chapter present no
simple picture of Fundamental Education; they offer no doctrinaire solutions to its many problems.   They raise, indeed,
or raise more sharply, questions which have not fully appeared in the earlier and more concrete accounts of Fundamental Education in action.   If this were to result in dis-
couragement, in any halt or hesitation in the attack on our
problem, that would of course be regrettable; but we are
persuaded that a careful reading of the chapter will have
no such effect.   We believe, on the contrary, that it will inspire fresh enthusiasm in this universal cause, and for the
very reason that these essays bring into clearer light the
meaning of what is to be done.   They emphasise its novel
and revolutionary character.   They present it as a phase or
aspect of the immense human struggle for a shared and conscious control of the common life of mankind.   Intensely
realistic with respect to difficulties and the need of skill, of
study, of the adaptation of the work to differences of environment and culture, and of prolonged, devoted effort,
they yet agree that the task must be undertaken and that it
can be accomplished.   Even where they differ as to the precise nature of the outcomes to be sought or expected, they
differ rather in emphasis than in their views as to the general
direction of the movement.   These essays deal with Fundamental Education in a serious and scientific spirit, and thus
in a way that is sobering and steadying, that lends force to
the pleas for research and careful planning, but that makes
still more evident the deep and enduring worth of this great
new responsibility of international leadership.

For I remarked that men commonly do not speak but babble; that is, they transmit not as from mind to mind things on the sense of things, but exchange between themselves words not understood or little and ill understood. And that not only the common folk do this but even the half-educated also, and what is more to be grieved at, the well-educated themselves for the most part; . . . for which reason whatever language a man may speak, whether rude or cultured, it maketh slight difference since we are all nought but sounding brass and tinkling cymbals so long as words, *not* things—(*the husks of* words, *I say, not the kernels of* meanings)—*be in our minds. Such a book, said I, could it be constructed aright, would be a kind of antidote-universal to ignorance, misunderstandings, hallucinations, and errors. (Such were my hopes.) Yea, to the stinting of that complaint sometimes heard abroad that of the necessaries we are ignorant because the necessaries we learn not.*

COMENIUS, 1641.
quoted by OSCAR KOPOSCHKA in
The Teacher of Nations—ed.
JOSEPH NEEDHAM, F.R.S. 1942.

POLICIES AND METHODS

The Special Importance of This Chapter

In some sense Fundamental Education forces us all to be pragmatists. At least we must face in the end two questions which bring all theory to the test of operation: *What to do;* and even more pointedly, *What to do first?* The wise choice of means, the order and relation of procedures, and the temper and spirit in which the whole enterprise is approached are matters of such vital significance that no descriptive account of contemporary endeavour and no conceptual analysis will have much value unless it is productive of sound decisions on these points. This chapter cannot offer final answers to these practical questions; but it can raise them in the sharpest form now possible, and it can offer the counsel of experts on some of them.

The pragmatic approach has its limitations, to be sure. When it comes to a question of values, other considerations enter in. The most important thing to do may not be the thing to do first. It may be the last thing to be done, as the climax to all that has gone before. Or it may be no one thing at all, no single act or series of acts, but a spirit or atmosphere pervading the entire work—or the mere fact that someone cares enough to do the work at all.

Chapter IV does not deal with policy for Unesco. That final problem is reserved for Chapter V. Unesco's policy involves issues not only of Fundamental Education in its own character but of international relations and the place of the Organisation in the structure and operation of the United Nations. What is here in question is policy and method in

Fundamental Education at large, viewed as an undertaking within national areas.

But the suggestions to be offered and the definitions of the issues to which they apply cannot here be put in national terms. This volume cannot offer direct advice to Governments, nor criticise their policies, nor cast doubt upon the value of what they have so far accomplished. Our treatment must still be general, suggestive of action which may or may not fit the situation and the national purpose in any particular instance. Here we simply have to do our best to make the statement of the issues clear, their weight and impact apparent and inescapable, and the suggestions presented by our contributors fully meaningful in the setting provided by what has gone before. This requirement dictates the content and arrangement of this chapter.

An Outline of Issues

It is possible to separate issues of policy from issues of method but it is quite impossible to reach wise decisions on policy without taking the requirements of method into account. If it is necessary, for example, to begin the attack on illiteracy in a native language, this requirement will affect vitally the policy to be adopted in the recruitment of teachers. If fundamental education, in order to be useful in practice, must begin on the level of local interests, that necessity dictates a policy of general democratic development rather than one of selection of an elite for the sole purpose of buttressing a bureaucracy. Quite obviously, on the other hand, decisions of policy, especially financial policy, affect the possibility of any major success at the level of method. If the best way to undertake the task calls for large expenditure, the money must be raised somehow, or else a second-best way must be adopted. It then appears that the raising of funds itself involves, as a process, a decision of policy which is far-reaching in its practical effects; for partici-

pation by the people themselves comes into question; and
the discussion of what is to be done, the enactment of decisions, and the execution of plans, including financial plans—
all these will depend, at bottom, on the amount of direct
popular action required and engendered. Thus policy and
method interplay, and their separation in fundamental education, as in so many other social matters, is mainly for convenience in thinking.

With this interconnection in mind, we may bring up the
issues to be discussed in the present chapter without trying
to separate them sharply from one another or decide which
are matters of policy and which are matters of method. The
order which seems most to commend itself is as follows:

I. THE SCOPE OF FUNDAMENTAL EDUCATION
    Here we are concerned with two questions: (1) *who* is
    affected—i.e., what persons, of what ages, of what stages
    of advancement? and (2) *how* are they affected—i.e.,
    how far does Fundamental Education go and where
    does it shade off into other educational territory?

II. THE CONTENT OF FUNDAMENTAL EDUCATION
    Since it is clear that more than literacy is involved, of
    what should the actual substance of the desirable teach-
    ing and learning in Fundamental Education consist?

III. THE STATE AND VOLUNTARY AGENCIES
    What is the role of government, of other agencies, and
    of the people themselves, in starting, continuing and
    governing Fundamental Education, and paying for it?

IV. THE PROBLEM OF LANGUAGE
    Shall instruction be in the native tongue, a foreign
    tongue, or both? How can alphabets be simplified for
    the purpose of mass instruction? How can language
    itself be made more effective for educational ends?

V. THE PROVISION OF READING MATERIAL
    Here libraries, newspapers, and magazines are in view,
    as well as books.

VI. MASS COMMUNICATION THROUGH SENSE AIDS; AND THE
"ACTIVITY PROGRAMME" IN COMMUNITIES

Radio, films, film strips, slides, diagrams, charts, etc.,
are all in question. What are their uses in the process
of instruction in school? What are their direct uses in
the community? What is the need for new types of programmes; for better distribution of instruments? What
can be accomplished through group activities among
young people and adults, aside from schooling and beyond the use of mass media?

VII. THE PROBLEM OF INCENTIVES

How can the values of Fundamental Education be revealed to those who need it; how can they be moved by
a new and more intelligent desire to accept it and to
meet its requirements?

In dealing with these seven major issues of policy and
method, this chapter will be held within limits by reference
in various places to material in Chapters II and III. Where
new material is presented, it will sometimes go beyond the
heading under which it first appears; but this will be clearly
indicated. In general, the issues just listed will be treated
consecutively and—if the references to preceding chapters
are taken into account—with enough fulness to bring out
their importance.

I. THE SCOPE OF FUNDAMENTAL
EDUCATION

(a) *WHO is to be educated: what groups are involved, of
what ages, at what stages of advancement?*

1. Preceding chapters make it abundantly clear that
Fundamental Education is largely concerned with "backward peoples" but that "backwardness" is in no sense a term
derogatory to national groups nor even significant of the
same characteristics in all groups alike. Complete illiteracy
does, to be sure, mark any individual as a person who is in

need of the kind of education we have here in mind; but there are persons of various degrees of literacy whose need of fundamental education is no less definite. Even full literacy in a single language would not exclude some groups, whose "backwardness" might be due to illiteracy in a second language which is required for effective participation in their culture, or to a failure of formal schooling to make the group in question more than a bureaucratic element—in some cases a retarding element—in the progress of their people.

The reader is here referred to Laubach 1, in Chapter II, p. 24; Charton 4, in Chapter III, p. 129; Read 1, in Chapter III, p. 163; Baez 1, in Chapter III, p. 178. Other contributions bear on this point more or less emphatically.

It should be noted that very advanced nations—the United States of America is an example—may include fairly large numbers of people, whether in particular areas or scattered through the population, whose need for fundamental education is unmistakable.

Cf. Mead 1, Chapter III, p. 150; note also in Hellman and Whyte 1, Chapter II, *passim*, that the Asiatic, Coloured, and Native populations of the Union of South Africa are backward elements in a society otherwise advanced. Furthermore, even remarkable success in fundamental education, as in the U.S.S.R. leaves some islands of illiteracy and backwardness still untouched by the floodwaters of national educational effort. Cf. King 1, Chapter II, p. 122.

2. No exact references need be given to bear out the statement that fundamental education is concerned both with children and with adults. The material on China in Chapter II shows how the work may be divided as between these two main groups; and there is ample testimony throughout the two previous chapters that the education of either group lags unless the other group is included.

(b) *HOW (that is, how far) are such groups affected by Fundamental Education?*

1. Fundamental Education is groundwork. It is not necessarily, however, groundwork for mere adjustment to the environment; for that may already have been accomplished. A primitive people may have achieved discipline, responsibility, command enough over their material resources to meet simple needs, confidence in themselves, self-respect. Yet they cannot be said to be a part of the modern world; nor can they face famine, disease, or disrupting contacts with the exploiting elements of advanced civilisations, whether these are greedy individuals or officials bent on domination. In such cases the primitive group must be started on the road to participation in the life of a scientific age and protected against the loss of what was good in their earlier stage of culture. Fundamental Education is one aspect of that beginning. It is groundwork for a new way of living; and if there is some loss that is regrettable—of simplicity, steadiness, and loyalty—fundamental education is still an inevitable process, which may lead in the end, if it is wisely directed, to the retention of much of the good in the old way of living, as well as some mastery of the science, the technology, the legality, and the wider perspective of the new.

These points are brought out in Charton 1, Chapter II, p. 38; in Charton 4, Chapter III, p. 131; in Mead 1, Chapter III, p. 139; in Read 1, Chapter III, p. 158; and in King 1, Chapter II, p. 113.

2. No extended argument is needed to make it clear that fundamental education merges with other educational work at more or less definite points. For children, specialisation, selection, and vocational guidance lie outside the limits of fundamental education—though not outside its motivating interest. We believe, indeed, that the measurement of intelligence and aptitude should have its beginnings while

fundamental education is still in process. Educational guidance, guidance in health, moral guidance—these are simply aspects of education itself at any stage at which education is to be truly effective. When adult education is in question, technical training in agriculture, industry, sanitation, or government is not a part of fundamental education itself, though fundamental education may be abortive without it.

Dr. Huxley's statement, quoted in Chapter I, p. 14, is here in point. The reader is referred in this connection to other projects advanced by the Education Section of the Unesco Secretariat in Chapter II of the Final Program Report of the Preparatory Commission.

3. Is there a form or standard of living which can serve in a realistic sense as a goal or objective of Fundamental Education?

In seeking an answer to this very basic question, we may remind ourselves of certain facts and recall certain points of view. The greater number of groups whose needs have been presented in Chapters II and III are rural; they are farmers or herdsmen. Other groups, however, cannot be ignored, although they may not have been discussed in these pages; mine workers, migratory labourers, fisher-folk, refugees, and some of the submerged poor in city slums. If a stable life on some pre-conceived level is what is ultimately in view, Fundamental Education will not only start in the realities of the local environment but will tend to stay there. It will be chary of stimulating so much ambition as to lead to widespread discontent or even the desire to travel far from the native heath. It will in most cases—since mose cases are rural—magnify the values of village and agricultural life.

Out of this situation an issue emerges that can hardly be ignored—the issue put as a question at the beginning of this section; but it may be suggested that this issue will resolve itself in practice if certain generally accepted requirements of the actual work are faithfully observed. These are *first,* that Fundamental Education shall make itself thoroughly a part of the present life of those concerned—starting where they are, in their homes and fields and communities; *second,* that it shall not fail to stimulate them to the improvement of their own dwellings, their farms, their local governments, and their resources for recreation and expression; *third,* that it shall raise their eyes to the wider horizons of modern life, in science, world-relationships and art—but without imposing on them an impossible burden of detailed academic learning.

The vast majority of the people of the world must live simple lives and engage in activities that are humble and largely repetitive. Few can be "leaders in the strife". This fact is not due solely to mass production methods; it is not a new thing in the world, and it does not seem likely that it can be changed in any predictable future. But the alternative to leadership and the excitements of travel and wide cultural contacts does not have to be the life of "dumb, driven cattle". If democracy must face the fact that opportunity for living at high levels of perception and action is not equally available to all individuals—nor indeed the capacity and the desire to enjoy it or to use it wisely—there is still no reason why the total distribution of that opportunity and of that capacity cannot be lifted to a higher baseline. The annals of the poor need not remain forever short and simple. Peasant communities have often nourished the lives of "Olympians in homespun".

On this issue attention is directed first to Read 1, Chapter III, p. 157; then to Baez 1, Chapter III, p. 176-7; and to Mead 1, Chapter III, p. 154.

The requirements of modern living call in some instances for educational insights and discriminations of policy that are not yet fully understood—certainly not everywhere put into effect. Adequate knowledge of the consequences of very early training is a case in point. The beginnings of Fundamental Education must be made in the home and in the preschool years. The general programme of Unesco touches lightly on this period; but for Fundamental Education it may be a period of great importance. And back of the problems of the first years of child life lie the problems of maternity care, the general problems of health, and the problems of population.

Cf. Mead 1, Chapter III, p. 147; also Chetsingh 1, Chapter II, p. 82; and Hellman and Whyte 1, Chapter II, p. 71.

II. THE CONTENT OF FUNDAMENTAL EDUCATION

(a) *Literacy is not enough*

On this there is unanimous agreement. There can be no possible doubt, however, that the attack on illiteracy can neither be omitted nor long delayed—if indeed it can be delayed at all. Literacy and direct education without benefit of print go together.

Cf. Kandel 1, Chapter III, p. 179; this contributor has pointed out in a memorandum not included in this volume that the most effective work in agricultural education in the United States has been done not through books or other reading material but through the demonstrations and field work carried on by the U.S. Department of Agriculture. The extension work of the Agricultural Colleges, the formation of the 4H Clubs among young people of farming areas, and various other direct contacts with farm people should also be mentioned; but this work has been done with people who are able to read—at any rate in the overwhelming majority of cases. See also Read 1, Chapter III, p. 172.

(b) *The content of reading; topics of direct instruction through books and through other media*

Fundamental Education cannot rely on interests already so developed that there will be much independent effort to seek out new knowledge. Such interests will be present in some individuals, to be sure; but fundamental education deals inevitably with large groups of people who are overworked and underfed to the point of apathy. The content of reading, the teaching, and the mass communication provided in fundamental education must be stimulating, interesting, hopeful and challenging in relation to the immediate problems of those to whom it is presented. It is equally true that it must lead up from and out of their narrow environment and their purely personal or communal concerns.

We are here concerned with the *substance* of the materials used—not the way they are to be handled; and our interest at this point is to define, however roughly it may have to be done, the limits of Fundamental Education in terms of what we hope both children and adults can be induced to learn. It should be emphasised that factual knowledge is not all that is in view, nor indeed can large areas of such knowledge be considered especially important in the premises. Attitudes are involved; habits are to be formed; desires are to be stimulated. But the range of factual knowledge, the ideas and points of view, the attitudes, habits, interests and attachments—all the reactions we may hope for in Fundamental Education—can perhaps best be suggested in terms of topics which might appear in a curriculum—if only that curriculum is clearly understood to be not merely a plan for lessons in school but a broader programme of activities and incentives.

For the purpose in hand, therefore, we will content ourselves with a recital of topics or subjects of instruction. To correct at once the impression that we are forgetting mass communication, or activity programmes in school or village, or the concept of community-centred education, we ask the reader to look forward to the sixth section of this chapter (the section on Mass Communication and the "Activity Programme"). To illustrate the range of topics which may be handled in fundamental education we present excerpts from two manuscripts placed at our disposal.

The first of these manuscripts is one from which we have already presented an excerpt in Chapter II. It is a description of the programme developed in India by the Wardha Conference, describing the "Wardha Scheme". The manuscript reads as follows:

The Committee was not satisfied with the existing educational system because of its failure to meet the real needs of the Indian villages. They reported that there is "a demand from all sides for the replacement of the present system of education by a more constructive and human system, which will be better integrated with the needs and ideals of national life, and better able to meet the pressing demands. Any scheme of education designed for Indian children will in some respects differ radically from that adopted in the West. For, unlike the West, India has adopted non-violence as the method for achieving peace with freedom. Our children will therefore need to be taught the superiority of non-violence over violence."

Some of the principles and objectives of the Scheme can be summed up as follows:—1. Evolve a system of education which will be in harmony with the genius of the Indian people, and solve the problem of mass education in a practical way and within as short a time as possible; 2. Enable the child to acquire not the superficial literacy which implies, often without warrant, a capacity to read the printed page, but the far more important capacity of using hand and intelligence for some constructive purpose; 3. Therefore, give greater concreteness and reality to the knowledge acquired by children by making some significant craft the basis of education; 4. Produce *workers,* who will look upon all kinds of useful work—including manual labour, even scavenging—as honourable, and who will be both able and willing to stand on their own feet; 5. Give the citizens of the future a keen sense of personal worth, dignity and efficiency, and strengthen in them the desire for self-improvement and social service in a co-operative community; 6. Enable the children to carry the outlook and attitudes acquired in the school environment into the wider world outside.

The Course of Study: 1. *Length:* seven years; 2. *Age-range of pupils:* Seven to fourteen; 3. *Sex:* Boys and girls—(In general outline, the syllabus of studies will be the same for boys and girls up to the 5th grade of the school. In grades 4 and 5 the syllabus in general science should be so modified as to include Domestic Science for girls. In grades 6 and 7 the girls will be allowed to take an advanced course in Domestic Science in place of the basic craft.); 4. *Subject-matter:* Basic Crafts—(Spinning and weaving, Carpentry, Agriculture, Fruit and Vegetable Gardening, Leather work, Any other craft); Mother Tongue—(Reading, Writing, Speech, Composition, Literature); Mathematics—(Arithmetic, Practical Geometry, Book-keeping); Social Studies—(History, Geography—World Geography, Civics, Current Events, Comparative Religion); General Science—(Nature study, Botany, Zoology, Physiology, Hygiene, Physical Culture, Chemistry, A knowledge of the Stars, Science stories); Drawing—(Illustration of readings, Pictorial representation, Design and Decoration, Mechanical Drawing); Music—(Songs, Musical Appreciation, Rhythm, Group or Choral Singing); Hindustani—(Scripts, Urdu and Hindi, Reading, Speech, Literature).

Our excerpts from the second manuscript consists of selections from a set of topics on which Dr. Frank C. Laubach has prepared a book of readings for the teaching of English. The book is called *Making Everybody's World Safe.* It is a Second Reader in a series of texts aiming to enable the student to read newspapers, magazines and books with ease. In this series the First Reader, called *Streamlined English,* aims at teaching English phonetics. The author says, "If the student has mastered the very easy phonetic principles in the First

Reader, he will be able to pronounce every word in the
present book without any help". Our excerpt is not intended to describe Dr. Laubach's method of teaching English, which is not here in point, but to give the topics treated
in this book as an indication of the possibility of using subject-matter of a very wide meaning even in the teaching of
children or illiterate youth and adults. An examination of
the book in which these topics are treated will show how
very simply some of the most far-reaching ideas can be presented. It is to be noted that the sub-title of Dr. Laubach's
book is "Helping the United Nations". The topics follow:

The Nations Have United; The United Nations Organisa-
tions; The World Is Getting Smaller; One World Or No World;
The Atomic Bomb; The Radio; We Must All Help The UN;
We Must Share What We Know; How To Share This Book With
Others; We Are One; Learn To Like People Who Are Different;
Differences Make The World Beautiful; Thoughts Build The
World; Good Thoughts Build A Better World; It Could Be A
Good World For Everybody; Food For Everybody; How Farmers
Can Help Save The World; The Value of Co-operatives; Have A
Garden; Land That Is Too Wet Or Too Dry; Why Men Who
Fish Are Important; Good Homes For Everybody; A Beautiful
Home For Everybody; A Well Furnished Home; Where Wives
Are Queens; The Queen Of The Kitchen; Good Cooks Are Im-
portant; How Everybody Is Dependent Upon Everybody Else;
Those Who Make Clothing Are Important; Where Clothing
Makers Got Their Raw Materials; The Men Who Work Un-
derground; Health Of A Child's Mind And Body; The War
Against Disease; Keeping Fit; Teachers Are Very Important;
Industry Can Make A New World.

It is obvious that these excerpts do not constitute a comprehensive treatment of what may be taught, whether in class
or in out-of-school activities, in a programme of Fundamental
Education. The reader should turn in this connection to the
article by Dr. I. A. Richards given later in the present chap-

ter. What to teach in a programme so revolutionary as that of Fundamental Education is very obviously not easy to determine. Our treatment of this problem here can be no more than suggestive.

III. THE STATE AND VOLUNTARY AGENCIES

A complete discussion of the issues implicit in this topic would call, no doubt, for a new volume on political science, or on educational administration in relation to general government. Our necessarily modest treatment of the problem can touch on only a few main points.

If Whitehead is right in his philosophy of freedom (*Adventures of Ideas, Part I*) the basic demand upon all social organisations, including governments, is that they shall stimulate and elicit the spiritual energies of men and guide them in accordance with "the insights of enlightened wisdom". This generalisation might be accepted easily enough by most modern thinkers, if it were not for differences as to what the "insights of enlightened wisdom" actually are. Among those who give serious attention to education there is now but little disagreement on the proposition that state action shall enlarge the boundaries of the individual life, lift its horizons, and call forth the powers of each person for satisfying and socially useful ends. The extent to which these ends shall be determined in advance and the extent to which individual activity shall be channeled into established modes and forms by social authority is always the controversial question. There can be no doubt that individuals cannot be educated without some determination of the attitudes, values, and objects of endeavour that are to be presented to them as desirable or undesirable. Some "cake of custom" (a phrase used long ago by Bagehot) is a necessity: as one of our correspondents (Dickson 1) has pointed out—and as many others agree —when primitive loyalties, disciplines and modes of social

uscfulness are abandoned or disrupted, others must be sub-
stituted or the individual is left to an empty liberty which is
no better than a slavery to chaos. "Me this unchartered freedom tires, I feel the weight of chance desires." Governments cannot abdicate, in the hope of making education effective by the mere avoidance of dictation. Leadership is a
necessity: the problem is how to give it the character of
persuasion rather than domination, the form of freedom
within the substance of truth, the quality that induces willing commitment to shared and common good.

There is also the persistent problem of the *seat* of leadership—whether it shall be in the local community, the province or subordinate state, or the nation, or partly in all of
these, partly in some world organisation yet to be perfected.

Educators cannot solve these problems. They are obliged,
however, to recognise them and not only to confess that their
own activities are profoundly affected by the solutions
reached or in process but to insist that the essential character
and requirements of education shall be taken into account in
the search for solutions. These problems are ancient; the
progress of humanity is largely a history of man's attempt to
meet them. What the educator can say, and with hope for
the future, is that the purposes of education are more and
more fully recognised in the counsels of statesmen. In the
present connection it is enough to point out that education
cannot be effective unless it proceeds with an increasing understanding on the part of the people who are to be educated
and their increasingly full participation in the entire process,
including the meeting of costs. If this is not the entire gospel of education in relation to government, it does go close
to the heart of the matter. "A people which is becoming
conscious of its own identity", says the Report on *Mass Education in African Society*, (Colonial 186, p. 28, British),
"should come to regard a mass education system as its own
and as a powerful instrument for its own advancement.

Hence its views about present conditions and its own conceptions of a more satisfying life must reach and affect those who direct educational work".

More concretely, the question arises as to the recognition of voluntary agencies, both those that are external—as for example, missionary societies—and those that are indigenous. Quoting again from the Report just cited, we present the following as a productive approach to this question.

"Provision must be made for the stimulation of the community's interest in each aspect of its own life and for giving it a true conception of its own capabilities and needs. Traditional tribal governments in process of adaptation to present-day needs, local governments and other bodies which may be regarded as representing a community, may be considered as sufficient provision for the purposes we have mentioned; and obviously the co-operation of all such bodies should be sought. But apart from these, there are other organisations, such as progress or improvement associations, clubs and literary societies, which have been founded by the initiative of local private individuals who are capable of viewing their community in a more or less critical and objective fashion. These public-spirited individuals are more or less clearly aware that neither traditional nor imported forms of Government, nor voluntary societies originating from overseas, are by themselves capable of leading the community in the task of adjustment and regeneration which is imposed by the assault of new conditions and of diverse alien cultures. We are of opinion that these truly indigenous and popular societies should be given the fullest recognition in the organisation of a mass education system. It is true that they may be vigorously critical of both local and central Government, alleging inanition and lukewarm interest in the welfare of the community, and suspecting that no more than polite attention is given to their views and programmes. Their resentment may be intensified by a belief that they are re-

garded as ignorant and troublesome aspirants to a position
and influence far beyond their merits. But we are convinced
that officers in charge of mass education would find many of
them potest allies. It is essential to establish mutual confidence so that this progressive African Opinion is appreciated
by the mass education officers, on the one hand, and on the
other, that they give help to Africans in the discussion and
study of local problems."

In this connection, Cf. Hellman and Whyte 1, Chapter II, p.
73; Read 1, Chapter III, p. 172; and also other contributions,
such as that on China and that on Mexico, which recount governmental effort following upon the work of voluntary agencies.

The question of resources for paying the costs of Fundamental Education presents grave difficulties. What becomes
apparent upon analysis is a relatively simple but very important conclusion: voluntary agencies cannot support large-
scale educational effort which aims at immediate or very
early results; government support is imperative. It must be
added at once that government support must not suppress
or obviate local initiative and local participation. Help
must be adequate but it must not be stultifying.

It is of great interest to note that in our contributions to preceding chapters there is general agreement in principle on the
matter here discussed. Despite marked differences in ultimate
aims, the U.S.S.R. does not approach local groups in ways that
are basically divergent from those used in American Republics or
those advocated for British colonial dependencies or members of
the British Commonwealth. French education in overseas territories has the same guiding concepts with respect to the raising
of funds and the enlistment of community participation. Passages in point are Charton 2, Chapter II, p. 59; Hellman and
Whyte 1, Chapter II, p. 63; King 1, Chapter II, p. 117; the introductory material on China, Chapter II, p. 75; Caballero 1,
Chapter II, p. 30; and Read 1, Chapter III, p. 168. Other contributions bear out the testimony here referred to.

The recruitment and training of teachers and school officers, also of social workers, youth leaders, and educational personnel in Mass Communication, is a closely related problem. Government training schools are essential, but it may be a long time—although it should not be, if progress is to be rapid—before the training of teachers becomes comprehensive enough, varied enough, deep enough, flexible enough, to meet all the needs. If teachers' salaries are not increased, if administrators are not properly prepared, if educational workers for mass communication agencies are not trained, nor educational social workers in considerable variety, a far-reaching programme in Fundamental Education cannot be successfully conducted.

Cf. Torres 1, Chapter II, p. 43; King 1, Chapter II, p. 120; Chetsingh 1, Chapter II, p. 83; Hellman and Whyte 1, Chapter II, p. 65.

IV. THE PROBLEM OF LANGUAGE

(a) *Shall instruction be in the native tongue, a foreign tongue, or both?*

There would seem to be no single comprehensive answer to this question. The question itself must be asked in the light of circumstances and also in the light of general aims, partly political in character. We can do no more than point to answers provided in some of the practices reported in this volume.

1. In the U.S.S.R., the dominating aim of a social order in process of revolutionary change prescribes an immense effort to promote native languages, along with an effort to make Russian, in a modern form, a second language for most. Cf. King 1, Chapter II, p. 114.

2. In French overseas territories the same general process is going forward in some places; in others, French is made the sole language of instruction, either because it has already superseded the native tongue or because the indigen-

ous linguistic confusion is so great that it must do so. Cf.
Charton 1, Chapter II, p. 38; Charton 2, Chapter II, p. 57.

3. In Mexico, Indian languages are being studied but
Spanish prevails and seems likely to become eventually the
sole medium of instruction. Cf. Torres 1, Chapter II, p. 44.

4. In Africa, the language problem outside of French ter-
ritories is even more complicated than it is within them. Cf.
Hellman and Whyte 1, Chapter II, p. 60; Charton 2, Chapter
II, p. 52; also the Report on *Mass Education in African
Society,* (Colonial, 186, p. 33, British).

5. General considerations bearing on this problem may
be found in Mead 1, Chapter II, p. 139.

(b) *The simplification of alphabets and related problems*

These are problems of great technical difficulty. We cannot present here a full discussion of their complexities but
must be content, first, with a reference to the most comprehensive and determined attack on them which has come to
our attention; and second, with the presentation of an article
on the general linguistic problem in China, where it takes a
peculiarly trying form.

The reference is to the work of Dr. Frank C. Laubach, of
the Committee on World Literacy and Christian Literature,
Foreign Missions Conference of North America, 156, Fifth
Avenue, New York 10, N.Y. Dr. Laubach's views and methods are described in *Toward a Literate World,* N.Y., Columbia University Press, 1939, $1.75; *India Shall be Literate,*
1940, R.1.12; *The Silent Billions Speak,* N.Y., Friendship
Press, 1943, $1.00; *Helping the United Nations by Making
Everybody's World Safe,* in preparation; *Streamlined Lessons
in English, and Teachers' Manual* (in typed form, to be
printed shortly).

The contribution on the language problem in China
(Chao 1, pp. 1-26) is given in full, as an illustration of what
must be done by way of analysis and invention to solve the

language problem in one of its most complex and difficult manifestations.

This memorandum is intended to be an analysis of various problems concerning language education in China. Existing practices and proposed projects have been examined and evaluated in terms of the objectives aimed at, but no final conclusions are given here in the form of specific recommendations.

It will help clarify our ideas if we distinguish various types of problems involved in what is generally regarded as language education. They are: 1. Learning the Chinese language; 2. Learning *kuoyü* or the standard Mandarin; 3. Learning *wenli* or the literary language; 4. Learning a system of writing in which to read and write Chinese in any form.

1. *Learning Chinese.* In China, as elsewhere, the learning of the basic linguistic makeup of one's mother tongue is the least important problem in language education. Before the age of formal education, a child usually has acquired enough command of his native speech to communicate with everybody else in his immediate community. Some problems exist in the following marginal cases: (a) In some groups in Sinkiang and the southwestern provinces and in the territories, there are citizens of China whose native languages are not Chinese. In so far as they have occasion to communicate with the rest of the Chinese population, they will have to learn Chinese as a foreign language. (b) Some Chinese born abroad returning to live in China may not know any of the language and will have to learn it as a foreign language. (c) Deaf-mutes and to a less degree, persons with speech defects, such as lisping and stuttering, will need special training for using their own language. But by and large, the learning of Chinese by the majority of Chinese in China presents no educational problem.

2. *Learning Kuoyü or Mandarin.* There have been divergent dialects in the Chinese language throughout history. In the present state of the dialects, the greatest divergence, such as exists between Cantonese and the Peiping dialect, is comparable to that between French and Spanish or between German and Dutch. The fact that there is one common system of writing and

one common literary tradition masks the great divergence. In most other cases, however, the divergence between dialects is much less marked. The greatest dialectal variation exists in the South and Southeast, including the southern half of Kwangsi, Kwangtung, most of Hunan, most of Kiangsi, the southern end of Anhwei, the south-eastern part of Kiangsu, Chekiang, and Fukien. In the other provinces, and in the Chinese-speaking population of Manchuria, Inner Mongolia, and Sinkiang, in other words, in about three-quarters of the area and two-thirds of the population, there is enough similarity in all the dialects to group them under the general term of *Kuoyü* ("National Language") or Mandarin. The similarity is such that a shop clerk of Harbin in Manchuria can talk with one in Kunming, Yunnan, without great difficulty. This is of the order of difference between a native of, say, Kentucky and a London cockney.

The actual great currency of the Mandarin type of dialect has made it the general instrument of oral communication between people from various provinces (including those in the S.E.). It has long been called *p'u-t'ung-hua*—"ordinary speech." This type of speech also acquired prestige through the fact that the capital was for most of the last six centuries situated in this region. Hence, it is also called *Kuan-hua* "Official speech," whence the English term "Mandarin."

There was no official action to recognise any standard of speech until the early days of the Republic. In 1919, a system of *Kuoyin,* or "national pronunciation" was promulgated by the Ministry of Education and the language spoken according to this system of pronunciation was called *Kuoyü* or "National language." The system was based on the pronunciation of Peiping, with some eclectic modifications to incorporate a few dialectal features, such as the so-called fifth-tone and the use of the "broad o," to make it more universal. Because of the difficulty of getting any teachers to speak in this artificial system of pronunciation—that was before the days when one could multiply one person's voice a thousand times through broadcasting—the artificial system was revised and, in 1932, the eclectic features were abolished and the pronunciation of Peiping city has since been established as the standard of national pronunciation.

The government action was not so much for standardizing the pronunciation as for promoting the use of standard Mandarin throughout the country, especially in regions where the dialects were of the non-Mandarin type. The instrument used was a system of 39 National Phonetic Letters (37 since the 1932 revision), consisting of simplified parts of characters representing sounds. By making special signs for very frequent sound groups, for example a sign for *en,* one for *ang* (cf. *x* for ks), it is possible to spell any Chinese syllable with at most only three letters. This makes it possible to place the pronunciation at the side of characters in a character text, so that any reader who has learned the sound values of the 37 symbols can read the text in the standard pronunciation. The tones are indicated by schematized time-pitch graphs on the vowel, for example, e, é, ě, è for high-level, high-rising, low (circumflex)-rising and falling, respectively.

The work of promoting the spread of Mandarin speech through the use of the National Phonetic Letters has been assigned to a Committee on Unification of National Language, which is under the Ministry of Education. In the elementary schools in the country up to the sixth grade, textbooks are written in the standard dialect and pronunciation is indicated by having the National Phonetic Letters at the side of the characters.

With all the official recognition and encouragement given to the unification of the national language, it must be admitted that the net result has not been very great. There are several reasons for this. In the first place, the need, real as it is, is not as great as it is sometimes supposed to be. A substantial majority of the population already speaks some form of Mandarin. Among people from the southern and southeastern provinces, those who have travelled a little or have dealings with people from the other provinces usually pick up some Mandarin by ear without bothering to use the strange phonetic signs. Secondly, there is no difference in social standing between Mandarin and any of the southern and southeastern dialects. A speaker of

Cantonese does not feel ashamed for not understanding Mandarin or for speaking Mandarin with a Cantonese accent. It is an inconvenience or a nuisance for a Cantonese not to be able to talk with a speaker of Mandarin, but it implies no social inferiority. It is only in very recent years, perhaps for the last ten or twenty years that people have begun to apologise for not being able to speak Mandarin. Thirdly, there has been a lack of trained personnel for carrying out such a vast programme involving the teaching of a new way of talking to more than 100 million people.

All in all, the result of teaching speakers of sub-types of Mandarin to speak the standard Mandarin of Peiping may be said to be nil, the result of teaching speakers of non-Mandarin to speak Mandarin is slighty better—because they take it more seriously—but still very meagre in proportion to the size of the population involved, and it is only among the overseas Chinese, such as Chinese residents in the South Seas, in Hawaii, and continental United States that there has been a noticeable increase in knowledge of Mandarin.

3. *Learning the Literary Language.* The literary language or *wenli* (a Chinese term used by foreigners only) is not a separate language or dialect, but an idiom of the whole Chinese language used in all China and actualised in the pronunciation of all dialects. Before the ninth century A.D., possibly people had been writing more or less as they spoke—that is still a moot question. But since then, there has been a cleavage in vocabulary and idiom, and, to a less degree, in grammar, between the literary and the colloquial. Most writing since then has been in the literary style while most talk has of course been in the colloquial. But, while the colloquial language has been represented by widely divergent dialects, differing (1) in pronunciation, (2) in the choice of high-frequency words (for "I," "you," "he," "this," "what," "eat," "see," "give," "corner," "home," etc.), and (3) to some extent in grammar, the literary language, because there has been a common body of literature read throughout the country, is the same everywhere, (1) in the vocabulary, (2) in grammar; and it varies from place to place only in pronunciation.

There is no separate literary pronunciation (apart from a small number of exceptions) as such. Over and above the phonetic system of the dialects, scholars have reconstructed the ancient pronunciation for various periods, but non-linguists, including literary and other professional people, do not know about these reconstructions, not to mention using them. The situation can be compared with that of speakers of French and Spanish if they were to read and write exclusively in Latin, in their modern French and Spanish manners of pronouncing Latin, and talk only in French and Spanish.

Such is the nature of the literary idiom. Why should it be taught in an educational system? There are three reasons: (1) It is the only common idiom used in all China, with no dialectical variation in the choice of words or in grammar, differing only in pronunciation. And since pronunciation is not indicated in the writing, the same text can be understood by readers of all provinces who have learned this common idiom—each in his own dialectal pronunciation. (2) It is the language in which practically all older books were written and half of contemporary books are written and in which all official and private business is transacted, all news items are reported, and more than half of personal correspondence is carried on. (3) It is the idiom in which practically all of the cultural heritage is recorded, and contact with the past is bound up with a knowledge of this idiom of the Chinese language.

Useful and important as the literary idiom is, it has two very serious drawbacks. One is that it is not spoken by anybody in any dialect. To continue our analogy with French and Latin, it is as if all French literature were in Latin, and every French child had to learn Latin in order to read and write: he does not, however, have to learn a system of pronunciation, but pronounces words of the literary idiom using nothing but familiar sounds in his own speech. The other drawback is that the literary words are usually monosyllabic and abound in homonyms, whereas the units of syntax in the speech of all dialects contain a great many polysyllabic combinations. This makes it difficult for a literary passage to be understood when heard alone. Consequently, one could not make the literary idiom the standard medium of oral and aural communication even if it were made so by decree. This is less true of contemporary literary idiom in newspapers and business language, because of the frequent use of dissyllables. This fact, as we shall see later, will have a bearing on the problem of writing reform.

It was the idea of freeing the school-children of the country from the burden of having to learn an unspoken and unspeakable additional idiom and the idea of writing in one's living speech that were the main motives of the vernacular-literature movement of 1917 led by Hu Shih and others. From the preceding discussion, one can see two great difficulties in this movement. In the first place, since there is divergence in the choice of words and a slight divergence in grammar, as well as divergence in pronunciation, if everybody wrote as he spoke the result would be a breaking up of the linguistic unity which has so far been embodied in that common literary idiom. It is a truly linguistic unity and not merely a common system of visual signs representing ideas. For, although the literary idiom is never spoken, it is commonly read aloud and even composed aloud or *sotto voce*. The great difficulty is that it is not native to the speaker of any dialect and has to be learned as if it were a new distinct dialect. The second difficulty with the vernacular-literature or vernacular-writing movement is that the great body of Chinese literature in all subjects has been in the literary style, and if only the vernacular is used for writing and reading, there would be a break of continuity with the past. The actual facts of the case, however, are rather more complicated. But the complications have all been to the good.

In the first place, the divergent major dialects are not on an equal footing. As we have seen, the Mandarin group of dialects already had wide currency over three-fourths of the area and two-thirds of the population before the beginning of the Unification-of-National-Language Movement. For the last thirty years there may have been an increase of something like the order of one-twelfth of users of Mandarin, that is, there may now possibly be three-fourths of the population who can speak Mandarin. However, let us be conservative and still count it at two-thirds. Since textbooks up to the sixth-grade have been written in Mandarin, two-thirds of the school children can read and write more or less as they talk. To the remaining one-third of the country's children, Mandarin will be as strange an idiom as the literary idiom and will have to be learned anew. Instead, therefore, of requiring everybody to learn a new idiom, there will be a saving of the efforts of two-thirds of the population. It is true that for the one-third of school population there has not been enough personnel to teach them Mandarin pronunciation, even with the help of the National Phonetic Letters on the side of the characters. What has happened is that the teachers and pupils in one-third of the country have changed over from teaching the literary idiom, in their local pronunciation. Formerly, if a native of Canton wrote a book in the literary idiom, as people always did (composing *sotto voce* in his Cantonese pronunciations) people all over the country who had learned the literary idiom would be able to read it in their respective pronunciations, and would not be able to tell what part of the country the author came from. Now, when a native of Canton writes an editorial in the Mandarin idiom, as people often do (composing *sotto voce*, in his *Cantonese pronunciation* of the characters for the Mandarin text), people in one-third of the country who have learned the Mandarin idiom will be able to read it in their respective pronunciations, and people in the two-thirds of the country, who already speak some sort of Mandarin, will get the illusion that the writer speaks good Mandarin. He may. But more often than not, all he can do is pronounce his Mandarin words with the cognate Cantonese pronunciation. All in all, the changing over from the literary to the Mandarin has contributed to the unification of the National language by one major step. Formerly one-third of the people had to learn (1) the Mandarin idiom, (2) Mandarin pronunciation, in addition to (3) the literary idiom (in local pronunciation). Now they learn (1) the Mandarin idiom well, (2) the Mandarin pronunciation badly or not at all, and (3) not the literary idiom until after the sixth grade. The great advantage, then, is that two-thirds of the people already know the Mandarin idiom and a more or less Mandarin style of pronunciation in their mother tongue.

As for the second difficulty in the vernacular movement, that

of having to break away from the traditional culture, the dis-
continuity is rather relative than absolute. In the first place,
more than half of the vocabulary is the same for the literary
idiom and the dialects, including the standard dialect of Peiping
or Mandarin. For example, the words for "man," "sky," "have,"
"one," "come," "go," "place," "divide," etc., etc., are the same,
apart from difference in pronunciation. In the second place,
colloquial speech did have a certain amount of literature,
though only a small portion of the total. It was in fact from
such literature that we have been able to detect a divergence of
speech from the literary style in the 9th century A.D. Some of
the Buddhist lectures of the T'ang dynasty, some of the philo-
sophical writings of the Sung dynasty, parts of plays of the Yuan
dynasty, and most of the novels of the Ming and Ch'ing dynasties
were written in colloquial Mandarin.

The Vernacular-literature Movement did not, therefore, start
from nothing. It had as initial capital a dominant dialect, a
partially common stock of vocabulary between the literary idiom
and all dialects, and a certain amount of existing literature in
the vernacular. What the literary revolution did was to make
the writing of the vernacular respectable, and even fashionable,
and to recognise the teaching of colloquial Mandarin in schools,
up to the sixth grade, as legitimate and educative.

Has this movement been successful? Yes, to a degree. Nearly
half of the books, of articles (popular or learned), and of personal correspondence are now written in the Mandarin style.
Because of the greater ease of the idiom for two-thirds of the
population who already speak Mandarin, the reading public of
books in the vernacular has increased enormously. Publishers
report that the sale of books by authors in the vernacular, such
as those by Hu Shih, are of the order of ten times that of books
by authors like Lin Shu, who translated dozens of Western novels
in the literary idiom and was the most popular writer in the
1910's. Advance in general literacy has no doubt been a contributing factor, but the change of style must have played a very
important part.

But the so-called revolution is by no means complete. There
are several explanations for this. (1) The forms of official and

private business, legal terminology, forms of salutation, acknowledgment, request and conclusion in correspondence, etc., etc.,
have long been established and nobody has taken the trouble to
change such forms from the literary to the spoken style. One
finds the paradoxical situation that all newspaper language is in
the literary style, with the exception of the "literary section",
which is often in the colloquial style. (2) There is also a political reason for the continued use of the literary style. As Hu
Shih has often pointed out, all national movements tend to be
retrospective. One must remind one's countrymen of the glories
of the past as a source of patriotic sentiments and the past is
recorded mainly in the literary style of the language. Hence the
emphasis laid on the literary idiom by the majority of the leaders
of the National Party. The vernacular is all right for spreading
popular education and facilitating elementary education, but
after the sixth grade, that is, beginning with the junior middle
school, the children are introduced to the literary idiom, so that
they can begin to read books and read newspapers. (3) There
is also a peculiar linguistic situation that favours the use of the
literary idiom. Since the literary idiom is very close to, if not
identical with, forms of ancient speech, and since ancient speech
had a richer variety of sounds, the literary idiom takes fewer
words to say the same thing than any of the modern dialects.
But as the sound distinctions have been lost in the way in which
the literary idiom is now pronounced, no matter in what dialect,
it is not always auditorily intelligible. Actual speech in Mandarin, or any other modern dialect, is always more wordy in
order to be auditorily intelligible. But the written characters,
on the other hand, have not undergone such wear and tear of
usage through the ages as the sounds have. As a result, a sentence in the literary idiom is often more intelligible when seen
than when only heard. If it is sufficient to write concisely and
still be clear enough to the reader, why does one need to write
out more characters in accordance with the spoken idiom, which
must of course be auditorily intelligible? Hence the general
tendency on the part of a writer to use the more concise literary
idiom, or, if writing in the vernacular, to modify his style toward
the literary idiom and save the writing of more characters than

necessary. (4) Since the literary idiom lingers on, because of the factors favouring its continuance mentioned above, it is still to a very large extent the medium of everyday reading and writing. It is, then, of practical advantage for any one to learn as much of it as possible as soon as possible.

Although, therefore, the vernacular is to be taught throughout the first six grades according to the official curriculum, actually there has been a tendency on the part of parents and teachers to get the children on with the literary idiom as soon as possible, in order to get them on in life as soon as possible. Admittedly, it would be to the advantage of the nation if the vernacular were universally adopted. But so long as it is still not so, why should one retard the children's advancement in life by making them contribute to this change? Hence the tendency, on the part of parents, teachers, and compilers of elementary textbooks to introduce literary usages much earlier than they are supposed to and often with the result of teaching an idiom which is neither natural speech nor good style in the literary form.

4. *The Learning of a System of Writing.* In the preceding section, I have dealt with the literary idiom as a special form of language which, though not usually spoken, is something read and composed aloud or *sotto voce,* and I have reviewed the movement to replace it by the Mandarin form of colloquial speech. The fact that both the literary and the colloquial idioms of all dialects are written in characters has important bearings on the problems, but it was not the subject of discussion there. Moreover, all the statements made above would hold true if Chinese writing had been an alphabetic writing spelling ancient Chinese sounds but pronouncing them now with the modern sounds. In short, the topic of the last section was essentially a linguistic one. Now we shall consider the problem of writing, as a system of symbols to record the Chinese language, whether literary or colloquial.

First of all, one must dispose of the common misconception that the Chinese writing system consists of signs which are direct symbols of things or ideas. At one stage in the history of Chinese writing, as one finds in the oracle bones of the Shang dynasty, one does find symbols for ideas with an ambiguous correspondence with different words for saying the same idea. It is as if one were to write "i.e." and says indifferently "id est" or "that is." But such examples, common as they were, represented far fewer than the majority of words even in the Shang dynasty, and are much rarer through most historical times. A Chinese character, as pointed out by Du Ponceau in 1836, is not a pictograph or an ideograph, but a logograph, a graph for a spoken word. A small proportion of Chinese characters were schematized pictures of the things *whose names* they represent, but are not direct symbols of the things, with a pronunciation added as if it were an afterthought. A character which consists of a picture of the sun and a picture of the moon, does not have to do with brightness in general but is the conventional symbol for writing the particular spoken word *ming* for "bright" and no other. There is another word *liang* also meaning "bright" but it is written differently. Thus, synonyms are written with different characters because they are different spoken words. Moreover, homonyms, i.e., words with different meanings pronounced alike, are often written alike (irrespective of whether they originate from the same word or from unrelated words). For example, the word *ch'iu* "fur coat" was written with a picture of fur. There was also a word *ch'iu* meaning "to seek." Since it was difficult to picture the idea "to seek" the same symbol was used for writing it. Thus, homonyms were written in one form because they were identical in speech. This practice went on for centuries in the early history of Chinese writing and has still been going on, down to the present day. If this practice had been given free play, Chinese writing would have become a phonetic writing, with one written symbol for one spoken syllable. It would have been less analytic than an alphabetic system of writing, where one symbol represents approximately one sound, but it would nevertheless have been phonetic at the logographic level.

Actually, however, the history of Chinese writing developed in a new direction. Because of the desirability of distinguishing homonyms in writing, the two words *ch'iu* "fur coat" and *ch'iu* "to seek" were differentiated in writing by adding some distinguishing element to one or both of them. To the picture which would be sufficient as a picture of the fur coat, the character for the word *i* "clothes" was added and so a new character became the specific form of writing the word *ch'iu* "fur coat." Note that there is no change in the language itself. For with the introduction of the new character, there was no corresponding new word *ch'iu-i* or *i-ch'iu*. If one did want to say ch'iu-i "fur-coat clothes" as a phrase or a compound word, it would be written as two separate characters; and the first appearance of the form has nothing to do with the spoken word, but only serves to make the character of the first word more specific. On the other hand, the original character has now come to be used only for the word *ch'iu* "to seek".

This process of differentiation has been applied sometimes to homonyms derived from unrelated words and sometimes to different extensions of meaning from words etymologically the same. In the vast majority of cases, however, no differentiation in writing is made for the ramifying extensions of meaning of the same word, such as exist in the words of every language. Thus, the same character is used for the word *fang* meaning "square"; "method", "formula"; "locality", meanings so remote from each other that it is difficult to trace the semantic relationship between them. By chance, however, that extension of *fang* "square" to *fang* "square" (as the name of a market place or street) happens to be differentiated in writing.

Without going into further technicalities, it will serve the purpose of the present discussion to make it clear that Chinese writing consists of symbols for writing unit words with occasional, but historically fortuitous, differentiation of homonyms or of extensions of meaning.

In former days, when a child began school, he was taught the characters and was soon introduced to the learning of the literary idiom (in the local pronunciation) by studying two or three easy texts and then going on to the regular classics, usually in the order of *The Great Learning, The Doctrine of the Mean, The Analects of Confucius, Mencius,* and so on through the standard classics which were all written from the fifth century B.C. to the third century A.D. Since no one was supposed to write in the spoken idiom, and it took long years to learn the literary idiom, especially as only the more ancient form of the literary language was taught at first, it usually took five to eight years before a child began to compose anything himself.

In the present curriculum for school children they are taught (1) the characters, (2) the National Phonetic Letters (usually indifferently), (3) the Mandarin idiom, as used in the elementary textbooks, and (4) after the sixth grade, the literary idiom. For two-thirds of the population, which already speak some form of Mandarin, both in pronunciation and in vocabulary, teacher and pupil usually find the National Phonetic Letters an unnecessary nuisance, and, up to the sixth grade, the main task in school will be the learning of the characters for reading and writing the language which the child already speaks. In the relatively few cases where the National Phonetic Letters are properly taught, the pupil has the advantage of being able to get the pronunciation of the text from the phonetic spelling on the side of the characters or from the list of new characters, if the *whole* text is not phonetically marked. Thus reading during study hours is facilitated. For the remaining one-third of the population, the children will have to learn a new dialect, both as to sound and as to idiom, in addition to the characters. Actually, they usually just learn the idiom in their own local accent, treating Mandarin as if it were a new kind of literary idiom. This is all to the good, since they will be able to read in at least one living speech, and if there is occasion or necessity for coming into contact with speakers of Mandarin, they will be that much farther ahead and need only to improve their pronunciation instead of having to change both pronunciation and diction. After the sixth grade, when the literary idiom begins to be taught, the situation is the same for all parts of the country.

The great number of characters a child has to learn before he can read and the consequent retardation in education has been a problem for which many solutions have been proposed and tried. It is a well-known symbological principle that the more analytical a system of symbols is, the fewer *different* elementary symbols will be required, but each complex will require a larger number of elements to represent it. Thus, in an alphabetic writing, in which speech is analysed into individual sounds, it takes four letters *t-s-a-n* to write the syllable *Tsan*. In the semi-alphabetic writing of the 37 National Phonetic Letters, in which frequent combinations like *Ts* and *an* are represented by individual signs, the syllable *tsan* is written with two signs; but then there are more signs to learn. In a system of writing in which each *syllable* is written with a unit sign, many more *different* signs will be needed for writing all the syllables. There are about 1,300 different syllables in Mandarin (including difference in tone, which is as truly a part of the word as consonents and vowels). But as we have seen, homonymous words, and often even varying extensions of meaning of the same etymological word, are written with different characters. Without considering the large dictionaries of 40 or 50 thousand characters, most of which are obsolete, we get an idea of the number of common characters from the fact that the regular telegraphic code book has nearly 10 thousand characters, that a typewriter has on its drums about 5,400 types and that a minimum list of characters to be used in the first four grades prepared by the Ministry of Education consisted of 2,741 characters. The composition of characters is of course not all madness and no method. "The first thousand are the hardest". But the succeeding thousands will also have to be learned and cannot be reasoned out from sound or meaning.

The persistence of efforts in reforming the Chinese writing system is symptomatic of the actual difficulty of the system itself. In discussing these writing reforms, it will help keep our ideas clear if we distinguish between efforts in simplifying the writing and efforts in simplifying the language itself. The vernacular-literature movement is a movement to reform the language itself. It aims to abolish, for the purposes of present-day writing, an idiom of Chinese which is no longer spoken anywhere in the country and substitute for it the spoken language of two-thirds of the country's population. The unification movement is also a language movement. While it has never aimed at abolishing the non-Mandarin dialects, it does aim at adding the acquisition of a new kind of speech. The National Phonetic

Letters were designed for helping learn the pronunciation of Mandarin, not as a substitute for the characters as an independent system of writing. The simplification of the language and the simplification of the writing are of course not unrelated, as we shall see, but it is well not to confuse one with the other in dealing with either.

We can conveniently divide writing reforms into two main groups: (1) simplifying the characters and (2) devising an alphabetic writing in place of the characters.

The 1,000-word list used in the mass-education movement of Yen Yan-chu ("Jimmy Yen") is of type (1). Actually, the list consists of about 1,200 characters, chosen largely on the basis of frequency of occurrence in a number of representative texts in the vernacular. They are, and are meant to be, a useful list for beginners in the study of characters. Since a child or an illiterate adult actually uses many more words in his speech than are represented in the 1,200 characters (popular conceptions always underestimate the speaking vocabulary of illiterate persons), that list cannot be, and is not claimed to be, a system of writing for writing all of one's speech. The idea is rather to teach a limited vocabulary in order to lessen the burden of learning too many characters. Consequently, special reading material, often containing useful information about farming, citizenship, etc., had to be composed for use by those taught this basic list.

Another list containnig 1,100 characters, compiled by the playwright Hung-Shen, was chosen on a somewhat different principle. The idea there was to choose a vocabulary which would serve the purpose of all ordinary purposes of communication. Because of the greater grammatical flexibility in combination of elements, the resulting texts written within the scope of this vocabulary read much more naturally than the English style of Basic English. Being based on a selective list from the total vocabulary, it does not include the whole vocabulary of the spoken language, even for the speech of children and illiterate adults. Hung-Shen's basic list has not been followed up by himself or others.

About ten years ago, the Ministry of Education started a movement for simplified-stroke characters. There are currently a

number of variant forms of characters different from the usual
forms found in the regular type fonts. Most of these variants
are in the direction of reduction in the number of strokes. They
are of various levels as regards social standing. A small fraction
of the variants are archaisms of respectable standing. The majority are popular simplifications still frowned upon by school
teachers, especially those who do not know the history of Chinese writing. Since (as the advocates of this movement reasoned) both the accepted forms and the variants are met with
in practical life and a child will have to learn them sooner or
later, one might as well teach the simpler forms to start with
and encourage their use, leaving the more complicated forms
to be learned later. There was, however, so much opposition
on the part of the purists among influential government officials
that the Minister of Education had to give up the programme
after a brief trial. The printers were also relieved because they
had no types for most of the simpler forms of characters.

Here is the place for the writer to present his suggestion of
a list of basic characters as a half-way measure which might be
useful for the next 20 or 50 years. We have already noted that
standard Mandarin, based on the Peiping dialect, has about
1,300 syllables. In most cases, one of these syllables corresponds
to two or more homonymous words which are totally unrelated
to each other and are differentiated in writing by being written
in different characters. Moreover, in a great number of cases,
even what is etymologically the same word is written with different characters according to which one of a number of extensions of meaning is being used. This is what multiplied the
number of characters from 1,300 to a practical minimum of
something like 6,000, which is what one would need to know
in order to read a newspaper. The suggestion that the present
writer offers is to stop with the second step, namely, to differentiate the syllables if these are etymologically different words
under one syllable; but if a variety of characters are now used
for *extensions of meaning* for the same word, then either the
simplest one or the most frequently seen one will be chosen to
write that word, irrespective of which extension of meaning is
used. For example, there is a syllable *yuan* under which there

are the homonyms (1) *yuan* "round" and (2) *yuan* "primary, first, origin, source, spring". The present proposal is to write the symbols for *yuan* "round" differently from the symbol used for the other meanings; but for the latter, instead of writing three different characters for the five related meanings, use only one character for all of them. This differs from actual usage. But that it is "respectable" is shown by the fact that in ancient texts, and occasionally in current writing, one character was used for all the extensions of meaning and not limited, as that character now is, to "primary, first".

The reason for writing *yuan* "round" differently from *yuan* "primary", etc., instead of entirely on the basis of the Mandarin syllable *yuan,* is as follows: At the present stage of the unification movement, many speakers of the one-third minority of dialects have learned to speak Mandarin after a fashion and the remaining two-thirds already speak Mandarin of sorts. But there still is, and probably will be for a long time, a divergence in the phonetic systems of their actual pronunciaton of Mandarin. Since the phonetic system of standard Mandarin is one of the poorest in distinctive sounds, it happens in a great many cases that what are homonyms in standard Mandarin are different-sounding words, not homonyms, for most people. If a speaker who has not acquired an exact standard Mandarin habitually pronounces *yuan* "round" as *yuan,* but *yuan* "primary", etc., as *gnüan,* it would puzzle him to have to write two different *spoken* words by one and the same character. In general, etymologically different words which sound alike in standard Mandarin usually have some corresponding difference in the actual speech in one or more parts of the country. Because all dialects are descended from one common ancestral language, these distinctions hold parallel in wide regions of the country. Thus, of the three words A *hsi* "thin, fine", B *hsi* "a play" and C *hsi* "relation, system", if A is written differently from B and C, it suits the natural distinction in speech for Southern Hopeh, Shensi, Honan, Southern Kiangsu, Kwangtung, Fukien, S. W. Yunnan, and other places. If B and C are written differently, it suits Southern Kiangsu, Chekiang, Kiangsi, Hunan, Kwangtung, and many other places. But if the etymologically identical word C *hsi* "relation, system" is written one way as "relation" and another way as "system" it suits nobody in particular, because the distinction between "relation" and "system" is purely by semantic extension and corresponds to nothing in the language, ancient or modern, north or south.

The present suggestion is to put Chinese writing in characters on a strictly logographic basis, not at the level of standard Mandarin, but at a level which shall be convenient for speakers of all dialects. It is not meant to change the standard of pronunciation from that of Peiping to a more complicated system based on ancient or dialectal distinctions. People are expected to, and they certainly will, go on talking in their dialects, in poorly pronounced Mandarin, or in pure Mandarin, but the writing based on such a linguistically basic list of characters will distinguish a lot of homonyms which are not homonymous for a large proportion of the population and at the same time avoid the expensive luxury of adding characters for haphazard, hit-or-miss distinctions of extensions of meaning of the same word, which can always be clear from the context in which the word is used.

The writer has not made a survey of the total vocabulary of the Chinese language as to the exact numbers of words involved. As a rough estimate, probably around 3,000 characters, or 2,500 if rare words are excluded, will cover the entire range of the Chinese language.

If no more than 2,500 characters are taught in the schools, it will shorten the time for acquiring literacy by two or three years. It is true that actual books and the actual writing by people who know the usual characters will not be limited to this basic list. But since the majority, though not all, of the simplification consists in taking off additional parts, a normal text will be fairly legible to a person instructed only in the basic list. It should be noted in passing that this idea is not merely to "take off radicals". If *kung* "work" and *hung* "red" are written by different characters, they are kept this way, since *kung* and *hung* are different spoken words.

So much for reforms concerning the simplification of the characters. The other group of proposals has to do with schemes for writing the Chinese language with some sort of alphabet.

Shortly before the 1911 Revolution, two systems of alphabetic writing (1) *kuan hui tzu-mu* "Mandarin alphabet" and (2) *chien-tzu* "simplified writing" (not to be confused with *chien-pi-tzu* or "simplified-strokes characters" of the 1930's) were devised and tried for teaching the illiterate. They were systems of phonetic writing for Mandarin, consisting of initials, medials, and finals, very similar in principle to the National Phonetic Letters of later years both in system and in graphic form. Missionaries in different parts of the country have also devised systems of romanization, notably for the dialects of Canton, Amoy, Foochow, Ningpo, and Shanghai, had Bibles printed in them, and taught illiterate persons to write letters in them. These systems have not claimed the attention of the literary class, and their use has not spread far because of their limitation to local dialects. In the early days of the National Phonetic Letters, it was in fact the intention of many who took part in their promotion to use it as an alphabetic system of writing.

In fact, the immediate cause for the official adoption of that system was that the Minister of Education had seen one of his maidservants read a newspaper printed in that system. However, there was so much general opposition to any system of alphabetic writing that it was adopted only as a system of symbols for help in the learning of the standard pronunciation of characters and not as an independent system of writing. It is in this spirit that in texts with these symbols on the side of characters, they are usually printed small while the characters are printed large. The missionaries have also been interested in promoting the use of the National Phonetic Letters, but they print them large and the characters small. The government has sanctioned the unification of the national language, the use of the colloquial idiom in elementary schools, the use of the National Phonetic Letters as an aid to unification of pronunciation, but has never sanctioned the use of an alphabetic system of writing, even as an alternate system for teaching children or illiterates.

Two systems of alphabetic writing with the Latin alphabet

for Mandarin have been devised. One is National Romanization and the other is Latinxua, which means "Latinization".
National Romanization was devised by the present writer in
collaboration with Lin Yutang, Liu Fu, Ch'ien Hsuant'ung, and
other members of the Ministry of Education Committee for
Unification of National Language. It was intended to be an
alternate system of writing, but, because neither the public nor
the government was ready to try any alphabetic writing, it was
given the same recognition as the National Phonetic Letters
were, and was incorporated in the official dictionary of standard
pronunciation of 1932 side by side with the National Phonetic
Letters. Some private organisations in Shantung have tried
teaching it in classes, some periodicals have been published in
it, a number of instruction books have been published by W.
Simon of the London School of Oriental Studies, and the writer
has taught spoken Chinese with it in the army classes at Harvard
University.

Being devised originally as a possible system of writing, great
emphasis was laid on the convenience of final use at the expense
of more difficult initial learning. In an intensive 12-month
course for foreigners, it usually takes about ten days to drill the
student in the fundamental elements of pronunciation, three
or four days to learn the system of romanization, and eleven and
a half months to learn the spoken language. With the National
Romanization it takes about ten days longer to learn the orthography, but the gain in ease of writing and sureness of the Chinese
tones will repay the extra effort many times over in all subsequent use of the writing.

As for Chinese learners, the main problem of learning to spell
is to know the pronunciation accurately enough to know what
sounds to write down. It is a quite different situation from that
of oral communication between speakers of different dialects.
For two-thirds of the population, people can understand each
other if the sounds are approximately alike and the words used
are the same. But to have one uniform spelling, the distinction
of sound will have to be much finer. The speaker of a non-
Peiping dialect, even if he is from Paoting, only about 100 miles
away, will have to learn the pronunciation of a great many

words, before he can spell correctly in any system. The practical thing to do is, of course, not to force everybody to learn fine shades of pronunciation, which is neither possible nor necessary, but simply to learn that such and such words are spelt in such and such ways, just as in the interest of a uniform orthography of English words, *sure, shore* and *Shaw* are spelt as they are, even though in the speech of certain parts of Southern England they are all pronounced alike.

The complicated feature of National Romanization referred to above is the spelling of words of different tones with different letters, thus doing away with diacritical marks and giving more individuality to the physiognomy of written words. For example, to write the four totally unrelated words *māo* "cat", *máo* "hair", *mǎo* "the 4th double-hour", *mào* "hat" with the same letters differing only in diacritical marks (or with superscribed figures, as in the Wade-Giles system of romanization) is very confusing and the learner or reader is likely to neglect the tone signs. But in the National Romanization these words are *mhau* "cat", *mau* "hair", *mao* "the 4th double-hour", *maw* "hat". All tones are implied in the spelling.

The other system for Mandarin, that of Latinxua, was devised by A. Dragunov, a Soviet sinologist, who designed it for use in citing Chinese words, as in the Wade-Giles system of romanization used by writers in English. It was taken up by the Communists in China as a system of writing and a certain amount of literature has been printed in it and taught to illiterates. In the use of letters for sounds, it does not differ greatly in principle from any of the other systems of romanization for Chinese. However, it does not distinguish tones in its orthography except in a few cases of very frequent words, such as *na* "that" or "which?" and *mai* "buy" or "sell" where the spelling is varied after the fashion of National Romanization. Now tones in Chinese do not play the part of expressional intonation in a non-tonal language like English. *Believe me* and *Believe mé!* with both differences in stress and intonation, certainly have very different implications, but they are still the same words. Two words like *mau* "hair" and *maw* "hat" have absolutely nothing to do with each other, and the unsophisticated China-

man of the street has no idea of what consonants and vowels
are any more than what tones are. They are just different
words, as obviously and indescribably different as *bad* and *bed*
are to the native speaker of English and as elusive to foreigners.
To be sure, with enough context to suggest what is being talked
about, it is always possible to get the idea across by giving less
information than is actually in the speech. If, for instance, the
names of different things are being talked about, *This is c'ld
water* obviously means "This is called water". But if the tem-
perature of things has been the topic of conversation *This is
c'ld water* will probably mean "This is cold water". Now once
the speaker understands what the word is, he cannot help supplying the vowel distinction between *called* and *cold* in his
native speech. Similarly, a reader of a Chinese Latinxua text,
once he gathers from the context what the words are, cannot
help supplying the tones that are in his speech anyway. You
can make a Chinese write without tones, but you cannot make
a Chinese talk without tones any more than you can make an
Englishman speak without vowels or always with the same vowel.

Now, it is a generally recognised fact that the average style
of speech in every language is conditioned by the nature and
number of available significant phonetic elements. The number of sounds or words is usually sufficient to get the message
across. Some speakers are more concise, others more wordy, but
on the whole, they gravitate towards an average. Since tones do
form a major category of word-forming elements, the normal
style of speech would not be so wordy as if there were no tones in
the language. If English had no vowels or used only one vowel,
then one would have to say and write things like *This-here-is-
being-called-named-water* (vs. *chilly-cold water*). That is exactly
what writers in Latinxua are advised to do: use more words
where fewer words are used in the normal style of speech. Since
the normal verbosity or conciseness is already established by
one's use of the mother tongue, which does have tones, this
advice is often not followed. Thus one is in the dilemma of
either writing stuff that is not clear enough to read or in an
artificially padded style of language which nobody speaks.

There is also an educational problem involved in this lack of tones. It is very important that a child shall be able to learn new words from reading. A child learns the meaning of words in their active use much better than in isolation. If the text does not write the tones, the child will not be able to pronounce a new word in Chinese—for what has no tone is not Chinese. He might guess at it, with a 25% chance of being right and a 75% chance of being wrong. But since other people in his community know the word and say it with tones, he would be saying it in a way that is not actually used in the language. To continue our English example, if a child of limited vocabulary sees the sentence *These flowers have been c'ld from the garden,* he would perhaps guess at the meaning of the word *c'ld,* but could never be able to say it in English as he could if the vowel were given and the word were written *culled.* The Communist critics of the National Romanization say that since tones are a feature of bourgeois poetry, they should be abolished. By the same argument, one could of course say that since bourgeois poetry makes use of alliteration and assonance, one would have to abolish all consonants and vowels. The fact is, of course, that if a system of writing writes the language, it would be as effective a medium for writing one ideology as another. If not, not.

A side issue concerning Latinxua does have a political bearing. While the National Romanization can be adapted to writing other dialects than Mandarin, it has chiefly been used to promote the unification of standard Mandarin. It has been the policy of the advocates of Latinxua, however, to encourage the speakers of various dialects to spell their local dialects rather than standard Mandarin. While there are many Chinese Communists whose outlook is largely national and who are interested in the unification of the language, others, perhaps the more influential, take a non-national point of view and would regard the Latin alphabet as a general tool to be used by speakers of all languages and dialects in writing their own forms of speech. It should be made clear, however, that the majority of Chinese, both Communists and non-Communists, are not much concerned with latinization or romanization and carry on their daily life of reading and writing in the good old characters, which "everybody",—alas, not everybody!—knows.

In speaking of the National Romanization as being adequate to write the whole language, we did not make it clear that it was only the spoken language that was meant. If the literary language is transliterated into romanization, then, since it is not always auditorily intelligible in the modern pronunciation, it will not be clear enough to read. Current newspaper and business style of the literary idiom may not have great difficulties, but much of the large body of past literature will not be auditorily intelligible. To make romanization serve all the purposes that characters do has been the objective of a very ambitious scheme (started in the early 1930's), known as Interdialectal Romanization, or "Romanization Interdialectique" as called by its originators les Pères Lamasse and Jasmin of Szepingkai.

Lamasse and Jasmin took over the reconstruction of ancient Chinese pronunciation of 601 A.D., as worked out by the Swedish sinologist Bernhard Karlgren, and, substituting ordinary letters of the alphabet and combinations of them for the phonetic symbols used by Karlgren, they constructed a system of romanization which can be pronounced in the ancient pronunciation. But that is not the purpose. Because most modern dialects are descended from this ancient system, there are regular correspondences between the ancient sounds and the sounds of modern dialects. For instance, they write a word *dzah* "to sit". In Mandarin, *dz* becomes *ts, a* after dental consonants becomes *o,* ancient rising tone (represented by *-h*) becomes Mandarin falling (4th) tone after ancient voiced initials (that is, *dz*). Therefore, the word for "sit", always written *dzah,* is pronounced *tso* in Mandarin. The same written form *dzah,* following similar rules of pronunciation for Shanghai will automatically give the actual Shanghai pronunciation, *zu,* and similarly *ts'o,* with low-rising tone, for Cantonese, and so on throughout the country. Each dialect will have two closely printed pages of rules of pronunciation, not including exceptions, which, for common words, will probably run to several hundred words. Books, dictionaries, and periodicals have been printed in this system. The writer has no knowledge of the number of people who have been taught this system.

Lamasse and Jasmin are extremely meticulous and methodic

in their work. The whole idea seems to be extremely promising. Unification of speech is desirable, but before it comes about, and independently of it, some such system of writing will free romanization from the limitation to the colloquial style and would bring writing to an alphabetic basis. For the great advantage of romanization is not such much that it is phonetic —in this form, it is, too, to a certain extent—but that it is alphabetic.

Because, however, Lamasse and Jasmin are not phonologists and have had limited experience with practical handling of educational problems, the actual working out of the scheme seems to be more complicated than necessary. They started too far back in the history of the language, so that some archaisms are preserved which do not exist in any modern dialect, for example, the use of the ancient *a,* which has become *o* in almost all modern dialects under easily definable conditions. In the actual orthography, some forms are a little too mechanically designed. Thus, the recurring of the tall letter *h* for ancient rising tone makes one fourth of all words end in a similar shape, thus obliterating the individuality of the physiognomy of words. But these are relatively minor points in comparison with the main promising character of the whole idea of Interdialectal Romanization.

The Chinese linguist Chou Bienming of Amoy has devised a number of experimental forms of romanization, at first nearer the National Romanization and recently adopting some of the ideas of the Interdialectal Romanization.

Another native of Fukien, Lin Feng, independently devised a system of phonetic characters on the interdialect idea and with it also a system of romanization. Not having had the same background of training as Lamasse and Jasmin or Chou, his actual results are quite insignificant, but it is interesting to observe that this line of thought seems to be in the air.

A striking fact comes out if we compare the idea of the basic list of characters, eliminating the luxury of differentiated extensions, with the idea of an interdialectal romanization. Since both have regard to the present status of the modern dialects, which go back to a common basis in the past, the results of these two schemes, when worked out on a comparable scale, will be largely quite parallel. Roughly 3,000 basic characters will correspond, item for item, to roughly 3,000 syllables in an inter-dialect romanization. There may be cases where one character will have two or three romanized forms and vice versa, but the correspondence, because there is a linguistic basis for it, is on the whole pretty close.

The (linguistic) basic characters and the interdialectal romanization, therefore, seem to be two promising lines along which further explorations might profitably be made.

Meanwhile, unification of the national language is being pushed, the vernacular is being written, characters are being taught with the aid of the National Phonetic Letters, and National Romanization continues to be recognised as the official form of transliteration. Now, if the progress of the Mandarin speech is so accelerated that not only the "literary section" of newspapers, but the news and advertisements and letters and everything come to be written in the spoken style of Mandarin and the major part of the classics is paraphrased into good colloquial texts, then perhaps we need not worry about loss of contact with the past and everybody will be able to get along with National Romanization, or possibly an improved form of it, and leave the study of characters and ancient texts to such less essential members of the community as philologists, to which class the writer belongs.

But as long as it is still economically and socially advantageous to the individual to know as many as possible of the unlimited range of characters which are still being used everywhere in the country, parents and teachers will continue to teach the reading and writing of them for perhaps twenty, thirty, fifty, or ninety-nine years to come.

(c) *How can language itself be made more effective for educational ends?*

On this question we present two contributions, one entire, the other in summary. The first (Richards 1, pp. 1-7) covers, as will readily be observed, issues far more broadly conceived than would be the case if mere technique in the teaching of language were the exclusive concern of the author.

The root cause of educational backwardness and illiteracy (as with the less stultifying technologic lags) is local acceptance of this condition as normal. While your friends and family feel that illiteracy is as natural as the weather, or the traditional diet, you can hardly make the efforts needed to escape from it—even if facilities are available. Recent experience has shown that a considerable shaking up (in military service, for example), temporary membership of communities in which illiteracy is looked down upon, or exposure to vigorous "revolutionary" movements is required if much real advance is to be expected. The needed incentives, in other words, are social and moral as well as economic, and commonly their development entails no little conflict with received local standards and *mores*. It is well to admit, at the start, that a successful literacy programme is a radically unsettling thing and to recognise that it carries with it an obligation to replace the disturbed modes of living with better. What should be provided through literacy is not merely an exposure to multifarious disintegrating influences, but knowledge, ideas and desires, so far as possible directly applicable and satisfiable. In other words, Fundamental Education—to deserve the name—must be not only a set of tools but an outlook and an ethic in action.

The implication of this both as to teaching personnel and as to early texts are far reaching. The most successful teachers hitherto have been missionaries in spirit (Christian or Communist). Without such zeal to support him, the teacher soon ceases to find the work interesting enough to retain him in the face of far better paid opportunities for his own advancement. Persons *able* enough to be good teachers far too often leave for commercial or government openings. This wastage is a well known feature of all primary education programmes. It suggests the need to support those who remain both with suitable visual aids (the point chiefly laboured later) and with texts accurately aimed at the would-be reader's immediate needs, physical and mental. Few teachers, however close to the problems they may be, can themselves prepare such materials. Still less can they, as a rule, address them justly to the learner's deeper hopes and fears—to the release of the drives by which his progress must be sustained. A programme in Fundamental Education must provide materials—from the earliest possible moment—which will give the learner—along with technical aids to improved physical existence—a clearer view of what he is and what his world is and of how to better both.

All this points to the enlistment of the best available ability in the preparation of materials for wide distribution to serve both as bases for local adaptation or supplementation and as *models* with which to raise the standards of primary education everywhere—as to "methods" and content alike. Unesco can do most for Fundamental Education, at present, by a bold attempt to improve quality at a few key points of design, rather than by encouraging attempts which are needlessly ineffective through being insufficiently criticised and thought out.

From these preliminaries I pass to the media of instruction now available through which such models can best be put where they will do most good. Chief of these is the sound motion picture when rightly designed. Second come radio and the recording when properly supported by a fully illustrated text.

Almost all sound motion pictures hitherto produced use language to elucidate the picture. In most phases of Fundamental Education the reverse should be the case; *the picture's function is to elucidate the language.* (I postpone for a few pages the uses of film in teaching the very beginnings of reading.) Granted only a modicum of reading ability, films which reverse this language-picture relation can be of immense aid to the early reader's struggles. Work recently done at the Graduate School of Education at Harvard with children beginning reading and with very badly retarded children does in my judgment establish this, though detailed evidence suitable for publication is not yet available. The pictures used were the series made for me by The March of Time. These present an organically graded sequence of simple sentences illustrated by unambiguous observable action. Vocabulary and sentence patterns alike are strictly controlled. Linguistic novelty is at a minimum, the continuous illustration from the actions of the picture maintaining the interest. The learner throughout sees what the words are saying as he hears or utters them. The written sentences appear at the foot of the picture. After a number of showings, varying with the audience, the sound track is turned off and the voices of the learners supply its place. Later, when they are more practiced, they manage, on the appearance of the written words, to 'beat the actors to it'. The actor's voice then comes as a corrective or confirmation of their own reading.

The effect of this type of reading exercise is remarkable. In some cases, teachers of retarded "special classes" have been almost unable to believe their ears: their pupils, who have hitherto been slowly tumbling through their sentences, word by disjointed word, come out with a natural speech rhythm at a reading tempo they have never before approached. Their vivacity and the heightening of their attention are also noteworthy. Another advantage is the number of pupils who can be exercised simultaneously by this means. I have used these films with as many as 700 students at once—the great majority fully participating in the chorus. These were men of the Chinese Navy at the U.S. Naval Training Center, Miami, Florida, in the spring of 1945. I have no question that mass teaching by such films to groups of some thousands at once is feasible. Road shows and open-air screenings are entirely possible.

It should, however, be remarked that the only way to judge the effectiveness of such films is to try them out with a group, large or small, of suitable learners. Without such a class in action, a non-participating onlooker is seldom able to imagine their effect. We are accustomed to be passive before the screen. The whole secret of their right use is in the fact that such films can generate intense continuous *activity* in reading.

So far I have only been able to use pictures offering an introduction to English, going no further than a few hundred words deep into the language, though the sentence patterns thus taught constitute the major part of the difficulty of gaining an elementary usable knowledge of it. I see no reason why such instruction by films should not be taken on to any desired point. In fact these earliest stages present by far the hardest problems of design. Nor is it probable that similar pictures cannot be made for other languages—for Chinese, French, Russian or Spanish, for example—though certain structural characteristics of English make that language peculiarly fitted for this mode of instruction. A glance at these may make the general problems of the design of elementary reading courses clearer.

English is peculiar in two ways: in the enormous amount which can be said normally and clearly with a very small outfit of structure words and syntax; and in the degree to which this central initial equipment in the language can be presented through pictorial means. For any early reading programme in *any* language every word is an investment. We have to ask what sorts of dividend it will pay. If it is not going to be continuously useful in reading it should be postponed in favour of a more repaying word. This is perhaps the aspect from which the lack of design in current early reading materials is most apparent. Let us not burden the beginner with words which are not going to be endlessly useful to him in his reading. But in choosing the most useful words we have also to ask how far we can *tie* the written form of the word not only to its sound and articulation but to visible, actable instances of its meaning (what it is doing in a sentence). Only such ties will make it *permanently meaningful and therefore memorable*. In the earlier stages the bond we have to establish is between the graphic form of a word and its *meaning,* rather than between print and sound. Later, as experience of reading accrues, spelling will represent (or misrepresent) pronunciation, but concentration too early on this is a very frequent cause of abortive effort.

English, I have suggested, is fortunate in the smallness of its essential structural vocabulary and in the measure to which the meanings of these words can be presented in action to the eye. The specific nouns which a man needs to read will vary with his interests. A farmer needs one set and a sailor another. But both need the same outfit of essential structural words—verbs of maximum utility, pronouns, prepositions, articles and conjunctions—if they are to be able to read any sort of exposition or narrative. It is these structural words, with a few general nouns and a selection of specific names varying with the learner's environment and pursuits, which a reading programme in any language should give him.

This essential outfit may be compared to an engine and chassis on which whatever special body and gadgets are required may be mounted. In English this outfit is surprisingly compact. Less than 250 words are sufficient. With this number and about 150 special nautical terms it was possible to put the entire range of the U.S. Naval Manuals—Gunnery, Seamanship, Ship's organization, Signals, Sonar, Rules of the Road, Medical compend, etc.—into a normal English for the training programme of the Chinese Navy. Less than this outfit of English was sufficient for all the lectures, demonstrations, instructional films and the rest used in preparing them to take their ships to sea. And it may be noted that a considerable proportion of these seamen were, at the start of an eight months course, illiterate in Chinese as well as in English. The very same structural outfit with about 50 aeronautical terms is enough to carry all air-ground radiotelephone communications in an equally clear and normal English. A farming or trading community, or a machinist, will probably need a larger addition of special technical words, but in all cases the chassis will be the same. And that chassis can be taught with fewer than 24 five-minute reels of film rightly designed and used.

It will be evident that these films teaching the minimum of essential structural words and sentence patterns can be supplemented with content reels, using the same outfit but dealing with special subjects of local importance—agricultural methods, soil erosion, hygiene, industry and so on. What every early reader most needs is practice in reading. It is one thing to hand him a book and wish him luck. It is quite another to sit him down before a picture which makes him continually test, improve and apply his reading ability. The power of a film to drive home the essential points of instruction to an unskilled reader is incomparably greater.

In all this there is no suggestion that the teacher is to be superseded. His role is somewhat changed, that is all. The more mechanical part of it is handed over to a machine which will in some ways do it better, leaving him free to give his time and energy to the problems of individuals—which no machine can handle.

I turn now from the early reader to the true beginner who doesn't yet know how to see a word. With him the uses of motion pictures are more problematic, being untried. There is, however, reason to believe that they may be considerable.

Success will depend upon sufficient simplification of the learner's problem. Let us assume that we are teaching the reading of an alphabetic language, though similar considerations apply even more to Chinese. The learner's chances of seeing a word clearly enough to favour recognition is increased by reduction of the number of different letters used in writing the sentences presented to him. There is little question to-day that we should start with short and simple *sentences* whose meanings can be clearly illustrated in picture and action. We can do this and yet employ in these sentences a minimum number of different letters—avoiding systematically the early introduction of letters which are specially apt to be mistaken for one another.

In practice it has been found—in experimentation during the last three years at the Harvard Graduate School of Education— that reading work in English may be begun with as few as seven letters. The sentences otherwise are normal. Further letters, one at a time, are then introduced, as increase of vocabulary becomes desirable, but the number of different letters used is kept below thirteen for a considerable time, until considerable facility in the optical movements of reading has been achieved. At the same time, a minimum of variety in the sentence patterns used is maintained—all in the interest of the greatest possible simplification of the learner's task.[1] By such means, which, even through text and film strip unaided by motion, lead to greatly improved results, it seems possible to arrive at problems of discernment simple enough for motion picture treatment to become sufficiently repaying. The argument for motion is that at these initial stages more than all others, the learner's attention needs to be energised by the utmost vividness, variety and relevant drama of presentation. And for this the sound motion picture

[1] The text used, *Words on Paper* by I. A. Richards and Christine Gibson, may be obtained from 13, Kirkland Street, Cambridge, 38, Mass.

has no rival. It may be worth adding that certain peoples reported to be unable to see still drawings as representative are alleged to follow actions in motion pictures without difficulty. On theoretical grounds, motion may be expected to assist the perceptional grasp of the configurations of words in a number of ways. Writing, in one aspect, is applied dancing.

Turning now to radio and recordings, the one point I wish to stress is the power of the combination of the voice (which either can supply) with suitable, *fully illustrated* text. (For example, *The Pocket Book of Basic English.*) I can again only refer to unpublished experimental work done at Harvard. This indicates, however, that a text in which each sentence as presented is elucidated by a drawing adequate to make its meaning clear can be used very fruitfully in conjunction with a recorded reading. There should be pauses between the sentences to permit repetitions by the learner. As with the sound motion pictures, great improvements in pace and in speech rhythm have been remarked in independent reading without the record afterwards. The fully illustrated text to accompany the voice seems to be possibly the answer to the problem of using radio effectively in a reading course. Where local teachers are in short supply, this might obviously be very desirable.

This paper, thus far, has touched on general considerations indicating the scope and need of the undertaking and on the place of modern visual media in it. Though what I have to say on these is necessarily incomplete and unsupported, being based chiefly on work in progress, yet some mention of them seemed essential to my argument. Few who realise the scale, the urgency or the difficulties of the problem of world education will contemplate an attack upon it with any cheerful hopes unless they also see what powers these recently developed instruments of instruction have given us. They dwarf past modes almost as the atomic bomb dwarfs our former instruments of destruction. If we can use them—for good—we need not despair. But they do not automatically work for good as some 19th century educators supposed. We are readier to-day to regard our suddenly increased powers (of any sort) with fear, and these newly emerged ways of affecting others' minds are already under heavy suspicion.[2] The more potent man becomes as a teacher the more deeply and carefully he must consider what to teach. We know very well that print and film and radio, when they are not a blessing, become, at best, a blight, at worst, a means of corruption. The responsibility is upon us—and not least upon the Delegates to Unesco—to do whatever is possible to turn these new powers to the help rather than the hindrance of mankind.

For backward and advanced cultures alike, the first threat to which widened communications expose man is confusion, soothed by triviality and dulled by indifference. The second danger—since such confusion is in the long run intolerable—is the sway of passionate mass suggestion hardening into group fanaticism. Modern nationalism in its dangerous forms is partly a product of mass exposure to more news, reporting, rumour and opinion, in more disconnection, than men's minds can either comprehend or ignore. Rapid, random "education campaigns," are very likely to increase these dangers of disorientation, disequilibrium and disillusionment—from which the only harvests are reaped by the pulp and publicity circuses or the demagogue.

It would be absurd to be pessimistic here, as absurd as to propose return to a state of dumb nature. We exposed ourselves to these perils when we developed speech. All I desire to do is to note that our recent titanic extensions of the range and powers of speech and writing, and of communications in general, should make us more than ever before beware lest in our efforts to extend the rule of reason we do just the opposite—subject more and more people to exploitation by suasion, commercial or political.

The Memorandum to which this paper is a response speaks (in Section 2, indicating the scope of Fundamental Education) of providing children and adults "with knowledge relevant to their needs and those of their country as well as with the tools (such as ability to read) which will make it possible for them . . . to extend their knowledge". One of the chief impediments to any considerable undertaking by Unesco will be a doubt in reflective minds as to the status and quality of much of the

[2] I have been told that Japan, which claimed 100% literacy, used Imperial propaganda in its first texts and tests.

knowledge which would thus be put into widened circulation. It is easy to list spheres of useful knowledge: Agriculture, Hygiene, Technology and so on. But in making these available you unavoidably make a million questionably useful things available, and it is well to recognise frankly that among these will be much that is regarded by one side or another as good or bad ideology. The only adequate remedy for these damping or obstructive considerations would be some agreement as to a certain range of key concepts—as to man, his nature and history, and the world he lives in—to serve as framework or co-ordinates within which the hoped-for diffusion of knowledge could take place. Those who know most about the diversity and tenacity of beliefs, and their connections with cultural and other ambitions, will least expect such agreement. It is wise, therefore, to set aside this 18th century notion of a common world philosophy and seek instead a compromise fit to serve as a basis of common action.

Some may wonder whether the planning of a project in Fundamental Education does really raise such fundamental issues. It is easy to dodge them, of course. But a project which will really elicit the energies needed to carry it out cannot dodge them. These energies are needed in the planners, in those who provide the means, in the teachers and above all in the students, who have the largest part of the work to do. It is impossible to excite a hunger for knowledge and thought except by feeding it, and, as the history of education at every level shows, the most fruitful food is speculation. It is Wisdom, rather than Cleopatra or Martha, who "most makes hungry where most she satisfies". The learner who will really benefit himself and the world, in return for his own and his teacher's toil, is seeking for more than a rise in his income. He is seeking for a juster part in the common purposes of men. It is upon such learners—the cream of the intellectually under-privileged—that the success of any project in Fundamental Education depends. Their influence with their less inquiring fellow is paramount. They are the local leaders.

It is a truism that if you are to teach people to read you must provide them with things they want to read. Those who wish to throw cold water on the project will point to the comics and

the pulps. They will be pointing, however, to the results of the
failure to conceive Fundamental Education adequately. Reading, properly conceived, is not a mechanical operation which
should ever be taught in disregard of the value of what is read.
It is so taught, widely, in many modern school systems. Whence
comes much of our disillusionment and our distrust of elementary education. It is elementary and mechanical merely, not
fundamental. It seeks to teach people only to read, not *how
what* to read. It forgets the end in pursuit of the means. Reading should least of all be so conceived in the case of the illiterates
or the child who is being introduced through writing to ranges
of experience far wider than are contained in his native culture. As every word, for him, at the start, is an investment
whose dividend should be considered, so, later, every page should
be similarly weighed. And the instruction he receives in reading
should equip him—to the full measure of his ability—to share
in the weighing.

With this the problem of selection arises and the issue which
called for a compromise is in sight again. But the necessity for
selection presses in from all sides; there will be shortages, any-
how, of books, time and energy: properly simplified and graded
reading matter takes much preparation, if it is to be worth the
reading; the need for choice is indeed glaringly plain. And
the principle of the working compromise which might guide
selection is in sight too, if we will admit that learning to read
should and *can* include learning *how* to read and *to judge* as
well.

Dissent will concern the *can,* not the *should.* Those with the
traditional primary school teacher in mind will shrug their shoul-
ders. To teach anyone *how* to read is to teach him how to think
—the hardest task, which needs the finest teacher. To tell him
what to think is comparatively easy, as has been pointed out
numberless times. Instruction in reading *as thinking* is no job
for most of those who are likely to be available as field personnel
in an illiteracy campaign, as such campaigns have commonly
been conceived.

Here, precisely, is the opportunity for an undertaking using
the new media discussed above, through which the finest teaching

ability can be put to work exactly where it is most needed. A really good text raises its teachers towards its own level of understanding of the pupil's problems. Still more, a really good instructional film, being a demonstration of the teaching art in operation, can actually make an indifferent teacher live up to to it. No doubt these powers of the teaching film are at present only in an incipient phase of development. But as certainly they are there to be developed. What is needed to develop them is just the opportunity which a project for Fundamental Education offers. Through such a project a stimulus could be given to the teaching film and to primary and mass education alike, to the designing of texts and to the techniques of presentation, demonstration and elucidation in all fields, such as education has not yet undergone in all its history. In judging the powers of the instructional film it is but prudent to bear in mind that no sustained experimental work comparable to the work put into designing and testing a new model of a car, a plane or a destroyer has as yet been put into the improvement of a teaching picture.

The proposal has further advantages. It is relatively compact, could make a modest start expanding with experience. It would remain within the control and subject to the close criticism of the directing body. It would make a contribution to the quality of world education at the point where the smallest expenditure would have the largest effect in raising standards, and where what is done would be most readily available for imitation, criticism, correction and improvement. Finally such a project would be truly supranational, it would be directed to the benefit of education everywhere. For the backward and the illiterate are not alone in suffering from inadequacies in the tools of thought. There is no country, however advanced its educational system, which is not grievously afflicted with mental malnutrition and disorders of the intellectual digestive tract.

The summary of the second contribution under this head raises the ultimate question of the achievement of intellectual independence and integrity *in spite of* the inherent tendency of language to obstruct thought. The quotation from Comenius which heads this chapter is evidence that a great mind, three centuries ago, ran in the same channel. The summary account of this paper (Lauwerys, on Ogden 1, pp. 1-2) reads as follows:

Although millions have learned to read and to write so that industrial nations are to-day, by and large, literate, yet this enormous advance in educational standards has not helped much to increase their happiness or to enhance their dignity. To a Benthamite this is a peculiarly important question, for his intellectual forerunners believed that progress would follow almost automatically the spread of education. In fact, education has not proved in practice a liberating force. Why not? The answer is: "Those who cannot read are the victims of some forms of verbal illusions. Merely teaching them to read does not free them from verbal illusions, but in addition makes them more liable to be exploited through print". It is of no use, therefore, merely to teach people to read; it is insufficient even, to give the people knowledge which is useful only in helping them to meet their material needs. If our aim is truly to liberate mankind we must arm them against the evils of word magic. We must prepare them to resist those who would exploit them by using words. If Unesco's international responsibility is to construct the defences of peace, then Unesco cannot content itself merely by giving knowledge useful in raising living standards. To provide knowledge which will help a people to industrialise itself is a national responsibility. Unesco's duty is to try to make people less susceptible to the influence of "words of power". From the pedagogical point of view our aim is not so much to teach people to read propaganda fluently, but to help them detect the ways in which their emotions can twist their thinking, how words sometimes refer only to imaginary fictions while those who use them think they stand for things. It is in that sense that language remains the chief peril to world citizenship—not because men speak different dialects but because they worship different idols.

Thus it will not suffice to teach people to read, or even to put at their disposal basic knowledge; we must take what steps we can to make them less susceptible to the insidious and pernicious kinds of verbal magic. Furthermore, if we accept the idea that all children everywhere must be taught to read their own mother tongue, and that all languages deserve encouragement, we shall be faced with such a medley and such a confusion that the situation will become inextricable. It would be more to the point to encourage the publication of a mass education library of general knowledge in a few major languages of the world—or to put out new and better dictionaries.

The author is against preserving many languages; he argues for "de-Babelization". He argues also for "vertical" translation —that is, for translation not from a high level of expression in one language, with all its complexities and chances of obscurity, to the same level in another, but for translation into simpler terms. "For this purpose the translator must be clear (without reliance on the particular words which happen to be used) about what is being said. . . . Knowledge of word-equivalents and phraseological niceties is not enough. Hence most of the defects of current vulgarisation—in itself a highly commendable thing, essential to most of Unesco's educational programme. . . . Mass education depends on vertical translation, and further research on the nature and possibilities of this form of linguistic activity is urgently necessary. [Consequently] . . . dictionaries, bilingual and multilingual . . . at all levels . . . cheap, illustrated, and co-ordinated . . . [are needed]. . . . Make sure that the foundations of a conscious campaign against word magic as a World Menace which debilitates the Will to Peace are well and truly laid. . . ."

V. THE PROVISION OF READING MATERIAL

A number of contributions given in previous chapters emphasise the fact that literacy lapses unless reading material is provided. It hardly seems necessary to cite these contributions in detail. The problem is universal, the need pervasive. Excellent definitions of demands and recommendations for meeting them are to be found in *Mass Education in African Society*, pp. 29, ff. The need is not alone for books, school texts, and materials on particular subjects but for general reading materials, including newspapers and magazines. Problems of printing and publishing are involved. The distribution of books and other materials; subsidy by governmental departments (its necessity in some cases as well as its dangers) as against reliance on commercial publishing; and the development of libraries; reading rooms, and reading circles—all these are to be considered.

The penetrating analyses of Richards and Ogden should be borne in mind in this connection. It may be in the production of "model" materials for teaching and for reading that Unesco can do most good by *direct* action.

A letter from Dr. Frank C. Laubach makes the following points, some of which concern other matters than reading material, but almost all of which have some implication as to this problem.

1. Arthur Mayhew, in his fine book on *Education in India* quoted a statement that the education of children in India is the most expensive per child in the world, because the children of illiterates lapse into illiteracy unless they have passed the fifth grade. The child of literate parents never lapses into illiteracy.

2. The home is the fountain of all social, political and economic conditions. Illiterate parents give their children illiterate viewpoints. Parents are teachers, the first teachers, and therefore must be literate.

3. Illiterates are totally unable to grasp the meanings of the new "One World" into which we have been plunged by recent inventions. Illiteracy has now become intolerable.

4. Literate people are far greater assets than illiterates, because they can participate in skilled and technical industry.

5. The work which illiterates can do can be replaced in large measure by machines, and can be done far more rapidly and better in most cases.

6. Unesco can become a clearing house for valuable literature, finding out what has been prepared all over the world and investigating whether it is adaptable to other areas. Somewhere

by somebody nearly everything has been well written, but it has
not gotten beyond local use in most cases.

7. Unesco can train excellent translators who will do far more
than make mere translations, will make adaptations, changing
names and illustrations to meet the needs of various countries.

8. Unesco can discover what people want to read that they
ought to read. People will not read what they do not like.

9. Unesco can discover and develop talented writers, who will
be eager to write *simply*—for this good writers have considered
beneath them. A tremendous number of writers who write
simply but for adults is acutely needed. Here is one of the
bottle-necks in literacy.

10. Helping writers to find publishers is very important, publishers who will not simply accept or reject, but who will
patiently assist in developing material until it is high grade.

11. Unesco should make a study of the entire problem of distribution in the illiterate areas—libraries, lending libraries, book
stores, book salesmen, printing presses. An important question
is whether the right kind of type is available.

12. Unesco needs specialists in the fields of *industry* and *agriculture,* to help prepare and appraise matter of great practical
usefulness to craftsmen, semi-skilled labourers, farmers, animal
raisers. Some of our science digests are full of valuable matter.
Farm journals and specialised journals contain valuable material,
all of which can be made available to the entire world only by
persons who are specialists in those fields.

13. Vocational guidance can be stimulated and made practical
by Unesco. This is of particular importance to young people
of teen age.

14. Studies should be made available to the whole world of
the gearing of schools into industry, illustrated by Antioch College, by the high schools of Williamsport, Pa., and Allentown,
Pa.

15. Very simple courses should be prepared for training people
in the larger meaning and the more scientific attitude toward
their own trades. For example, a course for policemen, another
for tax collectors, another for shoe makers, etc.—the list is tremendous. Dr. Fred Hosler, formerly in charge of adult educa-

tion of Pennsylvania, now Superintendent of Schools in Allentown, had some of these courses prepared.

16. There are three types of books needed for illiterates.

(a) First, books to teach the phonetic symbols, phonetics. In English this requires about twenty days. French would be the same. Arabic about twelve days, Thai about twenty days. Some other languages much, much less: Spanish seven days, Malay languages two days, Polynesian languages one to two days, African languages, two to five days.

(b) Books building basic vocabularies, after the pattern of Michael West and Faucett, or my book on *Making the World Safe by Helping the United Nations.*

(c) Very simple books and papers employing the simple vocabulary used in stage-two books, with a few new words added on each page.

Also simple (four-page) periodicals, articles a half-page long, sentences one line long or less, words well known, every sentence a bull's eye of interesting information, paragraphs short, theme of utmost interest and value. Every country where there is a literacy campaign should have these.

Unesco can be of immense usefulness by distributing information of world-wide interest to all such periodicals.

17. Unesco can best ascertain what its part in literacy is, by asking nations what are their bottle-necks, and then discovering whether and how Unesco can help at these points.

18. We have already proven that where the course is easy, swift, delightful, and cheap, every illiterate will learn with eagerness; and with proper stimulus, patriotic or religious, people will volunteer to teach.

19. *Still* lantern slides, with the accompanying explanations on phonograph records, could be a tremendous contribution to the cause of literacy. Unesco might set one person aside to develop this. Discovering what companies can do it is a task we are now working on in New York. We think we know, some at least. Motion pictures are, we think, too expensive, considering the wide usage to be made of the method. Still sets can be purchased for $10.

20. Unesco can hold literacy conferences in one country after

another, consulting about the preparation of lessons, their format, etc., as I am doing. But be sure to send a good artist along wherever you go, for artists are hard to find, hard to train, and slow about their work.

The differences among experts as to the best means and materials (witness Laubach's advocacy of still slides and Richards's argument for moving films) should serve only to encourage action by Unesco. Such differences are inevitable in any great movement: it is the function of a central organization to resolve them.

VI. MASS COMMUNICATION THROUGH SENSE AIDS; COMMUNITY ACTIVITIES

(a) So important for Fundamental Education are the newly developed means of mass communication that we are including in our final chapter (on the programme of Unesco) two rather long passages on this topic. We shall not cover the same ground here; but we ought to present at this point a fore-view of the reasons for dealing with mass media (or sense aids) in two passages instead of one.

The reasons are simple. In formal instruction—from the beginnings in the three R's for children to the most advanced teaching within the scope of Fundamental Education—sense aids are literally *aids*: they do not carry the full burden of instruction but come in at carefully chosen points to introduce, reinforce, expand, or even correct what is taught. It is possible, indeed, and often very expedient, to use sense aids as instruments of examination or testing—as when flash-cards or pictured objects are presented for identification, to see whether pupils can make the desired discriminations. In expert teaching, therefore, sense aids must be introduced at the right points and the right way in the total development of a topic or unit of instruction, and this becomes a matter of conscious decision in the light of the immediate aims of the teaching to be done.

The points brought out by Richards in the contribution presented previously in the present chapter should again be recalled in this connection: if there is a dearth of good teachers, we have a recourse of great promise in the new media—yet teachers who know how to use them are still required. Mass media do not teach without *persons* to fit them to their uses as instruments for teaching.

Mass communication, however, has its own aims; and these aims are not entirely educational—at any rate not strictly instructional. Sheer enjoyment is also in view—or persuasion—or wonder, admiration, and sometimes (unfortunately) fear: and if it may be argued that education is not entirely excluded from these uses of mass media, at least the necessity of adapting the aid in question to some unit of instruction in a larger curriculum is not dominant. Entertainment does educate, of course: what people do with their leisure, what forms of relaxation or edification they come to seek, what they learn to like or dislike—these are important revelations of their sense of values. Education has been defined as "learning to love what we ought to love and hate what we ought to hate"; and in this sense education must be thought of as including preaching, and if you like, propaganda. Mass communication as a means of education is properly described, at least in part, as propaganda for good ends; but if it is to be educational, even in this meaning of the word, it must not only seek to impress but must also follow through to action and check up on the expression of what has been "learned". This means that the use of sense aids for education, even when such use involves no gearing-in of the aid to the formalities of class teaching, is subject to study in the light of what we know about learning. The theory of learning (and of individual development) has made striking advances in recent years; and these advances may be checked against studies in mass communication with advantages in both directions.

For the reasons here given, we have suggested in Chapter V that Unesco shall study sense aids in Fundamental Education under two headings: sense aids in the teaching of reading and writing; and sense aids as means of stimulating progressive activity in communities.

(b) To illustrate how far beyond formal education a programme in Fundamental Education must go if it is to be complete and effective, we present at this point some comments and considerations brought to our attention by our colleagues in Mass Communication. These concern the day-to-day operation of mass communication agencies. Comic strips in daily newspapers are cited as having a bearing on the process by which children or adults may learn to read and, in addition, on the formation of their social attitudes. It is well known, of course, that the newspaper "strip" (whether genuinely "comic" or used for purposes of advertising or even of education) has become more and more widely distributed and is likely to be adapted to more and varied uses. Strips, film slides, moving pictures, and other graphic materials may all combine strong motivation to learn with decided effects on attitudes and interests. When they are brought into play in situations of extreme cultural isolation they constitute a means by which illiterates and newly literate groups make contact for the first time with many of the streams of world culture. Thus they condition to some extent the perception and apprehension of many ideas and values which will be quite new to "backward peoples". They become a part of the sudden disruption of the simplicity and conservatism of primitive cultures. In many cases they also become means of propaganda—a point well illustrated by the battle of radio propaganda which bombarded the Arab peoples during the recent war. Intrusions of this sort into isolated cultures are becoming increasingly frequent and widespread. It is obvious that there are explosive dangers in this process but at the same time great potentialities for the more rapid bridging of the gap between backward peoples and world culture. As G. B. Shaw has remarked— "The number of people who can read is small, the number of people who can read to any purpose is much smaller, and the number who are too tired after a hard day's work to read at all—enormous. But all except the blind and deaf can see and hear".

Because of these potentialities for good or evil, educators should not only interest themselves in the use of mass media as sense aids in formal educational instruction but also in the day-to-day operation of mass communication agencies, with all their intensity of appeal to young and old alike. Research is needed as to the techniques and effects of these means of communication and equally as to the shaping of their operation toward good outcomes and away from bad ones. The formation of taste in music, drama and art suggests itself: and here it should be remembered that native modes of expression and native uses of leisure have desirable features which must not be sacrificed while primitive peoples are learning more "civilised" forms of recreation and artistic activity. Through the Section of Mass Communication, Unesco plans to extend the facilities of mass media into areas which have not yet enjoyed their benefits nor suffered from their possible detrimental effects. Research on the flow of communication in backward areas, on the size and composition of audiences, on the effects of programmes and on their current operations will be conducted. Conferences will be held on press, radio, films, and other mass communication materials designed for children and for illiterates or newly literate adults. Close liaison with communication agencies will be maintained in order to provide a channel for the advice and suggestions of educators.

These activties, in which the Section on Mass Communication will take the lead, and in which the Education Section will co-operate, are referred to in the second of the two passages in Chapter V which are mentioned above.

It seems to us justifiable to press home here the point that Fundamental Education, like every other aspect or phase of education, cannot be limited to lessons learned in schools or classes. "Taking a course" is not the only way, nor even in many cases the best way, to learn a "subject"; seldom probably, the best way to become a better person. Again the advantages of informal and out-of school learning are suggested. Not only mass media but also many types of activities are desirable, in fact essential. When it is a question of educating a community—and it is always a question of educating a community in our field of Fundamental Education—schooling has its merits; for schools are communities and their community life teaches (or may teach) many lessons not contained in books; but the wider community which supports the school morally as well as financially must also be approached direct.

An excellent discussion of broadcasting and cinema appears in *Mass Education in African Society*. Colonial No. 186, pp. 38 ff.

The preceding chapters contain references to mass communication, but go into no detail as to the uses of radio, films or other aids. The reader will recall the remarks of Dr. Richards on the use of sense aids in the teaching of language (this chapter, p. 260). School houses are often the best centres for radio programmes, film showings, etc.

(c) There is an extensive and important area of Fundamental Education which is not covered either by instruction as commonly understood nor by Mass Communication as such. This is the area of group activities, whether conducted by the school staff or by mission workers or by welfare agencies or by self-organised groups of the people themselves. We discuss the "activity programme" here because it is nearer in character and aim to the mass communication programme than it is to formal instruction; but in truth it is different from either and properly merits a separate and detailed treatment. Although we are not able to deal with it here at length, we would emphasise its importance.

At the risk of being accused of a visionary approach, we start with a question as to the facilities at hand for group activity in a very advanced civilisation. What facilities would a large and self-sufficient cultural community have at its disposal? One can think off-hand of a considerable list: playgrounds; museums; libraries; churches; theatres; art centers; gymnasiums and facilities for water sports; medical centers; general public halls; parks and gardens; governmental offices; post offices, telephone and telegraph facilities; commercial and industrial facilities; banks and financial institutions; music centers; historic monuments; scientific laboratories; educational institutions of all grades; centers for youth activities and for adult classes, demonstrations, and exhibits; publishing agencies of all sorts; radio stations; transportation facilities; nature sanctuaries; experimental farms; a community forest. This list is purposely a *melange*, but it may carry its meaning. Large cities now have most of these facilities, although no single city, perhaps, has every one of them, or at least not in sufficient quantity or well distributed. But is it not fair to say that when and if many of these facilities are present and in wide, active, effective, and beneficient use, the community is civilised? Of course other things are also necessary—sewerage, for example, and a fire department. Perhaps someone will wish to add that the people must also be God-fearing and reasonably united—which may be granted. It may be granted, too, that some of the institutions in the list may be over-developed and distracting—witness athletics in some countries. The question to which this excursion into a listing of the institutions of civilised existence is intended to lead may at any rate be fairly apparent:

in poorer or more primitive communities, what can be done toward introducing a few of these agencies of culture and human expression—those that are most needed and in their most desirable forms?

It is not a far cry to the conclusion that the humble beginnings of civilised living (as so defined) lie in group activities among young people and adults, close to their homes and their work and their native forms of recreation. Such activities may be wholly natural, simple, and practical. They need not partake of the exciting and enervating quality of some of the more sophisticated activities of city-dwellers; they may, in fact, be more truly civilised, and they may point forward to no undesirable complexity of life. If a reading circle is started, that is a beginning of a library service. If an athletic group is formed, that is a start toward a playground. If a nurse comes in to teach maternity care, hospitals may some day follow. If the school or the public square is used for radio programmes and the cinema, better facilities, if they are needed, may come in the course of time. If groups are formed for canning, home improvement, or crafts, many valuable developments may ensue. If discussion groups are formed, the horizons of community thinking may be widened without loss of sobriety. If study groups are started, their members may learn more than a lecturer could impart. Native drama may be developed; native music may become more fully expressive without sacrifice of older forms, which may then have a retrospective or historical value. Schools are necessary, but they may be pale affairs beside the work that could be done in the community itself. Teachers may help, but they cannot possibly carry the whole programme. Education must have a larger scope and meaning than literacy or than the whole range of formal schooling, if it is to be Fundamental Education.

Among discussions of education in relation to primitive art, music, drama, and the dance, the best that has been brought to our attention occurs in *Mass Education in African Society*, Colonial No. 186, p. 49 ff. The contributions in Chapter II which have a bearing on what we have here called the "activity programme" are, among others, Torres 1, p. 43; Charton 2, p. 50; Hellman and Whyte 1, p. 68; Chetsingh 1, p. 85; and Laubach 7, p. 95. See also Read 1, Chapter III, p. 174. It would seem evident that missionary workers have been more keenly aware of the need for recreation and for æsthetic and spiritual expression than have government workers or even most secular educators. The techniques of group work have been carefully studied by psychologists, especially Lewin, for their effects on personal development toward independence or subservience. Such studies have an obvious bearing on group activities among primitive peoples. And see especially Mead 1, Chapter III, p. 140.

VII. THE PROBLEM OF INCENTIVES

What has gone before in this chapter bears throughout, at least in some measure, on motivation for learning and for constructive activity. Every teacher is aware that learning means effort and that effort called for in learning is normally a product of the desire to achieve a goal that is *felt* (if not clearly conceived) to be of value to the person concerned or to the group with which he identifies himself. The advancement at which Fundamental Education aims must be clearly revealed to the individual and to his group as having values which they can attain and which it is natural for them to want to attain. In some cases and for brief periods, compulsion may serve as a bridge to self-active effort; and learners, especially children, may be kept in their places and (more or less accidentally) learn a little, even if their hearts are not in what goes on around them. But so deeply is learning a product of desire that it is a waste of time to expect continuity in real work, that has clear results in personal changes of a beneficial kind, unless the work has both immediate and remote rewards. Recent studies in the theory of learning make more and more of *effect*—that is, of motivation to repeat an action, or to attempt a new action in the same series or of a similar sort, because of a satisfaction arising from an action already taken. Even first steps are taken with most vigour and are most likely to prove rewarding, if the satisfaction to which they may lead can be anticipated or if it can be observed in the case of another person with whom the individual can align himself.

The discussion of starting points for motivating group action among primitive people in Mead 1, Chapter III, p. 140, is here in point. See also Read 1, Chapter III, p. 165.

It would be useless to assume community or family motivations of a "high" order for the children of a backward area or for adults who are oppressed by poverty, superstition, diseases, and fears. The joys of "civilised" life cannot be so glowingly depicted to persons who are confined in narrow routines and burdened with direct necessities that they will neglect immediate needs and customary compulsions in order to work hard for uncertain ends or for goals that are hardly understood as having any relation to themselves. Not even glamorous moving pictures can be more than diversions and means of escape if they are not made pertinent to the present conditions of life among those who see them.

The requirement is clearly a connection between the end in view and the personal need or desire of the individual concerned. A "lower" motivation need not be "bad" motivation. Motivation that is completely "intrinsic", that is, satisfaction in the very activity itself, such as joy in reading or in the building of a house or the planting of a crop or the writing of a letter—is no doubt possible in many instances: but human motives are almost always mixed, and the anticipation of approval or some other *result* of the reading, the building, the planting, or the writing will normally bulk larger than the mere joy in the doing. In music, probably, there is more intrinsic satisfaction than in any more "practical" activity—and also in dancing, in games that are not played solely to win, and in dramatic performance (unless applause comes to mean more than the fun of acting). Even among primitive people—perhaps especially among primitive people—there is no better way to stimulate self-rewarding activity than through music, dancing and dramatic performance. These are native and usually well established. If they have lapsed under the impact of "civilisation", they can be revived and new forms attempted. (Witness the traditional theatre—which, to be sure, has never "lapsed"—and the modern theatre in China.) And activity in art-forms is likely to lead a general inspiration toward other activity and an upgrading of ambitions in general. Joy in one accomplishment, combined with pride in its recognition by others, may lead to the desire to conquer new worlds.

Competition should not be looked at askance. Pictures or stories of what has been done for prosperity in another village, or the demonstration that new methods have led to better crops in one selected field, or the clear proof that medicine and nursing have resulted in better health in one family—any such evidence of the value of education and new activity may lead to emulation. What is most to be sought by those who are trying to change old ways for new is a measure of success in the first effort. There is enough truth in the old adage that "nothing succeeds like success" to commend it to educators in all their undertakings.

It does not follow that remoter rewards should never be referred to while nearer satisfactions are pursued. "A boy's will is the wind's will and the thoughts of youth are long, long thoughts". Simple folks are not necessarily devoid of vision. If that process on which the world is started and for which Unesco stands—that advance toward human unity in which nations and persons will not lose their identity but gain in brotherhood—is to go forward, then primitive peoples no less than their more advanced contemporaries must share in some of the major "insights of enlightened wisdom". The greatest of these is the insight that all humanity may live in peace and share in weaving out of human action "a texture of persuasive beauty analogous to the delicate splendour of nature". Motivation toward so high a goal is not impossible in any society, if the goal is not presented as if it were antagonistic to more immediate personal satisfactions or to the relief of the real distresses of the present. Whatever heaven is within the compass of the primitive imagination—or for that matter, the imagination of a more civilised people—it is inevitably a witness to some discontent with life here and now. Heaven to some primitive groups may mean war rather than peace—as it did to many peoples, now "advanced", in their pre-Christian period and as it may have done very recently—and the "moral equivalent for war", may be hard to discover for any people. But the testimony of most cultures is in favour of the hope that the ideal of a peaceful world, expressing human aspirations that are not warlike or brutal, is not ruled out by any pre-determined character in natural man.

WE THE PEOPLE OF THE UNITED NATIONS DETERMINED

to save succeeding generations from the scourge of war. ...

to reaffirm faith in fundamental human rights, in the dignity and worth of the human person. ...

(Purposes)

to promote social progress and better standards of life in larger freedom. ...

(Article 55)

and international cultural and educational co-operation.

from the CHARTER of the UNITED NATIONS

CHAPTER V

SUGGESTED LINES OF ACTION

The Functions of Unesco in Fundamental Education

No nation of the world can say that soon it will "possess the mountain winds of truth"; nor is any nation fully able of itself to lift its common life above immediate and self-regarding interests to the level of world need, world hope, and world co-operation. National tasks that are broadly human in their character and aim require concerted thought and international planning.

Among such tasks are those of education; and if Fundamental Education is in truth a common ground for all peoples, its problems must be approached as universal problems, for which mutual aid and counsel are imperative. Nation must confer with nation. Individuals and groups that have garnered varied experience with but little oportunity to share it, must be brought together for their common inspiration and enlightenment. Facts and ideas must be made public property. Records of successes and failures must be analysed and made available to all. Connections must be made among workers, and needless duplication of effort avoided. The groups already valuably engaged must be encouraged and new associations brought into being. Some projects must be attempted, if only for experiment and demonstration, which have not been undertaken anywhere before. Unesco obviously has a part to play in all these ways of bringing Fundamental Education out of the sheer separation of narrowly national endeavour and raising it to its larger human stature as a world movement.

The Nature of the Proposals in This Chapter

The Editorial Committee presents in this chapter suggestions gathered from its collaborators and advanced in its own
discussions. They are not assigned to their various sources,
for they have been worked over in many meetings and sifted
into a form and order which is the product of the Committee's own deliberations. They are presented as materials
which may be found useful in determining policies and in
choosing those particular enterprises which Unesco should
undertake in this field.

The Editorial Committee ventures to point out that the
suggestions for action in Fundamental Education should be
considered in relation to the programme of Unesco as a
whole and especially in relation to other proposals for the
programme in Education. Thus it should be noted that a
Committee is recommended (in Chapter II of the Final Program Report of Unesco) for the study of "the methods . . .
and content of education . . . to foster international understanding in primary and secondary schools". The work of
this Committee, if and when it is established, would obviously have a bearing on the work in Fundamental Education. Similarly, the recommended conference of leaders in
Adult Education (Chapter II of the Report) would have a
bearing on the work in Fundamental Education for illiterate
adults. Whatever is done in Vocational Education, in Selection and Guidance, in Educational Statistics, in Youth Activities, and in the Training of Teachers will be of interest
to those who are concerned with Fundamental Education.

These examples are drawn directly from Unesco's suggested programme in Education; but other Sections of the
Secretariat will be undertaking studies which may be equally
pertinent. If, for example, population problems are studied
by the Social Science Section, the results of such studies
should be considered in relation to the programme in Funda-

mental Education. There is obvious need, also, of co-ordination between work in Fundamental Education and studies in Mass Communication. It will prove impossible, presumably, to divorce the programme in Fundamental Education from the programme of any of the major Sections of the permanent Secretariat.

Meeting the Major Needs

Fundamental education is ideally a part of democracy; and like democracy, it must be "of the people, for the people, by the people". In this conception there is, of course, no intimation that leadership, governmental or voluntary—or both—has no function. On the contrary, the very fact that fundamental education depends finally on popular response makes leadership all the more important. Popular demand, leadership, and popular response are all required and are required at the same time. In a word, the process through which fundamental education may be advanced with fullest vigour and success may be called Participation.

Participation calls for encouragement. If Unesco can encourage both demand and response; if it can provide means and materials for leadership which might otherwise be lacking; if it can spur enthusiasm when it begins to lag—whether because problems have multiplied, or because funds are inadequate, or because political interests bar progress, or for any other reason; if it can spread the news of successful efforts and arrange personal contacts through which the contagion of fresh purpose may be caught; if, finally, it can meet some of the harder technical issues by means of its own studies or experiments—then Unesco will have played its proper role in fundamental education as an act in the drama of human evolution. What world leadership can do by participating in a process inherently democratic, Unesco will then be doing.

The role of Unesco is not easy to determine in detail.

What can best be done at any given point must be decided in the light of all the information that can be obtained at the time. Consultation is required with other agencies of the United Nations, with governments, with voluntary agencies, and with individual students and workers. These requirements lead to the chief recommendation of this chapter, a recommendation which emphasises *flexibility of procedure*.

A Commission in the Form of a "Panel"

The Editorial Committee suggests the establishment, in the Division of Education of the permanent Secretariat, of a Panel on Fundamental Education. The term Panel is used to indicate a group of persons some of whom can be continuously in service at Unesco Headquarters in Paris, while others can be brought in for consultation at various times; and it is intended that all members of the panel—or selected members thereof, as circumstances may dictate—shall be available for conferences, consultations, demonstrations, and other contacts in various countries of the world, as well as in Paris, and for the study of achievements, issues, national needs, and the part that Unesco should be taking in the movement.

The suggested period for the operation of the panel, and hence for the budgetary provision to be made in the first instance, is five years. Continuance of the panel beyond the end of this period should, of course, depend on its accomplishments and on the situation as it then presents itself. We believe, however, that five years is the minimum period within which substantial results can be expected in a field so extensive and difficult as Fundamental Education.

We recommend provision for two or more permanent members of the panel, to work in collaboration with and under the general leadership of the Director of the Division of Education. They should be persons of some experience in fundamental education and of commanding reputation as students of educational processes and problems. If possible they should have come to the study of education from different backgrounds—perhaps from anthropology and sociology in one instance and from psychology in another. Of course, no exact specifications can be laid down until possible personnel for this permanent "core" of the panel can be considered.

In any case, however, the composition of the entire panel should tap resources in scholarship and practical activity which include anthropology, psychology—both social and individual—economics, and linguistics. Other fields of interest may well be represented also—as, for example, mass communication by co-operation with the Mass Communication Division of the Unesco Secretariat, and political science with emphasis on demography. Again the consideration of the personnel actually available will govern final choices. A proper distribution by region and culture is, of course, desirable.

The panel as a whole may well number at least fifteen. This includes the Director of the Division of Education and the two members in continuous service. As will apear in the further discussion of the suggested functions of the panel, budgetary provision should be made for expenses of travel as well as for salaries during specified periods of service, whether in Paris or elsewhere.

Suggested Activities for the Panel

(a) The present volume is at best a rough outline of what Fundamental Education is, how it has become a world-wide movement, what its problems and difficulties are, and what can be done by all concerned to advance it. The panel should first address itself, we suggest, to the fuller development and correction of information in this field. That is not, of course, a task to be finished before other tasks of equal or greater importance are undertaken. The end in view is nevertheless essential to the full success of Unesco's work: what the Editorial Committee envisages is complete documentation, and it is suggested that the titles in the catalogue should be arranged not only by author and name but by topic, including regional treatments of fundamental education. With this thorough documentation as a background, certain more immediate services of information may be undertaken—or rather, such services should be undertaken as they are needed, carried on as well as possible without the benefit of full documentation, and completed when the documentation itself becomes complete. These more immediate informational services will be discussed later in the chapter.

Documentation implies here not merely materials in print but also full records of films, radio programmes, diagrams, charts, maps, and other sense aids for teaching in schools and for the instruction of adults. As the panel plans this work, it will obviously be important to establish close co-operation with the Division of Mass Communication. In a rapidly moving enterprise like Fundamental Education, documentation can never be final; which means that it is of special importance to keep open all possible channels of current information.

How much of the actual material, whether in print or in other forms, should be collected, stored, and exhibited in Unesco House is a problem for the panel to take under early consideration. It will be necessary to work this problem out in consultation with the Division of Libraries, Archives, and Museums and with the Unesco Administration. Unesco should presumably have a comprehensive catalogue, but it will probably have to be content with collections which are less than complete. One of the problems to be studied would accordingly be the problem of selection.

Among the bases of selection it would be natural to include those practical undertakings to which the panel may turn while its documentary work is in progress. These will be discussed in the succeeding sections of this chapter. We may conclude the present section by noting the great usefulness of a central and comprehensive bibliography. Statesmen, volunteers, scholars, and writers should find in Unesco House a source of guidance and inspiration, practical help and enlargement of vision, which will be one of the most continuous elements in that encouragement of participation that is Unesco's main function. *Therefore, the first suggested activity of the Panel on Fundamental Education is documentation.*

(b) Not everybody who needs help in Fundamental Education can come to Paris. Correspondence will become extensive: special booklists will be requested; sources of supply for reading materials, films, and other instruments of instruction will be in demand; statistics will be of interest; and posters, diagrams, and maps will have to be supplied or referred to. If Unesco is to make the information at its disposal fully useful, it will have to do more than gather it, more than display it in its own quarters, more even than meet visitors helpfully when they come in person to Unesco House. There is a continuous activity for the Panel on Fundamental Education in the dissemination of lists, brochures, addresses, governmental enactments and general news. This means typing, duplicating, printing, mailing, expressing. Coordination of such work with that of other Divisions of the Secretariat and with that of many external agencies is clearly desirable. Help will be required, as well as given, by the Unesco staff.

A fairly full bibliography of selected, classified and annotated titles may prove immediately useful and might be widely distributed. Statistical material should be prepared for the proposed International Education Yearbook. General information on Fundamental Education should be included in the International Education News Letter or Review, if it is decided that such a journal is to be issued by

Unesco. Graphic materials—charts, diagrams, maps—should be prepared to show the progress of fundamental education throughout the world. These materials might well become a means of stimulating wholesome emulation among governments and voluntary agencies. Films and radio programmes on fundamental education could, if they were well constructed and well handled, carry the message of this movement not to the leaders only but also to the people themselves. No one who has seen the American film on the work of the Tennessee Valley Authority can forget its message—and it was in part the very message of Fundamental Education. To spread that message widely is a primary function of Unesco. *The second suggested activity of the panel is accordingly the planning of staff services of information.*

(c) No matter how much information is gathered nor how widely it is distributed—no matter, indeed what form it takes, even the liveliest and most impressive,—information is still no substitute for personal contact and for consultation, discussion, and study on the very spot where the work is going on. Hence the Fundamental Education Panel should be regarded as a team or set of teams which may be sent on invitation to various parts of the world. Their mission should be to learn as well as to teach and assist. They can report back to Unesco and request others to do so. By preparing in advance, whether through plenary sessions in Paris or regional meetings of smaller panel groups, they can bring to Unesco well-ordered information on points which require concerted study and analysis. They can make contact for Unesco with workers in fundamental education and link one worker with another, group with group.

It is possible that the Panel should not be built up to its full strength until some contacts of this kind have been made by a smaller group of earlier members.

Travel and personal contact should result—we may hope before the end of five years—in a general survey of Fundamental Education, which could be published as a Unesco volume, or made a major part of one of the Yearbooks, or printed serially in several issues of the International Education Review.

The occasion of some of the proposed trips by panel groups should be Regional Conferences. These could be conferences arranged by Unesco or conferences called by other agencies. The governments of a given region might request a conference or arrange one, or one government might do so. Contact with National Commissions will be in order; and there is obvious opportunity in these missions for consultation with governments, with United Nations agencies, and with voluntary organisations. Fundamental Education touches even the institutions of higher education through the training of teachers and educational administrators; and it requires liaison with health organizations, trade union educational departments, agricultural organizations, and religious and social welfare agencies.

Regional conferences may have a general scope and a world outlook. It may not be long before a World Conference on Fundamental Education will be of value, but it is suggested that a World Conference should be in the nature of a climax to a period of survey, consultation, and personal contact rather than a starting point for such activities. A World conference should, of course, enlist the official co-operation of the Governments of Unesco's Member States. In any event, *the third suggested activity of the panel is personal contact, through attendance at conferences and otherwise, with workers in the field.*

(d) Fundamental Education is not to be carried through to a successful conclusion solely by goodwill nor entirely by devoted and persistent effort. It is not quite so simple an undertaking. The issues and problems discussed in the preceding chapters of this document include a considerable number that require careful study, some that cannot be solved save by experiment, and some that must be attacked in different ways under differing local conditions. Unesco has a very important duty to perform in the encouragement and facilitation of the investigation and experimentation required in these cases; and it may prove possible for the panel to plan and even itself to conduct some, perhaps eventually all, of the necessary constructive enquiries.

Whenever Unesco receives an appeal for technical assistance and advice—which should be often, if Unesco is to look with any satisfaction on its work in this area—the situation should first be analysed to see what problems are involved. There are probably very few cases indeed in which nothing at all can be done until some general solution can be found for a perplexing problem such, for example, as that of a language not yet reduced to written form. In some instances it will doubtless prove that the best course is to delay action with respect to the language situation—and thus with respect to illiteracy—while that problem is under consideration by experts, but meanwhile to attack the task of fundamental education by measures other than instruction in reading and writing. Mistakes in such a matter may be costly. As one of our contributors remarks, "Education is easier than re-education". In any case, the panel should, we believe, initiate and conduct studies of its own on a selected list of problems which call for expert handling.

There are some studies, to be sure, which may be undertaken in a general form—that is, without reference to any single situation in which the problem has arisen and with respect to which Unesco has been asked to render assistance. Of this character might be the problem of financing fundamental education, or the problem of recruiting and training personnel or the problem of using mass media for adult instruction. Of course, in all general studies the concrete circumstances of various situations will be held in mind as premises.

More often, perhaps, studies will be undertaken in the first instance with respect to a particular appeal or with direct reference to the circumstances in a given region. On the basis of results in one case, the study of similar cases may be undertaken with greater expectation of prompt and satisfactory results.

We select for illustration six types or classes of problems which demand careful attention, all of them at the level of expert knowledge. If the panel is not itself so constituted that it can provide the personnel required, it should recommend the expansion of its membership to include, perhaps for the sole purpose of the study in question, men or women who have the necessary qualifications.

i. *The problem of language.* This is a single problem only in name; in fact it is a hundred problems—or a thousand. The present volume contains so full an introduction to some of its typical appearances that we need hardly press the point that studies of language difficulties in fundamental education should be a major concern of the panel.

There are, of course, general aspects of the problem, as well as specific—that is, strictly linguistic—difficulties, which must be dealt with language by language. Whether or not the mother tongue shall be used as the medium of instruction for literacy in primary schools is a problem of policy. Much depends on the number of people who speak the tongue in question, and there are other factors which affect a decision in any particular instance: but these can be partly generalised. It is even possible that studies already made by Dr. Richards, Dr. Laubach, the French educational authorities, and others will afford sufficient ground for an early summary on these more general features of the language problem. If so, the problems left for the panel will concern particular languages.

There is a problem of teaching which is semantic rather than strictly linguistic—how to teach so as to avoid enslavement to misleading general ideas: this problem should also receive attention from the panel.

Special linguistic problems must be assigned to linguists: but it is pertinent to remark that the object in view is not in every case linguistic perfection. Sometimes, on balance, the best solution will do no more than rough justice to the claims of the language itself, so that larger social aims may be achieved. A language may have to be abandoned, or its forms modified, in the interest of prompt action. The preservation of a language must be weighed against the introduction of important knowledge which the language itself may be unfitted to convey.

ii. *Reading materials for new literates.* If educational wastage is to be avoided, materials must be provided for reading, and occasions for writing, once the required skills have been achieved. Here there are two major needs.

One is the discovery and recruitment of writers who have a genius for expression in the simplest terms on topics which are worthy of the attention of adults and of the more mature and intelligent children in schools. Pupils in the earlier grades present no very difficult problem, although primary-grade materials for city children in advanced countries are not suitable for children of the same age in rural or primitive communities. But to produce for newly literate adolescents and adults materials of interest and value requires writers of special talent. The panel should consider how this may best be done. A "pilot" experiment might be undertaken at Unesco House, or in a selected region.

The second need concerns content rather than style or choice of words. Enough has been said in earlier chapters to make it quite clear that the immediate interest of the people themselves must be the starting point in fundamental education in all its aspects. Reading material must therefore first be local, domestic, occupational; it must, in short, be such that its meanings come home to the individual. Its value for him must not be obscure or remote. Yet it must also lead out—and without any considerable delay—into far wider topics. One can imagine newspapers or small magazines that carry articles of general interest—including news of the United Nations and its associated agencies—but leave space for items of particular interest to localities. Here is a problem for study by the Fundamental Education Panel; and quite possibly for the development of a few examples of a mode of procedure which would assure both local interest and the introduction of new ideas.

iii. *Sense aids in the teaching of reading and writing, both to children and adults.* The use of films, film strips, records, the radio, diagrams, cards, maps, "mock-ups", and other visual, auditory, and kinesthetic aids *in literacy work itself* is a special problem. It is not a problem of mass communication in general, but of the adaptation of new media to a specified instructional purpose. The panel should seek the aid of the Mass Communication staff in this matter, but it is likely to prove that such experts as Dr. I. A. Richards will have most to contribute.

In general, the *instructional* use of sense aids requires the adjustment of the aids themselves, or any of them, to the exact object of the unit of instruction in hand. A notable experimental study of the use of films in a particular unit in science was financed some years ago by the Carnegie Foundation for the Advancement of Teaching and conducted by Professor P. J. Rulon of Harvard. This study was published in book form by the Harvard University Press. It presented final proof of the value of films when they are fully adapted to the special requirements of a chosen subject in a particular school grade and in a particular environment. How to make adaptations similarly exact under very different circumstances is quite a different question; and costs must naturally be taken into account. What is needed is not a repetition of experiment to decide whether or not sense aids (or specifically, films) are useful for instruction, but the conduct of studies to determine *when* such aids shall be used, *which* aids are required, and *how* they shall be used. These are basically problems of method in teaching. They must be particularised, although one study may carry over in many respects from a first situation to others.

Experimental procedure in such matters is neither simple nor cheap. The panel may well consider how to proceed so that in any given situation the financial burden on Unesco or on a co-operating agency shall not be too great and so that the results obtained shall be as widely applicable as possible.

iv. *Sense aids and other incentives to progressive activity with adults and community groups.* This is definitely an area of interest for the Division of Mass Communication. The Fundamental Education Panel has, however, a primary concern in any measures taken to stimulate interest in health, home building, foods, crafts, local government, citizenship in nation, and social membership in the wider sense of international goodwill and human brotherhood. United Nations agencies outside of Unesco are necessarily involved; and this whole area is obviously one in which co-ordination of measures must be carefully worked out. We have historical evidence that literacy failed to fulfill the hopes of its earlier advocates, and we have recent proof that a highly educated nation may be led astray. Instruction in schools is not enough, even for fundamental education.

Meanwhile the new media have been developed. Will radio and films do for humanity what formal education has not done? It cannot be forgotten that they have lent themselves to evil purposes as well as to good ones—to the uses of demagogues as well as of educators; nor is the effect of mass communication on the tastes, interests, ideas, and attitudes of a people, especially an illiterate people, to be ignored. The radio and the cinema are forms of entertainment and as such affect profoundly, if unconsciously, an individual's and a community's sense of values. The panel will be deeply interested in the studies undertaken by Unesco in mass communication.

Personal contact, demonstrations, group meetings, festivals (religious or secular), drama, music, clubs, recreation centres, nursing, home projects—all these are also to be considered as means toward fundamental education when the work is viewed in its larger perspective. Nor is instruction in simpler technological processes—agricultural or industrial—outside the pale of the panel's interest when such instruction is needed to free any group from primitive methods of work and life. Here is an area for exploration and pilot enterprise.

v. *The financing of Fundamental Education.* It has already been argued at some length (in Chapter IV of this volume) that decisions as to method determine in large part the ultimate costs of fundamental education. If sense aids are to be used, for example, they must be produced and distributed. If a foreign language is to be a major medium of instruction, teachers must be recruited and made competent in that tongue for all the teaching involved. On the basis of decisions on such points, schools must be built and equipped, graded and inspected and administered. Policies must be adopted concerning the relation of education for children to education for adults and the relation of school instruction to out-of-school educational activities. In all these matters a necessary element in the problem is money. In determining where the money is to come from, the relation of governments to voluntary agencies must be considered; and the basic requirement at once apears that the people themselves must have an interest and a voice in the decisions.

Policy in educational finance may vary with circumstances, but it is not a mere "practical" matter, to be worked out in terms of the resources immediately available. Local initiative may be stifled by complete financing, with its consequent

controls, from a central government. If voluntary agencies
are relied on, or if local funds are the main resource, the job
may not be done because the funds available are not sufficient.

The panel should study the problem of educational finance
in Fundamental Education both in general terms and under
particular conditions. Such international resources for
finance as are available should not be left out of consideration.

vi. *The recruitment and preparation of personnel, both
for teaching and administration, and for out-of-school
activities.* It would be idle to conceal the fact that fundamental education throughout the world requires a very large
number of workers. In any of the countries or regions considered in Chapter II of this volume the number of workers
required is larger than the number available. Teachers in
far greater numbers must everywhere be found, trained and
paid. Nor should educational workers who are not teachers
in the usual sense be forgotten—recreational leaders, for example, demonstrators in domestic economy, and other important groups. It should be noted especially that school
officers—administrators of every grade—need preparation, as
well as teachers. Educational policy does not rise unbidden
or unled from among the teachers in the schools, or the
workers in youth-serving groups. Problems of finance, of the
curriculum, of organisation, of social relations, and of aim
are profoundly interfused with the actual processes of instruction and motivation. The preparation of personnel for
fundamental education comprehends work with all grades
of teachers, principals, and directors, both in the schools and
in the less formal educational agencies. There are problems
here for analysis by the panel or its associated experts.

*The fourth suggested area of activity for the panel is the
direct study of a considerable variety of problems in Fundamental Education.*

The Suggested Programme as a Whole

If Fundamental Education were no more than the endeavour to make the entire population of the world literate, each group in its mother tongue, the effort required would still be enormous. But even this definition of the task would be quite misleading, for the selection of a language of literacy —or of two languages—cannot be so slightly dismissed. And it has been repeatedly emphasised that Fundamental Education means far more than literacy. Upon the entire undertaking, furthermore, falls the pressing demand for substantial accomplishment within our own day and age. M. Charton is justified in his statement that this is a revolutionary undertaking. It may truly be said that education in its traditional forms has failed to save us from the scourge of war or to promote social progress in larger freedom. Now a new and more direct and comprehensive approach is in order.

Unesco is in its very nature an organisation which must face such revolutionary tasks. The United Nations will not succeed unless the minds of men are moved by new ideas, their hearts stirred by new affections, their wills enlisted to establish a new human unity. It is wholly appropriate for Unesco to engage in a task so novel and so far-reaching as Fundamental Education. The extent of the labours involved and the varied character of the difficulties to be met should not deter Unesco from the work.

Unesco might be doubtful of its mission, perhaps, if Fundamental Education were a movement inspired only by *noblesse oblige,* by charity alone, by sheer humanitarian zeal; far more doubtful, of course, if it were motivated by the will to dominate or to exploit. But this volume shows, if it shows nothing more, that Fundamental Education is largely a movement of the peoples themselves, democratic, inherently *de base.* It is for this reason among others that we venture to suggest a programme as extensive, as penetrating—and as flexible—as the programme here proposed.

We cannot suppose, indeed, that this programme is final or that we have included all activities—even some of major importance—which should have been discussed. Problems we have not foreseen are bound to arise. We may hope, however, that the suggested activities and the supporting accounts and discussions will establish the fact that Fundamental Education is an essential part of a new and lasting basis for peace and progress.

APPENDIX A

CONTRIBUTORS AND PARTICIPANTS

The contributors to this volume and those who have taken part in producing it are here listed with a brief indication in each case of the office presently or most recently held by the person concerned, his connection with Unesco, and the nature of his work on the volume itself. When work on the volume is not specifically described, it is to be understood as advice or assistance to the Editorial Committee. It did not seem necessary to include in the list those members of the administrative staff of the Preparatory Commission (Dr. J. S. Huxley, Executive Secretary; Dr. H. E. Wilson, Deputy Executive Secretary; and Sir Alfred Zimmern, Chief Adviser) who took an active part in guiding the work as a whole. Their leadership is here gratefully acknowledged. The Committee wishes also to record its sincere appreciation of the work of the various contributors. They responded promptly, often under serious pressure, to the request of the Secretariat for the manuscripts which give to this volume its chief claim to the attention of the general reader.

ABBAS, Mekki.
   Adult Education Officer, Bakht Er Ruda, Sudan Government.

Contributor.

ALLEN, H. B.
   Director of Education, Near East Foundation.

Contributor.

AWAD, Mohamed Bey, Ph.D.
   Head, Department of Geography, Fuad I University,

Egypt; Chief Publicity Censor, Egypt; Adviser to the Egyptian Delegation to the San Francisco Conference.

Senior Counsellor, Social Sciences Section.

BAEZ, Martinez, Ph.D.

Under Secretary, Health and Welfare Department, Mexico; Mexican Delegate to the World Health Organization, Mexican Delegate to Unesco.

Contributor and Member of the Editorial Committee.

CABALLERO, Augustin Nieto, Licencié-en-droit.

Colombian Ambassador to Chile; Director of Primary and Secondary Schools, Colombia, Rector, Universidad Nacional, Colombia; Rector Gimnasio Moderno, Bogotá.

Contributor.

CHAO, Yuan Ren, Ph.D.

Research Fellow and Chief of Section of Linguistics, Institute of History and Philology, Academia Sinica; on leave for research and instruction at University of Hawaii, Yale University, Harvard University.

Contributor.

CHARTON, Albert, Agrégé de l'Université.

Inspecteur Général de l'Instruction Publique, Ministère de la France d'Outre Mer, 1946.

Contributor and Member of the Editorial Committee.

CHETSINGH, Ranjit Mohan, M.A.

Editor, *Indian Journal of Adult Education;* Honorary General Secretary, Indian Adult Education Association; Head, Quaker Centre, Delhi; Lecturer in Sociology and Economics, Delhi College of Nursing; Member, Executive Committee of National Christian Council, National Council of Indian Y.M.C.A., All-India Federation of Educational Associations, etc.

Contributor.

COWAN, Grace.
Secretarial Assistant to the Editor.

DICKSON, A. G., M.A.
Education Officer, East Africa.
Contributor.

EASTER, Bertie Harry, B.A.
Director of Education, Acting Colonial Secretary, Grenada, Jamaica.
Contributor.

FARNELL, H. L., M.A.
Chief English Translator.

FARR, W. C., B.A.
British Ministry of Information, Films Division.
Counsellor, Mass Communication Section.

FREE, L. A., LL.B.
Director of Research and Planning, International Film Foundation; Editor *Public Opinion Quarterly,* Princeton University.
Senior Counsellor, Mass Communication Section.

GABRIEL, E.
Head of the Supervision Section, Rural Education Division, Haiti; Head of the Section of Urban Primary Education and Teacher Training, Haiti.
Contributor; Assistant, Education Section.

GRIFFITHS, V. L.
Principal, Bakht Er Ruda, Sudan.
Contributor.

GUHA, B. C., Ph.D.
Chief Technical Adviser, Food Department, Government of India; Professor of Applied Chemistry, Calcutta University.
Counsellor, Natural Sciences Section.

GUITON, J. W., Licencié-ès-Lettres.
Associate Professor, Bryn Mawr College, U.S.A.; Acting Head, Section of University Relations, Institute of Intellectual Co-operation, Paris.

Senior Assistant, Education Section.

HART, Donn V., M.A.
Research Assistant for the Study of American Teaching Materials on the Soviet Union, American Council on Education.

Assistant to the Deputy Executive Secretary.

HAY, Mrs. Hope.
Missionary, London Missionary Society; at present engaged in experiment in Mass Education for Northern Rhodesia Government.

Contributor.

HELLMAN, Ellen, Ph.D.
Member, Executive Committee, South African Institute of Race Relations and South African Jewish Board of Deputies; Chairman, Johannesburg Joint Council of Europeans and Africans.

Contributor.

HOLMES, Henry W., Litt.D., LL.D.
Professor of Education, Harvard University.

Consultant, Education Section: Editor.

HSU, Francis, L. K., Ph.D.
Professor of Social Anthropology, National Yunnan University, Kunming, China; Lecturer on Anthropology, Columbia University, N.Y.

Contributor.

JONES, J. D. Rheinallt, Ph.D.
Lecturer on Race Relations, University of Witwatersrand; Secretary, Witwatersrand Council of Education; Member of Advisory Council of Labour; President of

Sections E and F, South African Association for the Advancement of Science; Founder and Director, South African Institute of Race Relations.

Contributor.

JONES, Thomas Jesse, Ph.D.
Educational Director, Phelps-Stokes Fund, U.S.A.

Contributor.

KABBANI, Ismail, M.A.
Director, Institute of Education, Cairo, Egypt; Technical Adviser to the Egyptian Ministry of Education.

Contributor.

KANDEL, Isaac L., Ph.D., Litt.D.
Professor of Education, International Institute, Teachers College, Columbia University.

Contributor; Advisory Member of the Editorial Committee.

KENWORTHY, L., M.A.
Head of the Social Studies Department, Friends Central School, Overbrook, Philadelphia, Pennsylvania, U.S.A.

Assistant, Education Section.

KING, Mrs. Beatrice.
Specialist on Soviet Education; Chairman, Education Committee, Society for Cultural Relations between the Peoples of the British Commonwealth and the U.S.S.R.; Assistant Editor *Anglo-Soviet Journal.*

Contributor.

KUO, Yu-shou, Docteur-ès-Lettres.
Member of the Council of the Szechwan Provincial Government, Commissioner of Education, Province of Szechwan, Professor, National Szechwan University and West China Union University, Adviser to the Chinese Delegation to the United Nations.

Senior Counsellor, Education Section; Chairman, Editorial Committee.

LABOURET, H., graduate of the Ecole des langues
        orientales vivantes.
Former professor of Sudanese, National School of
French Overseas Territories, National School of Orien-
tal Languages, Institute of Anthropology, School of
Political Sciences; former Head of the International
Institute of African Languages and Civilisations.
                                            Contributor.

LAMBERT, R. S., M.A.
Supervisor of Educational Broadcasts, Canadian Broad-
casting Corporation; Editor, *The Listener* British
Broadcasting Corporation.
                    Counsellor, Mass Communication Section.

LAUBACH, Frank Charles, Ph.D.
Director, Maranaw Folk Schools, Lanao, Philippines;
teacher and leader of literacy campaigns in India, Africa,
Mexico, Central and South America, Philippines, etc.;
Special Counsellor and Representative, Committee on
World Literacy and Christian Literature, Foreign Mis-
sions Conference of North America.
                                Contributor and Adviser.

LAUWERYS, J. A., D.Sc.
Reader in Education, University of London.
                    Contributor and Consultant, Education Section.

McCONNELL, H. Ormonde.
Pastor, Methodist Church, Port-au-Prince, Haiti; Acting
Chairman, Methodist Churches of Haiti; General Secre-
tary, Haitian Government Committee on Illiteracy.
                                            Contributor.

MEAD, Margaret, Ph.D., D.Sc., LL.D.
Anthropologist, social scientist; Associate Curator of
Anthropology, American Museum of Natural History.
                                            Contributor.

OGDEN, C. K., M.A.
Linguist; Editor *Psyche;* inventor of Basic English;
Director of Orthological Institute, London.
Contributor.

RAVNHOLT, Henning, Ph.D.
Head of Education Department, Danish Co-operative
Wholesale Society; Lecturer, Borup Folk High School,
Copenhagen.
Counsellor, Education Section.

READ, Margaret, Ph.D.
Anthropologist; Reader in Education, University of
London.
Contributor and Member of the Editorial Committee.

RICHARDS, Ivor Armstrong, Litt.D.
University Professor, Harvard University; Director, Harvard Commission on English Language Studies.
Contributor.

RIVETT, Mrs. F. H. M.
Secretary, Translation Section.

SALMAN, Hassan Ahmed.
Director of Rural Education, Ministry of Education,
Baghdad, Iraq.
Contributor.

SCULLY, Sylvia.
Secretary, Education Section.

TEIXEIRA, A., M.A.
Professor of Education, Institute of Education, Bahia;
Director, Department of Education, Federal District,
Rio de Janeiro, Brazil; Professor of Education, University of the Federal District.
Counsellor, Education Section.

TORRES, Elena Cuellar.
Organizer and Administrator, Experimental Rural Education Mission, Agricultural Department, Mexico; Gen-

eral Supervisor of Rural Education, Ministry of Education, Mexico.

> *Contributor; Counsellor, Education Section.*

Van DIFFELEN, R. W., Ph.D.
Sub-Director of Education and Public Worship, Netherlands Indies; Ministry of Overseas Territories, Plein, The Hague, Holland.

> *Contributor.*

VENET, G. V.
Professeur Agrégé de l'Université.

> *Chief French Translator.*

VIVIAN, Frank Harvey, B.A.
Exchange teacher, Training College for Teachers, Bonn University, Germany; Assistant Master, Wellington College, England and Clifton College, England; Education Officer, R.A.F., P.O.W. Camps, Germany.

> *Counsellor, Relief and Rehabilitation Section.*

WANG, Cheng-su, M.A.
Professor of Education, National Chekiang University, China.

> *Contributor.*

WHYTE, Quintin, B.A., Education Diploma.
Assistant Director, South African Institute of Race Relations; Assistant Secretary, Witwatersrand Council of Education.

> *Contributor.*

WRONG, Margaret, M.A.
Secretary International Committee on Christian Literature for Africa; Editor, *Books for Africa.*

> *Contributor.*

YEH, Chu-pei, Ph.D.
Director of Metallurgical Research, Laboratory of the National Resources Commission, U.S.A.; Member Chinese Technical Missions to U.S.A. and Great Britain.

> *Counsellor, Natural Science Section.*

SOURCES

The manuscripts used in this volume, whether received in response to the request for contributions or otherwise obtained, are here listed by author. In the case of those manuscripts from which excerpts are given in the text, the place of the excerpt in the volume is indicated; in all other cases the manuscripts were used by the Editorial Committee in the general development of the volume. Each manuscript, in its full form as submitted, has been filed in the archives of Unesco.

ABBAS, Mekki.

1. *Fundamental Education in Arab Countries.*

ALLEN, H. B.

1. *Scientific Advisory Mission Report (to Director General, Middle East Supply): Section on Rural Education and Welfare.*   (Ch. II, p. 109.)

BAEZ, M.

1. *Fundamental Education as a Problem for Unesco.*
    (Ch. III, p. 175.)

CABALLERO, A. N.

1. *Post War Education.*   (Ch. II, p. 27.)

CHAO, Y. R.

1. *Problems of Language Education in China.*
    (Ch. IV, p. 203.)

CHARTON, A.

1. *Les Antilles Françaises.*   (Ch. II, p. 37.)
2. *L'Education de Base dans les Pays Français d-Outre-Mer*   (Ch. II, p. 45.)
3. *L'Indochine.*   (Ch. II, p. 99.)
4. *Les Problemes de l'Education Fundamentale.*
    (Ch. III, p. 128.)

CHETSINGH, R. M.
1. *Fundamental Education in India.* (Ch. II, p. 80.)

DICKSON, A. G.
1. *Fundamental Education in Tropical Africa—Some Doubts and Anxieties.* (Ch. IV, p. 199.)

EASTER, B. H.
1. *Fundamental Education.*

GABRIEL, E.
1. Article, *L'Ecole Rurale Haitienne* in *L'Action Laïque No. 81, Avril 1946.* (Ch. II, p. 35.)
2. *Le Developpement et l'Organisation de l'Education Rurale au Mexique.* (Ch. II, p. 40.)

GRIFFITHS, V. L.
1. *Fundamental Education in Arab Countries.*

HAY, Mrs. Hope.
1. *United Missions in the Copper Belt.*

HELLMAN, E.
1. Paper written in collaboration with Mr. Quintin Whyte on behalf of Dr. J. D. Rheinallt Jones of the South African Institute of Race Relations.
(Ch. II, p. 60.)

HSU, F. L. K.
1. Article, *The Problem of Education in Contemporary China* in *Transactions of the New York Academy of Sciences, Series II, Vol. 8, No. 2, pp. 82-90, Dec. 1945.* (Ch. II, p. 77.)

JONES, J. D. R.
1. Article prepared by Hellman, E. and Whyte, Q. (q.v.). (Ch. II, p. 60.)

JONES, T. J.
1. Memorandum, *Essentials of Education for American Indians.*

KABBANI, I.
1. *Outline of the Development of Modern Education in Egypt.* (Ch. II, p. 107.)

316   FUNDAMENTAL EDUCATION

KANDEL, I. L.
　1.　Letter to Dr. Kuo, August 26th, 1946. (Ch. II, p. 22.)
　2.　*Fundamental Education.*　　　(Ch. III, p. 179.)
KING, Mrs. B.
　1.　*Fundamental Education in the U.S.S.R.*
　　　　　　　　　　　　　　　　　(Ch. II, p. 111.)
LABOURET, H.
　1.　*The Problem of the Education of the Masses in French Tropical Africa.*
LAUBACH, F. C.
　1.　*Adult Literacy as a Means of Social Reorganisation.*
　　　　　　　　　　　　　　　　　(Ch. II, p. 24.)
　2.　*Report from the Rev. Richard Schaull, Colombia.*
　　　　　　　　　　　　　　　　　(Ch. II, p. 33.)
　3.　*Report from Mr. Alan Reed, Ecuador.* (Ch. II, p. 33.)
　4.　*Report from H. Dudley Peck and Dorothy M. Peck, Guatemala.*　　　　　(Ch. II, p. 35.)
　5.　*Report from Harold N. Auler, Honduras.*
　　　　　　　　　　　　　　　　　(Ch. II, p. 39.)
　6.　*Report on the Problem of Illiteracy in China from R. O. Jolliffe.*　　　(Ch. II, p. 79.)
　7.　*Report from Sam and Ethel Higginbottom, Allahabad Agricultural School, India.*　(Ch. II, p. 88.)
　8.　*Helping the United Nations by Making Everybody's World Safe,* (Book in process of publication).
　　　　　　　　　　　　　　　　　(Ch. IV, p. 198.)
　9.　Letter to Education Section, October, 1946.
　　　　　　　　　　　　　　　　　(Ch. IV, p. 235.)
　10.　*Making the World Literate,* (A Handbook for Literacy Campaigns).
LAUWERYS, J. A.
　1.　Summary of article by C. K. Ogden; other passages.
　　　　　　　　　(Ch. IV, p. 253 and elsewhere.)
McCONNELL, H. Ormonde.
　1.　*Concerning the Problem of Illiteracy.*

MEAD, Margaret.

1. *Some Problems of World Educational Planning.*

(Ch. III, p. 132.)

OGDEN, C. K.

1. *Language in Fundamental Education.*

(Ch. IV, p. 233, summary by Lauwerys, J. A.)

READ, Margaret.

1. *An Introductory Study of Fundamental Education;* other passages.

(Ch. II, p. 22; Ch. III, p. 155; and elsewhere.)

RICHARDS, I. A.

1. *Problems of Method and Materials in Fundamental Education.* (Ch. IV, p. 224.)

SALMAN, H. A.

1. *Illiteracy—Campaign and Liquidation.*

(Ch. II, p. 108.)

TORRES, Elena C.

1. *Fundamental Education in Mexico.* (Ch. II, p. 42.)

VAN DIFFELEN, R. W.

1. *Fundamental Education in South-East Asia.*

(Ch. II, p. 96.)

WANG, Cheng-Su.

1. *Some Thoughts on Fundamental Education.*

WHYTE, Quintin

1. Paper written in collaboration with Miss E. Hellman on behalf of Dr. J. D. Rheinallt Jones of the South African Institute of Race Relations.

(Ch. II, p. 60.)

WRONG, Margaret.

1. *Fundamental Education at the Elementary Level.*

INDEX

Act of Union, 1910 (Union of South Africa), 67

Adult education
approach to, 184-186, 197
British attitude to, 196-197
literacy campaigns in, 187-188
see also Parents and children

Adult Education Committee (Union of South Africa), 70, 75

"Adventures of Ideas" (A. N. Whitehead), 228

Afghanistan, illiteracy rate, 21

Africa, 16, 44-80, 147, 171, 188, 194, 210, 233

Africa, British, 196-201

Africa, French, educational policy, 45-52

Africa, French Equatorial, 52

Africa, French West, 52-63
economic, social and cultural characteristics of natives, 53-56
future educational plans, 63
human and natural environment of natives, 52-53
obstacles to educational plans, 58
policy of educational colonisation, 55-58
statistics, 58
use of French in schools, 59-61

Africa, North, 48, 49, 50, 60

Africa, West, 60, 196, 198

"Africans learn to be French," 49

Alexander, Father, of Rhodes, 114

Algeria, 46, 47

Allahabad Agricultural Institute, 99, 103

"Allah helps those . . ." (E. Muller), 122

Allen, H. B., 123

Allentown, Pa., 274

American Association for Adult Education, 19

"American Dilemma, an" (K. G. Myrdal), 22

American Indians, 163

Americas, the, 21-44

"Analects of Confucius," 245

Annam, 111-117, 120

Antioch College, 274

Apprenticeship Act (Union of South Africa), 74

Arabia, 21, 125

Arab League, 152

Archangel Province, 130

Argentina, illiteracy rate, 20

Asia, 80-125
French schools in, 50
illiteracy rate, 20

Assam, population density, 90

Australia, illiteracy rate, 20

Australian aboriginals, 167

Auxiliary Education Committee of the Indian Statutory Commission, 88, 90

"Backward" areas, types of, 186-187
see also Under-Privileged groups

Baez, M., 201, 219, 222

Bagehot, W., 228

Balinese, 163, 168-170

"Balinese Character" (G. Bateson and M. Mead), 168

Balkans, the, 146

Baluchistan
illiteracy rate, 21
population density, 90

Ban Methuat, 116

Bantu, 64, 71
illiteracy rate, 21

Bateson, G., 163-168

Belorussia, 134

Benedict, R., 169

Bengal, population density, 89, 90

Bengal Government Committee on Problems of Primary and Adult Education, Report, 89, 90, 92

Bombay, 90, 92

"Book of Civilisation," 194

Books, types of, needed for illiterates, 275
see also Reading material

Brazil, illiteracy rate, 20

British Army, illiteracy rate, 19

British Colonial Office Advisory Committee on Education, 210

British Guiana, illiteracy rate, 20

Broadcasting, 280
see also Radio and recordings
Brunauer, E., 7
Buddhism, 112, 117, 150
"Bulletin du Ministère d'Education Nationale," 211
Bulgaria, illiteracy rate, 19
Bureau of Education, India. Eleventh Quinquennial Review, 95
Burma, illiteracy rate, 21
Buryat-Mongolia, 130, 137
"Bush" schools of West Africa, 196-197
Butterfield, K., 98

Caballero, A. N., 27, 231
Cambodians, 111-120
Cameroons, 52
Canada, illiteracy rate, 19-20
Capacity to learn, 165-175
Cape Province, 63, 65, 74, 79
Capetown Technical College, 74
Carnegie Foundation for the Advancement of Teaching, 300
Carneiro, P. B., 6
Caste. See Rank and caste
Celi, A., 31
Central Advisory Board of Education on Post War Educational Development in India. Report. See Sargent Report
Central Provinces, India, population density, 90
Chao, Yuen-Ren, 233
Charton, A., 35, 45, 111, 145, 219, 220, 231, 233, 283, 304
Chaturvedi, 19
Chekiang, dialectal variation in, 235, 250
Chetsingh, R. M., 88, 93, 223, 232, 283
Ch'ien Hsuant'ung, 253
Children's education, approach to, 182-184, 207-208
Child Welfare Society, 77
Chile, illiteracy rate, 20
China, 21, 50, 111, 140, 148, 151, 157, 160, 193, 210, 231, 285
illiteracy rate, 21
language problem, 80, 84, 88, 233-259
national attack on tasks of fundamental education, 80-88
statistics of school attendance, 82, 83
traditional education and western influence, 84-88

China, Ministry of Education Committee on Unification of National Language, 236, 253
movement for simplified stroke-characters started by, 248
system of "national pronunciation" promulgated by, 235
Chinese Navy, training programme of, 262, 264
Chou Bienming, 258
Chukchi, the, 138
Cinema, 280, 282, 301
see also Sound motion pictures
Cochin-China, 46, 48, 111, 112, 114-118, 119
Colombia, 22-29
Colour bar in South Africa, 73-74
Comenius, J. A., 12, 270
Commission on Higher Education in British West Africa. Report, 193, 197, 198, 201
Committee on Adult Education (Union of South Africa), 70, 75
Committe on Unification of National Language (Chinese Ministry of Education), 236, 253
Committee on World Literacy and Christian Literature, 233
Communists in China, 254, 256, 257
Conference of Allied Ministers of Education, 3
Conference on the Cultural Development of Native Languages, 131
Congress Party, 98
Co-operative Societies in U.S.S.R., 134, 135
Coorg, density of population, 90
Cuba, illiteracy rate, 20
Cubberly, E. P., 211
Cultural Development of Native Languages, Conference on, 131
Cultural values, fundamental education and, 150-159

Dabu, Ivory Coast, rural training college, 62
Dahomey, 52
Dahomey, Lower, 57, 60
Denmark, illiteracy rate, 19
Diaz, P., 39
Dickson, A. G., 228
"Doctrine of the Mean, the," 245
Documentation, 293-294
Dragunov, 254
Drzewieski, B., 7
Du Ponceau, 244

Durban, 76
Dutch East Indies, see Indonesia

"Earthbound China" (Fei Hsiao Tung), 193
East Indies, 171
Economic development, and fundamental education, 187-189, 192-195
"Educational Reconstruction," English Board of Education's White Paper on, 211
"Education for Victory," 18
"Education in India" (A. Mayhew), 273
Egypt, 120-122, 210
  illiteracy rate, 21
Eleventh Quinquennial Review of the Bureau of Education, India, 95
English language, 262-265
Ecuador, 29-32
Evenki, the, 130, 138

Faidherbe, L., 46
Farm-schools, Haiti, 34
Faucett, 275
Federal Committee on Adult Education (Transvaal Teachers' Association), 76
Fei Hsiao Tung, 193
Films, 267, 270, 279, 280, 293, 294, 295, 300, 301
  see also Motion pictures, Sound motion pictures
Final Program Report of Unesco, 10, 221, 289
Financing fundamental education, problem of, 231, 297, 301
Finland, literacy rate, 19
First Five-year Plan, 137
Foreign Missions Conference of North America, 233
France, policy of educational colonisation, 45-63, 112-114
French Overseas Territories, 45-63
Fukien, dialectal variation in, 235, 250
Fundamental education, defined, 145-150
Futa Djallon, 55
"Future of Education, the" (R. Livingstone), 207

Gabriel, E., 32, 38
Galliéni, J. S., 46
Glen Grey, Cape Province, 79

Germany, illiteracy rate, 19
Gibson, C., 165
Gilbert Islands, illiteracy rate, 20
Girls' Training College, Rufisque, 62
Gold Coast report, 182
Goldi, the, 130, 138
Grant-in-aid system, in India, 105
"Great Learning, the," 245
Group activities, 218, 280-283
"Growing up in New Guinea" (M. Read), 168
Guadeloupe, 35-37
Guam, illiteracy rate, 20
Guatemala, 32
Guayaquil, 29-30

Haarhoff, I. J., 7
Haiti, 32-35
"Handbook of Suggestions for the Consideration of Teachers and Others Concerned with the Elementary School," 208
Harvard Graduate School of Education, 261, 265
Hawaii, illiteracy rate, 20
Hellman, E., 63, 219, 223, 231, 233, 283
"Helping the United Nations by Making Everybody's World Safe" (F. C. Laubach). See Making Everybody's World Safe . . .
Higginbottom, S., 98
Higher education in British West Africa, Report on, 193, 197, 201
Hjelmveit, N., 3
Honduras, 37-38
Hosler, F., 274
Hsu, F. L. K., 84
Hunan, dialectal variation in, 235, 250
Hung-Shen, 248
Hu Shih, 239, 241, 242
Huxley, J. S., 8, 221

Idenburg, J., 6
Igarka, 137
Incentives to literacy, 161-165, 218, 259, 283-286
India, 21, 50, 80, 88-107, 140, 151, 157, 210, 212, 225, 273
Indian Statutory Commission's Auxiliary Education Committee, 88, 89
"India Shall be Liberated" (F. C. Laubach), 233
Indo-China, 46, 47, 51, 60, 107, 108, 109, 110, 111-120

Indo-China—Continued
  communal schools in, 117
  elementary schools in, 116
  French policy in, 112-113
  pagoda schools in, 117-118
  pioneer schools in, 116-117
  population of, 111-112
  schoolbooks and teachers, 118
  statistics, 119
Indonesia, 92, 107, 108, 109, 110, 111, 147, 152
  illiteracy rate, 21
Ingushetians, the, 138
Institute of the Peoples of the North (U.S.S.R.), 138
Interdialectal Romanization, 257, 258
International Education News Letter, 294
International Education Review, 294, 295
International Education Yearbook, 294
International Institute of Teachers' College, Columbia University. See Teachers College, Columbia University
"Investigation of the Thought of Primitive Children with special reference to Animism" (M. Mead), 168
Iran, illiteracy rate, 21
Iranian Government Memorandum, 3
Iraq, 122, 125, 210
  illiteracy rate, 21
Italy, illiteracy rate, 19
Ivory Coast, 54, 62

Jamaica, 16
Japan, 5, 20, 152, 154, 171, 267
Japanese, the, 168, 169, 170, 172
Jasmin of Szepingkai, 257-258
Javanese, the, 166
Johannesburg, 73, 75
Juarez, B., 38, 39

Kabbani, I., 121
Kandel, I. L., 16, 205, 223
Karlgren, B., 257
Katibugu, rural training college, 62
Kazakhstan, 139
Kiangsi, dialectal variation in, 235, 250
Kiangsu, dialectal variation in, 235, 250
King, B., 126, 219, 220, 231, 233
Kirghizia, 137, 140

Komi, 130
Koran schools, 48, 50
Krupskaya, 138
Kultarmeitsi, 135
"Kummy Yen" (Yen Yan-chu), 248
Kuo Yu-shou, 5
Kwangtung, dialectal variation in, 235, 250

Lamasse, Les Pères, 257-258
Language, problem of, 217, 233-259, 296-298
  in Africa, 233
  in China, 80, 84, 88, 234-259
  in French overseas territories, 232
  in Mexico, 233
  in U.S.S.R., 130-134, 232
Language and script, relationship between, 166-167
Lantern slides, 275
Lao, 111, 112, 115, 117, 118
Latin America, 20, 60, 147, 148, 171
Latinxua, 253, 254-256
Laubach, F. C., 18, 29, 30, 32, 37, 87, 98, 103, 219, 226, 227, 273, 276, 298
Lauwerys, J. A., 271
Leaders, 161, 174-175
Leadership, 229, 290, 291
Leisure, use of, 200
Lenin, 94, 130
Leningrad Eastern Institute, 130
Lewin, K., 283
Libraries, Archives and Museums, Division of Unesco, 293
Lin Feng, 259
Lin Shu, 241
Lin Yutang, 253
Literacy campaigns, 198, 205
  question of priority, 188
  see also Adult education, approach to
"Literacy in India" (R. V. Parulekar), 92
Lithuania, 18
Liu Fu, 253
Livingstone, Sir Richard, 94, 207
London School of Oriental Studies, 253
Lopari, the, 130
Lyautey, L. H. G., 46

Madagascar, 46, 51
"Making Everybody's World Safe . . ." (F. C. Laubach), 226, 233, 275
"Making the World Safe by Helping the United Nations" (F. C. Lau-

bach), see "Making Everybody's World Safe . . ."

Malacca, 107, 110
Manchuria, 235
Mann, H., 12
Manus tribe, 168-170
Martinez Baez, M., see Baez, M.
Martinique, 35-37
Mass communication, 218, 225, 232, 276-283, 290
  see also Films, Radio and recordings, Sense aids, Sound motion pictures
Mass Communication Division of Unesco, 292, 300, 301
"Mass Education in African Society," 198, 200, 229, 233, 272, 280, 283
Mayhew, A., 273
Mead, M., 150, 159, 164, 168, 219, 220, 222, 223, 233, 283
"Mencius," 245
Meos, the, 111
Meston's Report on an Educational policy for India, 105
Mexico, 4, 20, 29, 38-43, 103, 210, 231, 233
Middle East, 120-126, 147, 151
Minimum standard of living, 179-180
Moga experiment, 210
Moïs, the, 111, 112, 115, 116, 118
Mongolia, Inner, 235
Moniz de Aragao, J. J., 2
Morocco, 46, 47
Moscow, 133, 137, 139
Motion pictures, 275, 278
  see also Sound motion pictures
Muller, E., 122
Muslim civilisation, 50
Myrdal, K. G., 22

Natal, 63, 65, 71, 76
National Christian Council, 98
National Education Association of the United States, 212
National Phonetic Letters, 236, 240, 246, 247, 252, 259
National Romanization, 253-259
Netherlands, illiteracy rate, 19
Netherlands East Indies. See Indonesia
New Guinea, 167
New Zealand, illiteracy rate, 20
New Zealand Educational Institute, 212
Norway, illiteracy rate, 19

Obregon, President, 40
Ogden, C. K., 271, 273
"On this foundation" (W. S. Rycroft), 20
Orange Free State, 66, 68
"Organization of an International Campaign against Illiteracy," 4

Pagoda schools, 117, 118
Panel on fundamental education, 291-303
Parents and children, 190-192
Parulekar, R. V., 91, 92
"Patterns of Japanese culture" (R. Benedict), 169
Perez, L., 4
Peru, illiteracy rate, 20
Pestalozzi, H., 12
Philippines, 92, 107, 108, 110, 166, 210
"Pioneer" schools, 116-117
"Pocket Book of Basic English," 266
Ponty College, 62
Porto Rico. See Puerto Rico
Portugal, illiteracy rate, 19
"Proposals for Public Education in Post-war America," 212
Provincial Financial Resources Committee (Union of South Africa) Report, 67
"Public Education in the United States" (Cubberly, E. P.,), 211
Puerto Rico, 20, 210

Quito, 31-32
Quoc-nghu, 114, 115, 119

Raadi, G. A., 3
Radio, 279, 280, 282, 293, 295, 300, 301
Radio and recordings, in the teaching of reading, 261, 266-267
Rank and caste, 164-165
Read, M., 18, 178, 219, 220, 222, 231, 283, 284
"Reader's Digest," 122
Reading material, provision of, 217, 272-276, 299
Rebsamen, E. C., 39
Recruitment of personnel, 303
Reed, A., 30
Rhadés, the, 115, 116
Richards, I. A., 227, 259, 265, 273, 276, 280, 298, 300
Rivera, Diego, 41
"Rotarian, the," 122
Rufisque, Girls' Training College, 62
Rulon, P. J., 300

Rural Reconstruction Centres, in India, 99-107
Rycroft, W. S., 20

Sáenz, M., 40
Salman, H. A., 122
Samoa, illiteracy rate, 20
Sargent Report, 91, 93
"Science, philosophy and religion" (G. Bateson), 163
Scientific Advisory Mission Report (Middle East), 123
Script. See Language and script, relationship between
Senegal, 46, 48, 52, 55, 57, 59
Sense Aids, 276-280, 293, 300-302
  see also Mass communications
Sepik basin, tribes of the, 167
Shantung, 253
Shaw, G. B., 279
Shop Employees Act (India), 94
Siam, 21, 108, 109, 166
"Silent Billions Speak, the" (F. C. Laubach), 233
Simon, W., 253
Singapore, 107, 109, 110
Sinkiang, 234, 235
Social and Economic Planning Council (Union of South Africa), 65, 70, 74
"Social Change and Cultural Surrogates" (M. Mead), 164
Social Science Section of Unesco, 289
"Some Professional Problems of Education in Dependent Countries" (M. Mead), 159
Sommerfelt, A., 6
Sotho tribes, 72
Sound motion pictures, in the teaching of reading, 261-266
South Africa. See Union of South Africa
Soviet Union. See U.S.S.R.
Spain, illiteracy rate, 19
Stanley, O., 208
Statistics, in specific countries:
  Afghanistan, 21
  Arabia, 21
  Argentina, 20
  Australia, 20
  Baluchistan, 21
  Bantus of South Africa, 21
  Brazil, 20
  British Guiana, 20
  Bulgaria, 19
  Burma, 21

Statistics—Continued
  Canada, 19-20
  Chile, 20
  China, 21, 82, 83, 84
  Colombia, 27
  Cuba, 20
  Denmark, 19
  Egypt, 21, 121
  Ellis Islands, 20
  Finland, 19
  French West Africa, 58
  Germany, 19
  Gilbert Islands, 20
  Guadeloupe, 36, 37
  Guam, 20
  Hawaii, 20
  India, 21, 90
  Indo-China, 108, 110, 119
  Indonesia, 21, 109, 110
  Iran, 21
  Iraq, 21
  Italy, 19
  Japan, 20
  Lithuania, 18
  Martinique, 37
  Mexico, 20
  Netherlands, 19
  New Zealand, 20
  Norway, 19
  Peru, 20
  Philippines, 108, 109
  Portugal, 19
  Puerto Rico, 20
  Samoa, 20
  Siam, 21, 109, 110
  Spain, 19
  Sweden, 19
  Switzerland, 19
  Union of South Africa, 68, 69, 72, 75
  United Kingdom, 19
  United States of America, 19, 20
  U.S.S.R., 139-140
"Streamlined English" (F. C. Laubach), 226
"Streamlined Lessons in English, and Teachers' Manual" (F. C. Laubach), 233
Student Social Service League, 103
Supreme Council of Education (Egypt), 121
Sweden, illiteracy rate, 19
Switzerland, illiteracy rate, 19
Szechwan, 81, 83

Tashkent Central Asiatic Co-operative school for women, 134

Teachers College, Columbia University, 41, 210
Teachers' training in Colombia, 23-25
Tennessee Valley Authority, 295
Thais, the, 111, 115
Thos, the, 111, 115
Togoland, 52
Tonking, 46, 47, 111, 113, 116, 117, 119
Torres, E. C., 40, 232, 233, 283
Torres Bodet, J., 2
"Toward a Literate World" (F. C. Laubach), 233
Transkei, 75, 79
Transvaal, 65, 76
Transvaal Teachers' Association, 76
Tubi, the, 130
Tungussi, 130
Turkmenistan, 137, 140

Ukraine, 134
Ulan-Ude, 137
Under-privileged groups, 179-181
see also "Backward" areas, types of
Unification of National Language, Committee on (Chinese Ministry of Education), 239, 253
Union Advisory Board on Native Education (Union of South Africa), 67, 69
Union de Artistas y Escritores, 29
Union Nacional de Periodistas, 31
Union of South Africa, 63-80, 219
desire for education, 71-72, 75
education of European children, 65
education of non-Europeans, 65-75
industrial colour bar, 73-74
lack of facilities for primary education, 70
population, 63-65
social and political status of non-Europeans, 78-79
statistics, 68-69, 72, 75
United Kingdom, 19
United Provinces, 90, 102
United States, 19-20, 158, 210, 219, 223, 237
United States, Department of Agriculture, 161, 223
Uprooted peoples, 171-176

Urals, the, 130
U.S.S.R., 126-142, 148, 157, 158, 209, 219, 231, 232
"Building Socialism in Russia," 126-129
language problem, 130-133
statistics, 139-140
work among women, 135-136
Uzbekistan, 134, 140

Vallon, H., 6
Van Diffelen, R. W., 107
Vasconcelos, J., 40
Vera Cruz, 39
Vernacular-literature movement in China, 241-243
Viet-Nam, 112
Village Centre Project, 99
Voguls, the, 130
Voluntary agencies, the state and, 217, 228

Wade-Giles system of romanization, 254
Wardha National Education Conference, "Wardha Scheme," 95, 225
Weir's report on village education in the United Provinces, 100
West, M., 275
West Indies, 46, 48, 60, 147, 171
West Indies, French, 35-37
Whitehead, A. N., 228
Whyte, Q., 63, 219, 223, 231, 232, 233, 283
Wilkinson, E., 7
Williamsport, Pa., high schools, 274
Women and girls:
education of (West Africa), 198
inferior social status of (India), 99
work among (U.S.S.R.), 135-136
"Words on paper" (I. A. Richards and C. Gibson), 265

Yakuts, the, 129
Yakutsk, 130, 137
Yen, J., 81
Yen Yan-chu ("Kummy Yen"), 248

Zimmern, Sir Alfred, 1